THE COST OF DUTY

First Published in Great Britain 2021 by Mirador Publishing

Copyright © 2021 by Max Carmichael

All rights reserved. No part of this publication may be reproduced or transmitted, in any form or by any means, without permission of the publishers or author. Excepting brief quotes used in reviews.

First edition: 2021

References to places and people are made with due respect. Any offence caused by references in the narrative is completely unintentional.

A copy of this work is available through the British Library.

ISBN: 978-1-913833-62-6

Mirador Publishing
10 Greenbrook Terrace
Taunton
Somerset
UK
TA1 1UT

The Cost of Duty

By

Max Carmichael

Forward

By, Brigadier R.G, Curtis AM, MC, (Retired).

When Max Carmichael, the author of "The Cost of Duty" contacted me regarding writing the Foreword to this book, I was interested to learn the protagonists were Trevor Leon Bawden, better known by all those who know him as Mick, and his wife Mardi.

Mick and I served together in the 9th Battalion the Royal Australian Regiment (9 RAR) during the Unit's preparation for, and throughout its operational service in South Vietnam. We both held the rank of captain at that time. What was equally compelling was that my future wife, Anne Holmes, who was born at Mount Gambier, attended the same school as Mick Bawden's wife, Mardi. They knew each other well. Together we became friends, drawn together by the mutual bond of the 9 RAR family.

I believe members of the 9 RAR family, like me, will recall with pride, some sadness, and even a little amusement the detailed events described in "The Cost of Duty" regarding 9 RAR. I was reminded of the intensive training we undertook that followed the raising of the Battalion; and of the operations we undertook during our 12-month tour of duty in South Vietnam.

Vietnam was an unpopular war. Numerous servicemen and women, including Mick, having done their duty, were ostracized and reviled by many within the Australian community. That was an unexpected and additional cost of their duty to be borne, along with the other physical and mental scars of their service in that brutal war. In Mick's case the battle with his personal demons began after he had ended his Army service, and like many other veterans of that war, it was sometime before he was able to receive any worthwhile help.

When Mick resigned from the Army our careers went in different directions. I stayed in the Army and Mick followed a new path in agriculture. However, I was not surprised to learn that he had found a way to continue public service. During his Army career, Mick understood and was conscious of the significance of the Royal Australian Regiment's motto "Duty First". That ethos had been imbedded in his psyche, and as a civilian he continued to apply that philosophy to life. He became a local government representative, a volunteer fireman, and took part in various other voluntary community organizations, including work with the Vietnam Veterans' Association of Australia. Throughout all of this Mardi's duty has remained steadfast, providing support to Mick and her children.

In writing this book, the author seeks to remind the wider community of the physical and mental issues faced by servicemen and women, and indeed by all first responders, in carrying out their duty. "The Cost of Duty" in relating Mick and Mardi's story shines a light on those costs.

INTRODUCTION

FROM THE TIME PEOPLE FIRST began to live in groups, successful societies have relied on the individual sense of duty as a means of creating and maintaining a moral, and law-abiding society. The performance of a duty is a deliberate, voluntary moral action undertaken by a person for the perceived benefit of others. However, this undoubtedly positive social concept is invariably undertaken at a cost to the person performing the duty.

The cost of duty is generally commensurate to the nature of the duty. For the majority of people, the nature of their duty whilst important is unexceptional, and the associated costs generally mundane. For example, the cost of duty involved in caring for a sick relative might be as simple as the time and effort involved. However, at the higher end of the "duty scale", there are people for whom duty is hazardous and the associated costs often extreme. This group includes the police, firefighters, paramedics, members of the armed forces and those others who choose to place themselves in harm's way to save or help another person. For these people the potential cost for their duty is injury or death.

This story explores the life experiences of Vietnam veteran Mick Bawden, and his wife and stalwart supporter Mardi. The story also broadly addresses the cost of duty paid by the Battalion to which Mick was assigned, the 9th Battalion Royal Australian Regiment, during the Battalion's operational tour of Vietnam.

It is important to note that the events outlined in this account are not unique. Thousands of other Australian families during that particular war, and other conflicts involving Australian forces, have lived through similar events and suffered similar costs for their duty. It is also important to note that neither Mick nor Mardi are heroes, although some of their duties have required them to exhibit courage and endurance. Rather, they are perhaps typical of the ordinary Australians who found their sense of duty involved them in an unpopular war, for which, regardless of whether they deployed to the war zone, or remained at home waiting hopefully for the return of a loved one, they have paid a high cost.

Prologue

THE 11ᵀᴴ OF DECEMBER 1967, the day the 9th Battalion Royal Australian Regiment (9 RAR) mounted its first operation in Vietnam. It was a cordon and search operation focused on the village of Xa An Nhut. In theory there was nothing new for the Battalion in this task, during its pre-deployment training back in Australia the Battalion had conducted almost countless cordon and search exercises. Every man was familiar with the role he had to play, however there was an air of tension in the Battalion, the difference between a training activity and an actual operation was now all too apparent. They were all acutely aware that at Xa An Nhut if there was a contact, the enemy would be a real person and he would fire real bullets at them, and the casualties they could suffer would be all too real.

The first stage of the operation, establishing the cordon around the village, and halting all movement to and from the village was successfully achieved. The second phase of the operation, the search, immediately followed on. During this second phase of the operation, every occupant of the village would be screened...a census carried out at gunpoint. In addition, the buildings and storage facilities within the village would be searched for contraband of any kind. Xa An Nhut was a known Viet Cong supply point for rice and other items the enemy required, and as a result a discovery of this kind was quite possible.

The search phase progressed...over 1000 occupants of the village were screened and several who were deemed to be Viet Cong suspects detained. Then as the village storage facilities were being searched, there was a moment of high drama. A Viet Cong soldier was discovered hiding in a large basket of rice. The enemy soldier was challenged, he attempted to resist and was subsequently shot and killed.

Soon after this incident the body of the dead Viet Cong was moved by armoured personnel carrier (APC) to an evacuation point. The dead enemy soldier was not a pretty sight and yet Captain Mick Bawden and several other 9 RAR personnel who were waiting at the evacuation point felt compelled to take a closer look at the Battalion's first kill.

It was a sobering occasion for Mick Bawden. Here at his feet was the major reason for the presence of Australian infantry in Vietnam…to close with and kill the enemy. So far as this particular dead Viet Cong was concerned 9 RAR had done its job all too well. However, Mick felt no elation at the death of this enemy soldier, only distaste at the death of another human being, and a degree of sad understanding that the dead man must have been in some ways very similar to himself…a soldier simply performing his duty.

Mick turned away from the body. The feelings the dead man had generated within him would not prevent him performing of his own duties. The dead Viet Cong had made his remittance for his duty…the cost Mick Bawden would have to pay for his was merely delayed.

Chapter 1

O, listen for a moment, lads, and hear me tell my tale –
How, o'er the sea from England's shore I was compelled to sail.
The jury says, 'He's guilty, sir,' and says the judge, says he
'For life, Jim Jones, I'm sending you across the stormy sea.' [1]

The Bawdens

IF MICK BAWDEN'S GREAT, GREAT, Grandfather John Charles Bawden, had not tried his hand at larceny, the Bawden family tree would certainly have had a very different shape, and his great grandson Mick Bawden might never have faced duty in Vietnam. John Charles Bawden was born in 1821, the eldest son of inn keepers John and Sarah Bawden of Bishops Hatfield in Hertfordshire, England. Compared with many children of Britain's Industrial Revolution, John Charles had a fortunate life. He had a roof over his head, he never starved and by the time he was 15 years of age he was working as a farm hand. However, it was during that employment that things went badly wrong for him.

For some reason, John Charles turned to crime. His motivation in this regard is unknown, however his crime was discovered, he was arrested, and on the 25th of July 1845, brought before the assizes court at Salop, where he

---

[1] Anon, <u>Jim Jones at Botany Bay.</u>

was found guilty and sentenced to 10 years prison. His sentence was to be served in exile in Australia.

At the time it was British Government policy to export many of the nation's convicts to Australia. Transportation reduced the stress on the home-based British prison system and gave the impression to the British public that the Government was fighting crime. However, it was not a seamless process. Logistically, transportation was a complex and time-consuming business. There were a limited number of suitable ships available in which to transport the convicts. In addition, it took a sailing ship almost a year to make the outward journey, deliver its human cargo, and return home. As a result, convicted people were often faced with a considerable wait in an English prison, before a ship was available to take them to the other side of the world. This was the fate that befell John Charles and he served 2 years in the Millbank Prison, before his transportation was eventually effected. Finally, on the 2nd of June 1847, John Charles along with 249 other convicts embarked on the prison ship the *Joseph Soames* for the long sea voyage to Australia.

There was little for the *Joseph Soames* human cargo to look forward to. It was well known that jail time in the colonies was extremely harsh. Indeed, conviction to transportation was closely akin to a death sentence, as few of the thousands who were transported in chains to the colonies, returned to their homes and families. However, as luck would have it, the preparation for the *Joseph Soames* June 1847 voyage, coincided with a radical change in the British Government's policy for the management of transported convicts.

The change came in response to objections raised by colonial authorities and some free settlers in Australia, regarding the number of convicts being landed on Australian shores. To counter those objections, the Government, through Queen Victoria, decreed that future convicts bound for Australia, and who met particular criteria, were to be granted conditional pardons on their arrival in the colonies. Thus, rather than exporting convicts, Britain was providing assisted passage to "free" settlers. This was a cynical political sleight of hand and it fooled no one.

In fairness the Government had no intention of extending the new policy to hardened criminals. Convicts to be transported under this scheme were carefully selected. Those chosen were of an average age of 28 years. Older convicts were excluded on the basis they could possibly provide a negative influence on the younger convicts, as were those who had committed serious offences such as murder. However, perhaps the most important criterion for a convict to be included in the new scheme was a record of excellent behaviour during their initial incarceration in Britain.

Millbank Prison had had a dramatic impact on the young John Charles, and it might safely be assumed, the experience put the fear of Christ in him. In fact, he became a model prisoner, and while this change in attitude had no effect on his sentence, the authorities found that he fitted the established criterion for the new policy. Subsequently he was chosen to be part of the *Joseph Soames* consignment of convicts.

At the time of sailing, the convicts on board the *Joseph Soames* were not aware of their good fortune and they completed their sea journey in fear and dread of what awaited them at their destination. To their surprise, on the 24th of September 1847 as the ship arrived at Geelong the convicts were advised of their changed circumstances. They had been granted conditional pardons, and were now, to all intents and purposes, free men. Potential employers were then invited on board the ship to negotiate employment contracts with the now *former* convicts. Most employment contracts were of one year's duration and were enforceable under the terms of the *New South Wales Masters' and Servants' Act of 1845*. The Act directed that an employee, who breeched his, or her, contract, could receive a fine or a prison term of up to 6 months. Those who chose not to accept an employment contract were required to leave the ship, where once ashore they were faced with the possibility of long-term unemployment, and of course the temptations that had led to their convictions in the first place.

John Charles was lucky. His previous experience in farming stood him in good stead and he was offered work as a station hand and shearer on Winninburn Station, which was located in what is now Western Victoria, near the village of Merino. He was to remain there for some years, before taking other similar work around the area and beyond. During his time at Winninburn he became a "gun" shearer, able to shear 129 sheep a day with hand shears. He also met a young Irish woman, Julia Murphy, a domestic servant at the Winninburn homestead.

Julia was illiterate, but her lack of formal education was not an indication of a low intellect. Station records of the time described her as being "as sharp as a tack". The two married on the 15th of June 1857, in a midnight ceremony, enabling the bride and groom to complete their employment duties on the day of their nuptials, and ensured they would be ready for work at first light the next day. There was nothing particularly remarkable in this edict. Duty to one's employer in those days was almost boundless, and it is possible John Charles' stint in prison reinforced his determination that he and his family would do the right thing in their new land.

Eighty-two years later, in the year 1939, one of John and Julia's many grandchildren, Byron (better known as Blinx) Bawden, had good reason to be thankful for his grand-parents devotion to duty. Byron's home town of Mount Gambier was prosperous, and as a butcher he was sharing in that prosperity. His wife Sadie (formerly Jessie Maud Steer who was always referred to as "Sadie"), had 2 years previously, produced the couple's first born, a son named Byron after his doting father, a happy and healthy young fellow; and Sadie was now pregnant with their second child. On the face of it, the Bawden family seemed destined for a comfortable and successful life. However, in spite of these reasons for optimism they had only to read the local newspaper or listen to radio news to realise the good times they enjoyed may not last long.

1939 heralded a very dark period for the world. In Europe, Adolf Hitler's Nazi Germany was threatening uncontrolled aggression and domination. Closer to home the expansionist aspirations of Japan had resulted in massive human rights abuses in China, destabilizing the whole Asian region. Other world powers seemed either powerless, or disinterested, in preventing the excesses of these two belligerent nations, and many feared the world had begun an inexorable slide toward another war. Australians viewed the international situation with concern, however most believed Australia's isolation would negate any direct threat to the nation. Besides, there were more localised events to take their attention.

January 1939 was particularly hot and dry right across southern Australia.

In Mount Gambier, the local newspaper, The Border Watch, reported on the 10th of January 1939 temperatures in excess of 107 degrees Fahrenheit (41 degrees Celsius). Every citizen of country Australia knew that temperatures such as these, in combination with hot, strong winds were a recipe for bushfire disaster. It would only take a lightning strike or a careless act, and the countryside would become a blazing inferno. Three days later across the border in Victoria, these conditions all came together, and a series of massive bushfires resulted in the deaths of 70 people. The citizens of Mount Gambier could only watch and pray they would be spared a similar catastrophe. On that occasion their prayers were answered, and the district was spared.

In April 1939 the international situation had further deteriorated with Italian troops invading Albania. Great Britain and France had guaranteed armed assistance to Greece and Romania, should they be attacked by Germany or Italy, however, once again events at home drew the attention of most Australians away from the international crisis, to focus on Canberra and the Federal Government. Prime Minister of Australia, Joseph Lyons, had died on the 7th of April, of a heart attack. Lyons was the first Australian Prime Minister to die in office. His replacement was the leader of the United Australia Party…Robert Menzies. Menzies, a staunch royalist and pragmatist, was strongly vocal in his support for Britain, yet at the same time he saw nothing wrong with selling the Japanese raw materials.

By May the international news was worse. Germany and Italy signed a formal alliance titled the "Pact of Steel" and The Border Watch ran a feature story on the Japanese incursion into the International Settlement at Amoy, in Fukion Province, China. The war that many believed to be unthinkable now seemed to be almost inevitable.

Even so, life in Mount Gambier continued to be prosperous. Potato farmers, of whom there were many in the Mount Gambier area, were receiving 4 pounds per ton for their produce, a good return for the time. A draught horse could be purchased for around five pounds, considered by many farmers to be a high price. The dairy industry was experiencing a boom in production and prices, and the Bawdens' butcher shop continued to do well. However, in the Bawden household, all of this was a mere backdrop to Sadie's preparation for her confinement.

On the 26th of May having been admitted to the Saint Neots Hospital at Mount Gambier, Sadie gave birth to her second son. The new baby was christened Trevor Leon Bawden, neither Christian name being relevant to either side of the family, apparently chosen simply because his parents liked the names. A family theory developed later, suggested the new baby's second name was in honour of his father's brother, Noel… "Leon" being "Noel" spelt backwards, but this seems unlikely. Naming aside, and in spite of Sadie's preparations, the existing members of the Bawden family were actually ill prepared for the new baby. Almost from the moment of his birth, baby Trevor was victim to a family situation many young families face…second child syndrome.

Psychotherapists have since hypothesised that second child syndrome occurs when the first child receives attention, privileges and responsibilities, by virtue of being the oldest, while the second child is often left with no clear role in the family. This was the case in the Bawden family. Sadie and Blinx were besotted with their first born, which is not to say they did not love their second child, but it is fair to say they struggled to come to terms with sharing the level of love they felt for Byron junior with young Trevor. However, at that time, particularly in rural Australia such theories were given little credence. Besides, there were much more pressing issues to be concerned with…the world was now poised on the abyss of yet another global conflict.

On 1st September 1939 German forces invaded Poland and on the 3rd of September Britain declared war on Germany. At 9.00pm the same day in a speech broadcast on every national and commercial radio station in Australia, the Prime Minister Robert Menzies announced the beginning of Australia's involvement in the Second World War:

"*Fellow Australians,*

It is my melancholy duty to inform you officially that in consequence of a persistence by Germany in her invasion of Poland, Great Britain has declared war upon her and that, as a result, Australia is also at war.

No harder task can fall to the lot of a democratic leader than to make such an announcement.

Great Britain and France with the cooperation of the British Dominions have struggled to avoid this tragedy. They have, as I firmly believe, been patient. They have kept the door of negotiation open. They have given no cause for aggression.

But in the result their efforts have failed, and we are therefore, as a great family of nations, involved in a struggle which we must at all costs win and which we believe in our hearts we will win."[2]

For most of the extended Bawden family, events following this dramatic announcement moved slowly. The war remained a distant phenomenon, but now that it had been declared it was widely assumed that Britain and her European allies would deliver the foe a swift and merciless beating. As for Australia's security it was assumed the British Navy, believed to be far superior to any capability the Japanese possessed, would keep the enemy at bay. Both of these assumptions proved to be woefully incorrect.

By May 1940 the war situation was extremely grave. France had fallen and the German military might threatened to invade Britain. Previously the Australian Government had authorised the raising of the Second Australian Imperial Force (AIF). This was relatively easily achieved, as many Australians of that era had been brought up in the belief it was their duty to serve their country in its time of need. Three divisions of this force, approximately 45,000 men were sent overseas to support Britain. By the end of the war 575,799 men and women had served overseas. The price exacted by the performance of this duty was high for of this number 39,429 died and 66,563 were wounded[3]. In South Australia, approximately 9.14% of the population elected to do their duty and enlist voluntarily in the AIF. Blinx Bawden did not immediately rush to enlist. Whilst the war news was far from good, the fighting was still many thousands of kilometres away, and importantly, he had a duty right here at home…a wife and two young children. However, one who did join those early volunteers was Sadie Bawden's brother, Gilbert Steer.

Gilbert Steer enlisted in Adelaide on 10th of June 1940 and allocated the Army number SX4979. After his initial training, he was deployed to the Middle East as a reinforcement. Gilbert's military career was to be a short one. Soon after his arrival in theatre he participated in the Siege of Tobruk. It

---

[2] Declaration of War – Menzies virtual museum.

[3] rslnsw.org.au/commemoration/heritage/the-second-world-war

was there he paid a high price for his duty. He was severely wounded, resulting in the loss of a leg, and was consequently repatriated to Australia and discharged from the AIF as medically unfit for further service.

In December 1941 Japan entered the war, aligning itself with Nazi Germany. The British Navy proved inadequate to quell the Japanese advance, and suddenly the war was moving alarmingly closer to Australian shores. This threat was far closer to home and Blinx Bawden now felt the focus of his duty was clear. He joined thousands of Australians who volunteered to participate in the defence of the nation. SX17094 B. R. Bawden enlisted on the 3$^{rd\ of}$ February 1942 and for the next 4 years he served in the South West Pacific campaigns fighting the Japanese. During that time, he saw little of his family, a cost of duty paid by all four members of the family.

When peace finally came, Blinx was demobilized and eventually arrived home at Mount Gambier. However, he took some time to readjust to peace and family life. The close attention of 9-year-old Byron junior, and a particularly lively 7-year-old Trevor, did not make Blinx's reassimilation any easier. To his two sons he appeared distant and a little frightening. They were far too young to understand their father's demeanour was a cost of the duty he had rendered, but they learned to endure his moods. Luckily, although the process was gradual, their father eventually adjusted to the peace and family life.

It was at this time that Trevor began to understand that not only was he placed second to his brother chronologically, but also in the extended family pecking order. His mother and father, his grandparents, uncles and aunts, all deferred to Byron junior's status as "number one son". Trevor was left to grapple with the feeling that he did not fit in anywhere. As a result, as the two boys grew, Byron lived in a happy utopia where his wants and needs were immediately catered for, whereas for Trevor…not so much. Adding to this situation a seemingly innocent, yet nonetheless life changing, event occurred.

Soon after Blinx's return from active duty, as young Trevor sat on his mother's knee, his brother remarked that Trevor looked like the cartoon character "Mickey Mouse". It was quite a joke with his parents, and encouraged by this positive feedback, Byron continued to refer to his younger sibling as "Mickey". In this he was not corrected by any senior Bawden family members, indeed his parents reinforced their eldest son's conduct by using Trevor's nickname themselves, and before anyone really understood what was happening "Trevor Leon" had all but disappeared from the family fold, to be replaced by "Mickey" Bawden. Years later "Mickey" would be shortened to "Mick" but to this day some of Mick's friends are still unaware of the identity of "Trevor Leon Bawden". However to avoid further confusion, from this point in this story, Trevor Leon Bawden will be referred to as "Mick"

His renaming did little to hold the Bawdens' youngest son back. By the time he had reached school age young Mick had developed into a competitive lad, perhaps even more so than his brother. School presented the younger Bawden with an area in which he could prove his worth. He attended the Mount Gambier Primary School and in spite of being 2 years junior to his brother, his academic potential was quickly recognised. He jumped a class and was placed in the year directly below his brother Byron, and in his final year in primary school Mick was second to the dux of the school. Indeed, had Fate not decreed otherwise, secondary school may have seen him go on to further achievements, but it was not to be…

On the 3rd of November 1950, following complications from an appendectomy the Bawdens' eldest son Byron died. He was just 13 years and 11 months of age.

Byron's death had a dreadful impact on the Bawden family. Profound grief engulfed Blinx and Sadie, a sorrow from which neither ever fully recovered. Their coping mechanism was to withdraw from everything and everyone that had once given them joy. Sadly, this included their surviving son, and the 11-year-old lad was basically left to his own devices. The fact that their surviving son grieved too was overlooked by his parents. He was fed, had a roof over his head, but he was denied the general and emotional support of his parents. Mick's need for that support was soon to be greater than ever.

As an after-school activity Mick had begun to attend the Mount Gambier Boys Institute where he was training in gymnastics, completely unaware that as he trained, he was being groomed by a sexual predator. When this paedophile judged the moment was right, he struck and his 11-year-old victim was faced with a situation no child should be expected to cope with.

Confused and alone, Mick found he had no one in whom he could confide. His parents, locked in their grief at young Byron's death, were unapproachable. Fear prevented him from going to the police, or his schoolteachers. Somehow, he managed to push the assault into the back of his mind, and to proceed with his life, however this was not easily achieved. Secondary school became a struggle, his behaviour deteriorated, and his grades suffered. If his teachers bothered to seek an explanation as to this reversal, they failed to pursue sexual assault as a possible reason. It was not until the 2016 – 2017 Royal Commission into Sexual Abuse of Children that Mick finally spoke of the assault, when he gave evidence before the Commission. At that time following some research of official records, Mick discovered that a number of other boys had fallen victim to the same predator. It was some small consolation to learn that prior to the paedophile's death, he had spent some time in prison for his crimes.

In spite of Mick's educational decline, at the age of 15, and as the youngest in his class, he managed to pass Year 11. No doubt he could have gone on to matriculate, however at that time none of the Mount Gambier schools offered Year 12. Those students who wished to progress to that level and possibly go and enter university, were required to move to Adelaide, and Mick's parents made it clear this was not an option for him. As a result, his formal education progressed no further. In fact, according to school friend Ian Marks, the education system was rather glad to see the back of Mick and several of his mates:

"We raised the spirits of our teachers of the three "Rs" by saying farewell to our school days, and in not too many years extended and developed an interest in the three "Bs"...Baseball, Booze and Birds".

After leaving school, Mick secured a junior position in the local branch of the Commonwealth Bank. Later, with some experience behind him he was promoted to a slightly more senior position at the Bordertown branch of the bank. It was a good job for someone who was inclined to such a life, but Mick was restless. Bordertown seemed a distant outpost, isolating him from his friends and family. He bought a sports car, a red Sunbeam Alpine, and driving this vehicle from Mount Gambier to Bordertown provided some distraction from his growing discontent with his lot. He also found some solace in sport, baseball in particular, and he involved himself in the Boy Scout movement. Baseball fostered a competitive spirit, while scouting nurtured an interest in outdoor activities and community service. He also enjoyed archery, hunting and fishing, outdoor activities that expanded his knowledge of bushcraft. In combination these interests almost led to disaster. A long-time friend, Sandy Haig had an almost pathological interest in explosives, and he convinced Mick it would be a good idea to arm an arrow with a stick of gelignite and detonator and to shoot this missile out into the ocean. Sandy Haig:

"One Saturday afternoon, with detonators, gelignite and fuses, Mick and I retired to the coast, I fixed the gelignite to the arrow and we cut the fuse for a short burn of one inch, or 2.7 seconds. Mick poised with the bow and arrow and on letting loose, the arrow dropped at our feet. Our dual shout of "Christ" was drowned out as the gelignite exploded".

However even with this kind of excitement Mick's after-hours pursuits were not enough to placate his search for a more fulfilling life. He decided to leave the banking sector and to join the family butchery business. Shortly after making this move, factors beyond the day-to-day work in the butcher shop were to influence his life.

In 1951 the Australian Government passed the National Service Act requiring all Australian males aged 18 years to register for 176 days of full-time military service and 5 years of service in the Citizen Military Force (CMF) the part-time Army and equivalent of the contemporary Army Reserve. While it was compulsory to register for service, the actual call-up was limited and subject to a ballot. Some young men saw conscription as an unwelcome impost on their personal lives, however many others during the immediate post-war period welcomed the chance to do their bit for the nation. In this the youth of the 1950's had the example of those who had served the nation during the two world wars and they were keen to show they had the same strong principles of service to the nation. Mick Bawden was one of these young patriots, and in 1957, having reached the age of eighteen, keen to do his duty as he saw it, he eagerly registered for National Service.

His enthusiasm was not rewarded. He was advised that he had been balloted out of the draft and would not be called up. Disappointed, he watched with envy as several of his school friends, who were conscripted, caught the Adelaide train bound for their initial full-time service at Woodside Army Camp. In spite of this setback Mick remained determined to pursue his duty through military service. He decided to enlist in the Citizen Military Force (CMF) as a volunteer.

Again, he was to be disappointed. The local CMF unit was limited in the number of volunteers it could accept, and when Mick applied to enlist the unit was at its authorised strength, and there were no vacancies for new recruits. He was placed on a waiting list and sent away. It was 12 months before his name finally bubbled to the top of the waiting list and he completed his enlistment.

In 1957 the CMF drill hall at Mount Gambier housed A Company of the 27th Infantry Battalion South Australian Scottish Regiment. Located in James Street, Mount Gambier, the drill hall was a corrugated iron shed which amongst its other characteristics, was freezing in the winter and stifling hot in the summer. Training consisted of a weekly 3-hour parade, one weekend a month (known as a 'bivouac') and one 14-day annual camp.

In spite of the sporadic nature of this training, the proficiency of the Mount Gambier soldiers was quite high. This was due to a number of factors. First the National Service members of the Company had had the benefit of 3 months of intensive full-time training, creating a strong foundation of proficient soldiers within the Company. Added to this, the Company still retained a number of 'old soldiers' with World War Two experience. Indeed, just prior to Mick's enlistment the Officer Commanding the Company was Captain Jack Burnett MM[4]. During World War Two as the Regimental Sergeant Major (RSM) of the 2/27th Battalion AIF, Burnett had won the Military Medal in New Guinea at the battle of Gona. Under the guidance of men like Burnett and in combination with the proficiency of the National Servicemen, CMF volunteers, such as the young Mick Bawden, achieved a higher standard of competence than might have been expected of their limited training curriculum.

---

[4] Military Medal.

Right then the only cost of Mick's military duty was his time, but this was hardly an issue for him as he thrived on his CMF experience. He enjoyed the camaraderie that builds within a group of like-minded people engaged in a single purpose. Soon he discovered he was quite good at basic soldiering and that others looked to him for leadership. Promotion followed. By 1960 Mick was a sergeant and 12 months later he began to study for his First Appointment examinations. Success in these exams generally resulted in the student being commissioned at the rank of lieutenant. At that particular time CMF officer candidates were not posted away from their home training depot to attend an Officer Cadet Training Unit. Instead, the candidates continued to parade as usual, studying at home, and finally sitting exams in a variety of subjects including minor tactics, administration, military law, and man management. Not every candidate passed, but Mick did, and in 1962 he was commissioned as a lieutenant.

Amazingly he had achieved this milestone in his career while being severely distracted by another aspect of life…he had fallen in love. This life changing chain of events began in 1961 when Mick was driving a motorboat on Mount Gambier's picturesque Valley Lake, for a lithe, dark-haired beauty named Mardi McPherson who was learning to water ski.

CHAPTER 2

Take a pair of sparkling eyes[5]

Mardi McPherson

MARDI MCPHERSON THE DAUGHTER OF flamboyant Master Butcher Albert Henry McPherson, and his musically gifted wife Alma, was born on the 26th of April 1944. Originally from Melbourne, the McPhersons had moved to Mount Gambier in 1946 where Albert had purchased a butchery business from local Commercial Street butcher Mr R. J. Maloney. Aside from the business the McPhersons established the new family seat at *Camelot*, 91 Bay Road, Mount Gambier a fine old Federation house which had been built in 1901. However, while the family flourished in their new home, it took some time for the business to thrive. At the time of sale, former owner R.J. Maloney had set a substantial value on the goodwill for the business, however, after the sale, the established clientele left in droves, apparently annoyed at the "fancy city bloke" that had taken over Maloney's shop.

Indeed, so far as rural, conservative Mount Gambier was concerned, Albert was certainly a fancy man. To start with he was a grand dresser, his stepping out attire generally consisted of white shirt, red bow tie, pin-striped, black suit with matching kerchief peeping from jacket pocket, and Fedora hat

---

[5] Sir William Gilbert, The Gondoliers.

worn at a slight angle. At Melbourne Cup time the Fedora was set aside in favour of a Homberg when he took Alma back to Melbourne for the race, an event the two attended regularly. He had a fondness for whiskey and having grown up among six sisters he was at ease in the company of women. All of this was hardly the image of the quintessential Aussie bloke that the citizens of Mount Gambier were used to having as their local butcher, so they had taken their business elsewhere. In a display of honour rarely seen today, on learning of this situation the former owner R.J. Maloney offered to repay the amount he had been paid for the goodwill of the business. Albert was grateful, but refused to accept the offer, no doubt Scottish pride played a part in that decision, for the McPhersons came from a fiercely proud Scottish ancestry.

While key member of the Bawden family, John Charles, had arrived in Australia in chains, records regarding Albert McPherson's forebears are sketchy. However, it is likely they made the journey as "free settlers". Even so, the nature of the McPherson exodus from their native Scotland was hardly less compelling than that which saw John Charles Bawden transported to Australia. The MacPhersons (or McPherson if the Anglicised spelling of the name is used) a once powerful clan of the Highlands of Scotland had the misfortune to back the wrong side in the 1745 Jacobite Rising, when they came out in support of Bonnie Prince Charlie. After the Prince was defeated, to avoid the vengeance of the English Government, many of his supporters, including numerous McPhersons, escaped overseas, mainly to Canada and America. Those refugees had fled from war, however for those who remained in Scotland an even worse set of circumstances was to come.

The Scottish clan system was founded in feudalism and subsistence agriculture, a way of life that was incapable of keeping pace with a modern market economy. The farming methods practised by the Scottish peasantry were particularly backward and in the wake of the rebellion, landowners (the lairds) began to employ improved farming methods and techniques. The new methods reduced the need for agricultural labour and relied more on the running of sheep. Loyalty it seems was not a two-way street for while the peasantry generally supported the Chief or Laird, the Chiefs and Lairds were more interested in profit. With no work, and facing the prospect of starvation, numerous clansmen, again including many McPhersons, opted to create a secondary wave of refugees bound for the colonies. The land left vacant by this new migration was quickly repopulated with sheep. So far as the landowners were concerned the depopulating of the Highlands was a remarkably successful program. There was however an unexpected consequence. In 1854 the Crimean War commenced, and the story goes that the Second Duke of Sutherland called a meeting of remaining clansmen in the hope of recruiting them for Army service. In this endeavour he was singularly unsuccessful as not one man stepped forward to take the King's shilling. Angrily the Duke demanded an explanation and eventually one old man stepped forward to provide a response:

"I am sorry for the response your Grace's proposals are meeting here today, so near to the spot where your maternal grandmother by giving some forty-eight hours' notice marshalled 1,500 men to pick out the 800 she required, but there is a cause for it and a genuine cause and, as your Grace demands to know it, I must tell you as I see none else in the assembly is inclined to do so. These lands are now devoted to rear dumb animals which your parents considered of far more value than men, I do assure your Grace that it is the prevailing opinion of this county that, should the Czar of Russia take possession of Dunrobin Castle and Stafford House next term that we could not expect worse treatment at his hands than we have experienced at the hands of your family for the past fifty years. Your parents, yourself and your Commissioners have desolated the glens and straths of Sutherland where you should find hundreds, yea thousands of men to meet and respond to your call cheerfully had your parents kept faith with them. How could your Grace expect to find men where they are not, and the few of them that are to be found have more sense than to be decoyed off by chaff to the field of slaughter. But one comfort you have, though you cannot find men to fight, you can supply those who will fight with plenty of mutton, beef and venison".[6]

Probably Albert McPherson's forebears were among those who believed it was their duty to their families to choose to leave the Scottish Highlands to the sheep, and to seek a better life in Australia. Perhaps they commenced that

---

[6] Michael Brander, The Making of the Highlands, Book Club Associates London 1980, pp 170-171.

perilous journey around about the same time as young John Charles Bawden had left on his marginally less comfortable voyage to the same destination.

The McPherson family possibly disembarked at Port Melbourne, although their voyage, like young John Charles Bawden, may have ended at Geelong as there is some evidence to suggest they lived in that location for a time. Later perhaps they joined other McPhersons who were lured to Ballarat in search of gold, but in any event the family eventually settled in Melbourne. It was there Albert was born on the 2nd of February 1901 and some 20 years later, where he would meet and marry Alma Duncan.

Alma, the daughter of John Joseph Duncan and Gertrude May Wood, was born on the 18th of June 1906. While there is no evidence to support the following conjecture, it would seem her parents were not in the happiest of relationships. When World War One commenced, her father, John Joseph Duncan, enlisted and was soon sent abroad to fight. He survived the war and returned to Australia, but not to his family. His wife, better known as Gertie, was left alone to raise her son Harold, and daughter Alma. This was certainly a duty Gertie had not bargained for; however, she did not shrink from the duty life had presented her with. With an often grim determination, she managed to feed and keep a roof over the heads of her family by buying and selling second-hand goods. A favourite story of Alma's regarding her mother was that she had once tipped the dinner out of a copper saucepan in order to sell the 'pan.

In spite of the difficulties Gertie undoubtedly faced, she was determined her daughter would receive a good education. An important part of that education was the study of music, and Alma went on to become an accomplished pianist. Mardi proudly remembers her mother's musical gift:

"She loved her piano, she could play for hours, the classics of her day - Black & White Rag, Nola, Tea for Two... all rolled into each other without a stop. When I was little, I used to lie under the piano and listen as she played.

My sister-in-law claims that Mother studied at the Conservatorium, but I don't know about that. She wasn't a concert pianist, but she loved the classics.

In the 70s when I lived at OB Flat, Dale Cleves the local Mount Gambier music man, had famous concert pianists come to his lounge room to give a concert to a handful of music teachers and Mum and I were privileged to be included.

She loved our piano and once loaned it to Winifred Attwell[7] for use in a concert in Mount Gambier. It was returned with a chunk out of it, and Mother vowed she would never loan her piano again..."

Alma grew into a clever, confident young woman, with a strong sense of responsibility, and it seems distaste for those who avoided their obligations. Aged 16 she was travelling in Melbourne on a tram when she recognised a man sitting opposite to her. "Are you John Joseph Duncan?" she inquired and on receiving confirmation of his identity she said..."Well I'm your daughter". The result of this confrontation is not recorded but her father played no further role in her life.

In her twenty-first year Alma's own sense of duty would be sorely tested. On her birthday she married Albert McPherson, however this happy occasion was somewhat complicated by other events. Her mother Gertie had fallen pregnant to a man named Cecil Goodson and late in 1926 she was delivered of a son whom she named Mervyn Cecil Goodson. Sadly, 8 months after Mervyn's birth Gertie died. The baby's father Cecil Goodson was conspicuous by his absence and Alma and Albert determined that they would raise the child as their own. So, after a 3-day honeymoon the couple returned home to Port Melbourne and baby Mervyn.

Alma and Albert soon had children of their own. Kenneth Albert was born on the 14th of May 1929, Graham Wallace followed on the 20th of May 1934, and Margaret who became known as Mardi was born the 26th of April 1944. Mervyn's place in the McPherson family was never in doubt and he was always referred to as Mervyn McPherson, never as Mervyn Goodson. To all intent and purpose, he was the eldest son, and Mardi grew up referring to him as her "first brother".

Albert was a bad asthmatic, this condition preventing him from service in the Second World War. He was not a well-educated man, having left school at Grade 7, but he was good at figures and during the war this skill, along with his butchery knowledge, enabled him to gain employment in a variety of

---

[7] Winifred Attwell was a Trinidadian pianist who enjoyed great popularity in Britain and Australia from the 1950s with a series of boogie-woogie and ragtime hits.

managerial positions. Under Alma's tutorage he polished up his handwriting skills resulting in his handwriting style being very similar to hers. For a time, it seemed Melbourne would provide the McPherson family with excellent prospects, however when the war ended the opportunities previously opened to Albert evaporated. It was this lack of prospects that led him to move the family to Mount Gambier.

It is entirely likely that Albert had anticipated the new butcher shop's initial downturn in clientele, for he quickly set about introducing innovative methods to win back his share of the market. An early initiative was to introduce Saturday morning opening. Prior to this Mount Gambier butchers were closed on Saturday. This piece of ingenuity did not endear Albert to his competitors, including rival butcher and Mardi's future father-in-law Blinx Bawden.

In another first Albert refrigerated his shop window display, the first such window display in Mount Gambier. Mardi recalls her father's enterprise:

"He would change the window arrangements. In one there was a baby pig which he dressed in one of my sun dresses and had it sitting up in a little deck chair".

The estranged clientele soon returned, and the renewed business became known as A.H. McPherson and Son. Ken, the eldest of Albert and Alma's own children, provided the "son" part of the business title. Ken was just 16 years old when he undertook this role and his father expected much of him. The second son Graham was at the time attending Mount Gambier High School. He had aspirations in life that did not include working in the butcher shop, but when he left school, he too entered the business, working unhappily under his brother's direction. As Albert's popularity grew, he became known as 'Macco' and at Christmas time, in yet another initiative, he produced a "Macco Ham". The "ham" was in fact made of mutton, a cheaper meat than pork, however once cured many believed just as tasty as the more traditional pork variety. Duty assumes many guises, and in spite of the frenetic energy Albert applied to the business, as Mardi recalls her father still made time for the family:

"He would take my mother her cuppa at 6am after he had cooked breakfast for the boys and sent them off to work..."

Mardi also recalls her mother's support for her husband and sons:

"…she would go to the butcher shop in the morning, always well dressed, to help the boys out, take the money and give out the change at the cash register, with a friendly smile, and a little small talk. She ran errands for them, the bank etc. She gave this supportive role throughout her life…"

The cost of these seemingly minor duties was little more than time and effort. However, like every family the McPhersons had their moments of trial. When Mervyn was 16, he discovered that he was in fact a Goodson and not a McPherson. Enraged and disappointed, he ran away from home for a while, but when he came back Albert set him up in a butcher shop of his own on Mount Gambier's Lake Terrace East, a few doors west of the cemetery.

In July 1949, Mardi began her formal education at Mount Gambier's Wehl Street Primary School. She seemed to have had some initial difficulty adjusting to Infant School, but by the end of 1950 she appeared to have got the hang of it as her report card indicated:

"…Mardi has improved considerably since the last exam, and her marks this time were very good. Her drawings show artistic talent…"

Her parents took note of the reference to "artistic talent" and when she was old enough, she was enrolled in special art classes in the Mount Gambier Institute building.

South Australia's capital works program had been unable to keep up with the post war influx of "Baby Boomer" children and to cope with overwhelming enrolments the Wehl Street School was forced to use the nearby Lutheran Sunday School as temporary classroom accommodation. Six years later as a big "Grade Sixer", Mardi and her fellow Wehl Street students were transferred to a brand-new facility, the Reidy Park Primary School where she completed her primary schooling.

Mardi's secondary schooling was completed at the Mount Gambier High School where she was streamed into "B Class" studying English, French, Shorthand, Typing, History, Geography, Maths 1 and 2. "A Class" took Latin, French, Maths 1 and 2, Chemistry and Physics, and "C Class" studied Art. Given Mardi's aptitude for music and fine art, "B Class" seems a strange choice of subject, however perhaps with an eye to her future employment prospects she persisted. However, on reaching Year 10 it was clear that a pass Year 11 Maths was beyond her and with a Year 11 pass in mind, she dropped Year 10 Maths and took up Art. The problem with this decision was that Mardi was 3 years of study behind the students who had originally chosen "Class C" for their stream. Mardi would have to make up the deficit by completing Year 8, 9, 10 studies in Art all in one year...no mean feat if she could achieve it, before attempting Year 11. She completed Year 8 Art in the first term, Year 9 Art in the second term, and Year 10 and 11 in the third term. However, the overall effort proved to be too much and at first attempt at Year 10 she failed. Undeterred, she elected to repeat the year and was rewarded by the achievement of being Dux of the year. Aside from her studies there had been piano lessons with local musician Frank Roberts, Highland Dancing under the tutorage of local expert Bessie Naughton, Art lessons in the old Institute building, and in the winter, she played hockey. This extremely busy schedule took a greater toll than she had initially anticipated and having passed Year 10 in such an emphatic fashion, she had had enough of education and opted to leave school without attempting Year 11.

In 1959 this decision would have been seen as sound economic sense, after all, who ever heard of a rich artist, and there were considerable advantages in a young lady having at least some form of financial independence. So soon after leaving school Mardi became a job seeker and was successful in finding a position in local government:

"...I secured a job as tea girl/stenographer at The City of Mount Gambier, firstly with Mr F Sharley, Town Clerk until his retirement, then Mr F.S. Laurie, really a pleasure to work for, then came Mr D.H.M. Roeger - I became his Secretary and had my own office. All this in only four years..."

Mardi never completely lost her love of art:

"In 1960 while visiting friends in Melbourne with my mother, out of sheer boredom I made a little girl sit still while I drew her – her mother framed and hung that drawing..."

However, art remained little more than a creative hobby, pushed further aside when on that fateful day, she went water skiing ...

CHAPTER 3

They're changing guard at Buckingham Palace -
Christopher Robin went down with Alice.
Alice is marrying one of the guard.
"A soldier's life is terrible hard,"
Says Alice.[8]

Full Time Duty

MICK'S LASTING RECOLLECTION OF THE water ski lesson is that he was immediately smitten with Mardi McPherson and he soon asked her out on a date. That event resulted in a variety of somewhat barbed comments from Bawden family members once it was realised he was dating the daughter of the opposition butchery. Mardi on the other hand claims the initial attraction she had for Mick was that red Sunbeam Alpine sports car he drove at the time. In any event romance blossomed and the two were soon seen as an item. On the 19th of May 1962 they announced their engagement and married on the 18th of July 1964 in Mount Gambier's Saint Andrew's Presbyterian Church.

For the first 12 months of married life, Mick worked at the butcher shop, applied himself as a Platoon Commander in the CMF, played sport, and

---

[8] A.A. Milne, Buckingham Palace.

participated in a variety of social activities. Somehow, he had also found time to successfully study for another series of Army exams, this time for promotion to the rank of captain. It was a particularly exacting time. Mardi, however, found she had time on her hands.

Local government at that time precluded married women from its workforce and as a result, once she was married her employment was terminated. Unfair…of course but that was just the way things were at that time. A second income would have been handy for the newly married couple, but that would have meant no marriage and living in sin, a practice that was frowned on in the early sixties. On the positive side however, redundancy enabled Mardi to further her musical studies and she began to study with local musical entrepreneur Dale Cleves.

At this time Mick's military career began to flourish. Promotion to the rank of captain came on the 9th of October 1964 and with it the responsibilities that accompanied appointment as the second-in-command of the Mount Gambier based Rifle Company. He received a brief congratulatory letter from the regimental colonel, Colonel R.A. Blackmore:

"Dear Mick.

I was very pleased to hear that you have been promoted Substantive Captain. Congratulations – this is a credit to you.

I look to you to be of all possible assistance to your Company Commander. Make it your business to master every detail of Company administration as soon as you can…"

Colonel Blackmore need not have worried…Mick was right into the role. However, he was becoming increasingly dissatisfied in his civilian occupation and by mid-1965 he had begun to actively consider alternative employment.

His timing was opportune. In September 1965 the position of adjutant with 10 RSAR became vacant. This position was a Regular Army posting and normally held by a captain, but because of the Vietnam War, the Regular Army had a shortage of suitable officers. As a result, in order to fill the 10 RSAR vacancy, the position was made available to CMF officers who were able to complete a period of Full Time Duty. Under the *Defence Act 1903*, a member of the CMF could make a voluntary undertaking to serve on a full-time basis for an agreed period and are accepted by the Army[9]. Mick recalls what was to be a life changing conversation with the Commander of Central Command, Brigadier Bleechmore:

"Brigadier Bleechmore raised the possibility of me doing the Adjutant 10 RSAR job. He said that a selection process would take place. I agreed to do the selection procedure and was successful".

Mick was extremely pleased with his appointment, but it was a big step for him and for his young wife. As Mardi recalls:

*"Mick was never happy being a butcher and working for his father, although I imagine Blinx (*Mick's father*) had in mind leaving him the business when he retired. However even then I believe Mick's ultimate plan was to become a farmer.*

I was excited by the notion of becoming an Army wife and thrilled to be exploring new territory. Having been born in Melbourne my school holidays were spent there with my lovely aunties and old family friends. Adelaide seemed to be a bit of a frontier town, right out of my comfort zone and I felt ready for the adventure of going to live there.

*Macco (*Mardi's father*) was quite supportive of the plan and saw it as part of our growing up, and he believed it would enable Mick to find his own feet away from the sheltered life living under the guard of his parents. I just had to tag along. I don't think either Macco or I for that matter, considered all of the implications involved with the idea, but in any case, he suggested that Mick should get a "safe" job in the Army…"*

Other advice and support were forthcoming particularly from A Company's Regular Army Cadre Warrant Officer Ray Baldwin. Ray recognised that Mick's enthusiasm for Army life would probably enable the young captain to succeed in the offered position and he urged him to apply.

Ray Baldwin[10] was a very experienced soldier. Prior to World War Two he had served in the militia as a member of the 48th Battalion. When war was declared he enlisted in the 2/27th Battalion AIF and deployed with that Battalion to the Middle East. Whilst in Syria the Battalion took part in

---

[9] Department of Veteran Affairs, compensation and support.
[10] Ray Baldwin was awarded the Medal of the Order of Australia in 2009. He died in December 2014 at the age of 93.

operations against Vichy French forces which included elements of the French Foreign Legion.

In March 1942 the Battalion returned to Australia, and in August of that year deployed to Papua New Guinea to fight the Japanese. During the fighting withdrawal along the Kokoda Track, at the village of Efogi, Ray and 13 of his mates were cut off from the main Australian force, and for the next 14 days, they attempted to return to their own lines. During that time the group was without food or shelter and were in constant danger from the Japanese. By the time they achieved a marry-up with the Australians, Ray was quite unwell.

After a short period recuperating, Ray was seconded to Chaforce, an ad hoc unit that was to have been deployed in counter attack missions. In November 1942, he was re-united with the 2/27th Battalion, and whilst taking part in one of the assaults on the heavily fortified Japanese positions at Gona, he was wounded and evacuated to Port Moresby for medical treatment. Later he served in the Markham and Ramu Valley campaigns. After the New Guinea campaigns, he fought at Balikpapan, and Borneo, before returning to Australia in November 1945 when he was discharged.

Ray found returning to civilian life difficult, and after several jobs, in May 1946 he enlisted in the fledgling Australian Regular Army. One of his first tasks was to escort German and Italian prisoners of war back to their home countries. Promotion followed and a tour of Malaya with the 2nd Battalion Royal Australia Regiment (2 RAR). In 1963 he was promoted to the rank of Warrant Officer Class Two and appointed as the Regular Army cadre instructor with CMF unit, A Company 1 RSAR, at Mount Gambier.

Ray was one of those Regular Army soldiers who did not look on his part-time comrades of the militia and later the CMF, with disdain. As a result, he was particularly successful in this role. The friendship and mutual respect that quickly developed between Ray Baldwin and the younger Mick Bawden was enduring, and Ray's influence on Mick…profound. Mick Bawden recalls:

"He was such a wonderful personality and good leader that he made soldiering fun. Ray's practical experience and skills were invaluable…"

Armed with Ray Baldwin's support, and with Macco's advice ringing in their ears, Mick and Mardi prepared for the move to Adelaide. It is difficult to overstate the enormity of that step. Mick was about to enter a world where the emphasis was not so much on having fun as a part-time soldier, but on performing an unfamiliar role as a professional Army officer. He knew there would be many, both CMF contemporaries and Regular Army associates, who would critically judge how he performed his duties as adjutant. Should he succeed there would be immense personal satisfaction and not a little kudos. Should he fail…the prospect of returning to Mount Gambier with his tail between his legs was not a pleasant one. Essentially though, it was all up to him.

Mardi faced a somewhat different world, one where she would be "of" the Army, but never part of it. This is the fate of every Army wife, and whilst some wives assume a status associated with her husband's rank and position, in reality the wives have no official standing within the organization. In the 1960's in many ways wives and children were given similar consideration to a soldier's baggage…items to be trundled along to whatever posting the soldier was assigned. So long as the wives accepted their lot in life everything would be fine. It would take some time for Mardi to fully experience this situation, but she got something of a hint as to what she might expect when Mick was sent to Adelaide without her and she was left to make the journey later:

"At almost every appointment Mick had, the Army sent him first and I followed later. I'm not sure if they did this because they hadn't organised a house for us, or if they just wanted to make the wives feel like stringers-on…I rather think it was the latter case and I must say they were rather good at it…"

The cost of duty is sometimes a bitter pill to swallow, however once the couple consolidated themselves in Adelaide, the Bawdens established a home in a Defence owned house in the suburb of Northfield opposite the local school. Defence housing at the time varied in quality from very good, to pretty awful, and the Northfield home was on the rougher side of the ledger. In its case the laundry floor had neither tile, nor linoleum covering, and the door had never been painted. Seeking to improve their home Mardi decided she would paint both the floor and the door. Unfortunately, after a short time the paint began to peel away in unsightly flakes. Add to this as a relatively new bride, Mardi was somewhat inexperienced in matters of domestic science as eh ruefully recalls:

"It was a learning experience, I was still only a child at that stage, I was about 21, and I hadn't actually lived in lots of houses. My mother had a house cleaner, so I didn't ever have to do any housework at home..."

Mardi's inexperience became a particular issue when boiling milk in their Northfield home. By trial and error, she discovered that if not carefully watched, the liquid would often boil over and seemingly disappear. Where the boiled over milk went was a complete mystery to her. The problem was solved at her first house inspection.

The Defence Housing authority had teams of officious inspectors who would assess the condition of the house at regular intervals, or when the client householder left for a new address. As Mardi recalls:

"We were only at that address a few months when we were moved to another house. As we prepared to leave the inspector came. He checked above the door frames to see if they had been dusted, and he looked at the windows, and for marks on the wall. He wasn't impressed by my housekeeping skills or by my paint work in the laundry, and then he got to the kitchen and pulled the stove to pieces..."

The problem of the vanishing milk was solved as a burnt and poisonous mass was revealed, hidden in the depths of the stove.

The young couple's next address was at 18 Joyce Avenue, in the suburb of Klemzig. This house was part of a new build with four homes sharing an area back-to-back. There was no garden of any kind, the houses seemingly grown out of the surrounding dirt. There was, however, a group of congenial neighbours, the Beales, the Raywards and the Butchers all with a direct connection to the Army. Patrick Beale was the adjutant of 27 RSAR another South Australian CMF unit. John Rayward was adjutant of the Adelaide University Regiment a CMF unit focused on university students. Chris Butcher had recently completed his studies in medicine courtesy of an Army undergraduate scheme, and he was serving out his return of service obligation[11]. The four families were of similar ages and strong friendships quickly developed.

These friendships were indeed opportune for Mick. He was acutely aware that in comparison to many Regular Army officers he lacked experience. However, he felt confident he could seek advice from these three friends. In this he found Patrick Beale's advice and support particularly valuable. The two became great friends, and in December 1965 when Patrick married his sweetheart Denise Trainer, Mick was Best Man at their wedding.

Patrick Beale was a brave, experienced, and astute soldier. He had previously served with the 3rd Battalion Royal Australian Regiment (3 RAR) during the Indonesian Confrontation of Malaysia and during that crisis he was awarded a Military Cross. The citation for that award read:

"Acting on unconfirmed intelligence Captain Beale led his Platoon through difficult, poorly mapped country to ambush a likely enemy supply route in the Bau district, Sarawak.

On May 25, 1965, leaving the remainder of his patrol in a defensive area, he led a small reconnaissance party of three men to establish the location of the ambush. During this reconnaissance which lasted for six hours, he had to avoid enemy parties heard in the area and thereby was prevented setting the ambush that day.

Together with 12 members of his patrol Captain Beale entered the same area on May 27 and successfully laid out the ambush, undaunted by the presence of the enemy in the area.

Shortly afterwards he ordered the ambush to open fire on a large enemy party approaching the area, killing at least 15 of the party. Having achieved this mission, Captain Beale coolly ordered the withdrawal of the ambush party, notwithstanding the heavy volume of enemy small arms' fire which was being directed at it, without loss".

Posted to the CMF Battalion 27 RSAR, a sister Battalion to 10 RSAR, Patrick Beale soon became Mick's unofficial mentor. Under his tutorage Mick quickly established himself in his position as adjutant 10 RSAR and

---

[11] The Army, having invested a considerable amount into an individual's academic or technical training, there is an expectation that the individual will serve a minimum period of time to repay the investment.

was soon busy supporting the city and regional based sub-units of the Battalion with their training programs, a task that was not without incident. Early in his tenure he accompanied his CO to attend a weekend training activity in the South East of South Australia. To save time in travel, a light aircraft was arranged to fly the two officers to the training area. A landing strip prepared the previous year by an ARA unit was utilized, but in the 12 months since its last use, the strip had fallen into disrepair. An extremely rough landing was experienced by Mick and his CO, and the two emerged from the aircraft shaken but relieved to be in one piece.

Mick's work was not limited to South Australia and the CMF. In 1966 along with two other Australian Army officers, he spent 6 weeks in Papua New Guinea as an observer to the Pacific Island Regiment (PIR). During this period Mardi was heavily pregnant with her first child, not perhaps the most opportune time for her husband to be absent. However, the issue was solved in the way of many an intelligent girl of the time…she went home to her mother in Mount Gambier.

Mick's work in New Guinea was part of an important Australian Government initiative. The Indonesian Confrontation of Malaysia continued, and Indonesian and Australian forces were still opposing one another in Borneo and on the Malayan peninsular. The Australian Government, at that time responsible for the protection and administration of Papua New Guinea (PNG), was concerned that Indonesian forces might infiltrate from Indonesian controlled West Papua into PNG. To counter this possibility, the PIR were engaged in patrolling the PNG border with Indonesian West Papua. These patrols provided an important aspect of Australia's international policy, but it also provided valuable experience for Mick and his two Australian companions. However not everything went to plan...

Traditional PNG society has practiced ritual payback a means of rough justice for real or imagined wrongs. "Justice" could be administered in the form of a bashing, but more commonly a transgressor would be killed. In an effort to avoid the tradition adversely impacting on the workings of the PIR, the Regiment tried to ensure soldiers from clans who were known to be seeking revenge on one another, were not posted to the same units. However, during Mick's time patrolling with the PIR, two soldiers from warring clans had accidentally been brought into close contact with one another. Before Mick's horrified gaze one of these soldiers delivered a massive blow to the other's head with his rifle butt, killing the man instantly. The offender was arrested and removed from the patrol, and in the inquest that followed, Mick was required to give evidence as a witness.

This tragic incident was a timely reminder of the frailty of life and the underlying violence of man. The cost of duty was beginning to reveal itself to Mick, and it was not confined to his military career, for while he was tramping through the wilds of New Guinea, Mardi gave birth to their son Byron. Mick missed the event and arrived back in South Australia in time to take Mardi and baby Byron back to Adelaide.[12]

The cost demanded by duty continued to rise. Throughout 1967 Mick found himself seconded to Regular Army exercises for 3 RAR prior to that Battalion's commitment to South Vietnam. Later he performed a similar function for the 8 RAR prior to its commitment in Malaysia. Each secondment lasted around 6 weeks, time apart that the young couple and their new born son could never retrieve.

Mick's role during these secondments was as an assessor. Attached to the exercising Company, the assessor's task was to observe the various aspects of Company training, and at the end of the exercise provide a detailed report regarding the unit's performance. This was an important role as an adverse report might well see an officer or soldier removed from the Battalion prior to its deployment. Mick felt some awkwardness with the task. A CMF officer assessing the performance of Regular Army troops might be expected to raise a few eyebrows among the ranks of the professional soldiers. Nevertheless, he managed to provide a positive contribution to the exercises on which he was employed. Little did he know that in a few short years he would find himself under similar scrutiny prior to his deployment to Vietnam.

As the adjutant of 10 RSAR, the bulk of Mick's duties while he was in Adelaide were not related to tactics and working in the field. Administrative responsibilities form a large part of an adjutant's role. It was during the

---

[12] 1966 proved to be a particularly busy time for the Army families of Joyce Avenue and its close surrounds. A total of seven boys, including one set of twins, were born to families living in the avenue.

pursuit of this side of his responsibilities that Mick discovered the RSM of 10 RSAR appeared to have been overlooked in the award of the Long Service and Good Conduct medal. The RSM position within a CMF unit was held by a Regular Army soldier, and at that time the 10 RSAR RSM was Warrant Officer First Class Percival.

Percival was a World War Two veteran, serving throughout the war with the 2/10th Battalion AIF, and then continuing his Army service after peace was declared. He was a gruff old fellow, but held in high esteem bordering on hero worship by all members of 10 RSAR. However, the time for RSM Percival to finally retire had come, and Mick was tasked to organize a parade to honour the occasion. It was during his preparation for the parade, that Mick discovered the discrepancy. The Long Service and Good Conduct medal was presented to soldiers who had completed a lengthy period of service and who had no record of misconduct. Mick felt that the parade presented an excellent opportunity to address what was clearly an administrative oversight. Mick's idea was generally supported within Battalion circles, but as the RSM had only weeks to serve, doubt was expressed that the medal could be issued in time. Mick appealed to those in Canberra who managed the issue of medals and awards, and after the situation was explained, Canberra agreed to fast track the issue of the RSM's medal.

Mick had also established the then Chief of the General Staff (CGS), General Daly, had served with RSM Percival during World War Two, when the two were in the 2/10th during the Syrian campaign. Determined to make Percival's retirement parade an event to be remembered, Mick pushed his luck and sent an invitation to the CGS to attend the parade and to present the medal to the RSM. The CGS graciously accepted the invitation and a triumphant Mick Bawden made the final arrangements for the parade.

On the day of the parade everything went according to plan. With due ceremony, the CGS called the RSM forward to be presented with the medal. Now, when a medal is presented, a small holder is attached to the shirt of the recipient. This holder enables the presenter to easily attach the medal without any embarrassing fumbles. The CGS attached the medal to the RSM's shirt but when the RSM stepped smartly back to salute…the medal fell off. The

CGS quickly recovered the situation by bending down and retrieving the fallen medal, handing it to the RSM who marched away. Save for this unusual moment, the parade went without a hitch.

It was only after the ceremony that one of General Daly's aides remarked it was a funny thing about the medal falling off, because in actual fact RSM Percival was not entitled to it. It transpired that during World War Two, the RSM had at some time, struck an officer and had been charged for the offence. As a result, he was not entitled to the medal. Canberra found out too late to prevent the award, and General Daly had no wish to embarrass an old comrade, so the presentation had gone ahead.

On another occasion, a situation arose that may well have had more serious consequences for the young adjutant. Mick had been invited to attend a mess function at the Adelaide University Regiment (AUR) at which the Minister for the Army, Malcolm Fraser was the guest of honour. AUR had at that time a mess tradition that any visitor to their mess should have their neck tie cut off with a pair of scissors, and then the visitor would be presented with a mess tie. The problem was no one thought to advise the Minister of this custom and before any explanation could be provided, the tie he was wearing was cut from his person and then passed around a gathering of young officers like some trophy of war. The Minister was not happy and while he accepted the mess tie, he left the mess soon afterward without saying goodnight. In the afterglow of the enactment of the AUR tradition, the actual wielder of the scissors was uncertain. Several candidates for this honour were nominated, a list which included (incorrectly) Mick, this nomination firmed when his friend John Rayward (the adjutant of AUR) jokingly congratulated Mick for the deed. However, the real culprit was never identified. The story quickly assumed fantastic proportions in the minds of the alcohol befuddled brains of the AUR junior subalterns and they ended the evening well satisfied with the turn of events.

The next morning, however, the situation took a turn for the worse. The Minister, still angry at the treatment he had been subjected to on the previous evening, had complained to the Commander of Central Command, Brigadier S.J. Bleechmore CBE, the most senior Army officer in South Australia. It seemed the Minister's anger stemmed from the fact that the tie cut from his neck, had been a gift from the President of France, Charles De Gaulle, and was therefore in the Minister's opinion, irreplaceable.

Sidney John Bleechmore was a very experienced officer. He had commenced his military career in 1933 as an officer cadet at the Royal Military College Duntroon, and he well understood the mischiefs that junior officers sometimes engaged in at mess functions. Under other circumstances he may well have ignored a "tradition" such as the AUR tie cutting, however an assault on the Minister for the Army could not be so easily overlooked. Even so, it would seem Bleechmore made no great effort to establish the identity of the Minister's assailant. He summoned Major Tony Gwynn Jones, the AUR Mess President and coldly advised him that an "abject letter of apology" might just restore what was, so far as those who had taken part in the episode were concerned, pretty mediocre military careers. The letter was written as required and no more was said through official channels.

There are two sequels to this story. The first occurred 2 years later in Vietnam when the Minister for the Army Malcolm Fraser made a visit to 9 RAR in the field. The CO of 9 RAR, who had heard of the neck tie cutting episode, with much amusement detailed Mick to host the Minister during his visit. Certain he would be recognised as one who had been present at the slaying of Charles De Gaulle's tie, a nervous Mick greeted the Minister as he stepped from the helicopter that delivered him to the 9 RAR position. However, if Fraser did recognise Mick, he gave no indication of having done so. Nor did he display any interest in meeting several 9 RAR soldiers who originated from his electorate. Mick was curtly advised the only person the Minister wished to speak to was the CO and that was that.

The second sequel took place some years later when Mick had left the Army and he was again brought face to face with Malcolm Fraser. By this time Fraser had risen to the dizzy heights of Prime Minister, lost an election and retired from politics. In Mick's case he had chosen a farmer's life instead of pursuing his military career. Like many men of the land in Victoria, Mick had become an active member of the Country Fire Authority (CFA) and in preparation for another bad fire season, he and his local CFA Brigade were taking part in a controlled fire brake burn along a busy road. Mick's job during the burn was that of a traffic controller and on seeing a car approaching the thick smoke generated by the burn, he stepped onto the road and ordered the car to stop. To his horror, grim faced and silent behind the steering wheel of the car was Malcolm Fraser. Mick prayed that smoke from the fire would swallow him up, but there was no need, for once again Fraser failed to recognise him. Thereafter Mick met Fraser on several occasions and Fraser never ever mentioned if he associated Mick with the necktie incident and Mick felt it would be inappropriate to raise the issue.

Aside from being an accessory after the fact to an assault upon a federal minister, Mick's tenure as 10 RSAR Adjutant was a productive time. Along with his day-to-day tasks and attending both CMF and Regular Army exercises, he attended professional development courses. A parachuting course was perhaps the most exacting of these, but Mick persisted and qualified, earning the right to wear the parachutist emblem on his uniform. Then late in 1967 he completed a Joint Warfare Course and a Ground Liaison Officers Course at the Airforce base Williamtown in New South Wales. Thus far duty had only demanded a relatively minor fee…short periods of absence from home…absence from the birth of his son, and a little discomfort when living rough in the bush, however that situation was about to change.

Late in 1967 he was granted a short service commission in the Regular Army and advised that in the following year he would be posted to the about to be raised 9th Battalion of the Royal Australian Regiment (9 RAR). For Mick and Mardi his acceptance into the Regular Army and a posting to a regular Battalion was an exciting prospect. First of all, it was confirmation that Mick's superiors believed he was doing a good job, a pleasing thought. There was also the slightly sobering knowledge that the new Battalion would be deployed to Vietnam, but in many ways, this actually added to the moment. Eagerly the couple awaited the new adventures they were sure the New Year would bring.

CHAPTER 4

"My army, O my army! The time I dreamed of comes!
I want to see your colours; I long to hear your drums!"[13]

The Regular Army

MICK'S OPPORTUNITY TO SERVE AS an officer in the Regular Army had not arisen by accident but was as a result of the Federal Government's decision to involve Australia in the Vietnam War. This decision had been generated by the fear of a rise of communism in South East Asia. This fear was fed by the Cold War contention known as the Domino Theory that postulated that should a communist government be established in one nation, communist takeovers would quickly follow in neighbouring states, each falling like a perfectly aligned row of dominos. Circumstances supporting this theory occurred in 1945 after the defeat of Japan and the French Government endeavoured to reclaim their former colonies in Indochina. The French return was strongly resisted by a communist backed organization known as the Viet Minh. This organization was led by Second World War Vietnamese resistance leader Ho Chi Minh. Under his leadership in 1950, the French were forced to concede that Vietnam would be governed by two separate administrations. In the north the Democratic Republic of Vietnam was

---

[13] Henry Lawson, My Army O My Army

recognised and supported by communist bloc nations such as Russia and China. In the south the State of Vietnam, an associated state in the French Union, was recognised and supported by the non-communist nations. The French continued to wage war against the Viet Minh until in 1954 at the Battle of Dien Bien Phu the French suffered a major defeat.

Following the Viet Minh victory, under the Geneva Accords of 1954, Vietnam was officially split on geographic lines, with the Democratic Republic of Vietnam in the north, and the State of Vietnam in the south. The Geneva Accord also imposed a deadline of July 1956 for the Governments of the two partitions to hold elections with the view of unifying the two into one nation. However, in 1955, following a series of political crises in the South in which the Prime Minister Ngo Dinh Diem deposed the President of the country and installed himself in the position, the situation took a new direction. Diem declared the South would not take part in the elections and as a result North Vietnam began a campaign of insurgency, subversion and sabotage aimed at toppling the Government of the South. This, it was claimed, was the living proof that the Domino Theory was valid.

In September 1957, President Diem visited Australia, a visit that received bi-partisan support in the Australian Federal Parliament. The visit was also enthusiastically supported by the Roman Catholic community. However, Diem's situation at home was rapidly deteriorating, and in 1962 he appealed to the United States of America and its allies for assistance in countering the growing insurgency.

The Americans first initiative was to deploy military advisers to South Vietnam. This action provided the North Vietnamese with a propaganda advantage as they were able to claim the South had become a "puppet' government of the Americans. To counter this assertion the Americans appealed to their allies to assist them with the provision of additional military support. Under the South East Asian Treaty Organization (SEATO) and Australian, New Zealand and United States (ANZUS) pact, the Australian Government agreed to involvement in the Vietnam War. As a result, between 1962 and 1972 Australia deployed almost 60,000 personnel to Vietnam, including ground troops, naval forces and air assets. In addition, large amounts of material were contributed to the war effort.

Prior to the Vietnam commitment, Australian troops had gained considerable experience in jungle warfare and counter insurgency operations in deployments to assist the British during the Malayan Emergency. The Malayan Emergency was a guerrilla war fought from 1948 until 1960. During that conflict Australian and other Commonwealth forces fought successfully against the Malayan National Liberation Army a guerrilla force, the military arm of the Malayan Communist Party, who were attempting to destabilise the newly independent Federation of Malaya.

As a result of Australian successes in Malaya, it was felt Australia could best contribute to the Vietnam situation by the provision of a team of advisers. To this end, the Government committed a team of thirty military advisers known as the Australian Army Training Team Vietnam (AATTV), or a shortened version of the title simply "the Team". The first members of the Team arrived in Vietnam in mid-1962. Warrant Officer Class Two Kevin Conway, a member of the AATTV, was killed on the 6th of July 1964, becoming Australia's first battle casualty of the war.

By the end of 1964, there were almost 200 Australian military personnel in South Vietnam, and it was clear this commitment was expected to increase. In November of that year the Australian Government introduced conscription in order to boost the size of the Army. All 20-year-old males were required to register for service, and for the duration of the scheme an annual "birthday ballot" was conducted. The ballot randomly selected those who were to be drafted into the Army for a period of 2 years' continuous service. After a period of initial training, the National Servicemen were allocated to various Corps across the Army including the Infantry. As a result, once the decision was made to commit Australian Infantry Battalions to the conflict, each Battalion contained a National Serviceman component.

It was in April 1965 that the Prime Minister Robert Menzies announced that following a request for additional military assistance to South Vietnam, and in consultation with the Americans, an infantry Battalion would be deployed to the war. The Prime Minister argued that a communist victory in South Vietnam posed a direct threat to Australia and the nation's national interests. Therefore, he concluded that an increased commitment to the Vietnam War was imperative.

The 1st Battalion Royal Australian Regiment (1 RAR) accompanied by a troop from 4th/9th Prince of Wales Light Horse (equipped with APCs) and some logistic personnel were the first to deploy, and throughout 1965 they undertook a series of operations in the Bien Hoa Province. 1 RAR deployment had highlighted the differences between Australian and American operational methods. The Americans fought a war of attrition relying on massive firepower, rapid mobility and the commitment of large numbers of troops in Search and Destroy operations. These tactics often resulted in heavy casualties on both sides.

On the other hand, the Australians emphasised patrolling, employing dispersed companies supported by artillery, APCs and helicopters. The Australian concept of operations was to separate the Viet Cong from the population and thereby slowly extending Government control.

The Americans saw Australian tactics as "pussy footing", the Australians saw the American tactics as foolhardy. As a result of these differences, it was subsequently agreed that future deployments of Australian combat forces would be undertaken in a discreet province where the Australians would be able to fight their own tactical war.

In April 1966 the 1st Australian Task Force was established in Phuoc Tuy Province based at Nui Dat. Phuoc Tuy Province was situated on the south coast of South Vietnam. The topography of the province included some hills and mountains, but the majority of the area was flat country with large sections of rainforest and rolling grasslands. The main industries in the province were the production of rice, and rubber. Access to the sea was via the port of Vung Tau.

The South Vietnamese Government administered Phuoc Tuy Province through the provincial capital of Ba Ria. However, when the first Australian troops deployed into the province the countryside beyond the capital was controlled by the Viet Cong. The communist forces had an extensive network of political and military organizations that penetrated every town and village. In addition, they had developed major bases in the province's mountainous areas and jungles. It was estimated that across the province the Viet Cong had approximately 5000 troops under arms. These troops were actively supported by many of the province's civilian population.

Eventually the Australian Task Force would consist of three Infantry Battalions, a squadron of armoured personnel carriers, a detachment of the Special Air Service Regiment (SASR), a squadron of Centurion tanks, a Regiment of field artillery, and various logistic supporting elements under the command of 1st Australian Logistic Support Group. A RAAF (Royal Australian Air Force) contingent including three squadrons – No. 35 Squadron flying Caribou ST OL transports, No. 9 Squadron flying UH-1 Iroquois helicopters and No. 2 Squadron flying Canberra bombers, were also deployed. The Royal Australian Navy also made a significant contribution consisting of a destroyer deployed on gun-line in a shore bombardment role, a helicopter flight, and a Clearance Diving Team. In addition, *HMAS Sydney*, an aircraft carrier converted to a troop-ship role, was deployed to convey the bulk of Australian ground troops to and from South Vietnam. Female members of the three services also served in South Vietnam, most at the 1st Australian Field Hospital which was established at Vung Tau as the Australian force expanded.

Such a commitment by such a relatively small nation as Australia placed considerable strain on its three services. The Army officer stream in particular was badly stretched, as existing training facilities could not produce the number of trained officers required. As a result, suitably qualified and experienced officers from the CMF were encouraged to fill the gaps. Mick Bawden, already serving on Full-Time Duty, was well qualified and in the right place at the right time.

CHAPTER 5

"...well trained soldiers can be brought to a state of readiness in quite a short time."[14]

Raising the New Battalion

1967 WAS A YEAR OF mixed fortunes for many Australians. Victorian and South Australian farmers and graziers were doing it tough in the face of a prolonged drought. In Tasmania massive bushfires impacted on the state's capital Hobart. Ronald Ryan became the last person to be hanged. The oral contraceptive pill received Government blessing. Aboriginal Australians received the right to be counted as citizens. The postcode system of addressing letters was introduced. Singer John Farnham's single "Sadie the Cleaning Lady" reached number one on the hit parade, as did the group The Seekers with their song "Georgie Girl".

Politically, the Government was beginning to face opposition to Australia's commitment in Vietnam. In January a visit to Australia by the Prime Minister of South Vietnam Nguyen Cao Ky was dogged by anti-war protestors, and in April the Roman Catholic bishops publicly declared their opposition to the war, a complete reversal of their 1957 stance.

---

[14] Extract of an interview with Major General Alan Morrison, AO, DSO, MBE, by Major Paul Rooney 1995.

There were other reasons for Australian public opinion to follow the Catholic bishops' lead and turn against the war. There was for instance, growing dissatisfaction at the lack of public consultation the Menzies Government took in making decisions about the conflict. There were also major objections being raised regarding National Service and the scheme's selective ballot based on birthdates. Many believed it would be fairer if all men in the target age group were called up. In addition, Australian casualties were beginning to rise and every night the television news brought the war into the average Australian's living room. To the shock of many, the war was nothing like the Hollywood portrayal of a battlefield and the public began to wonder if the war was winnable. However, in spite of this growing opposition to the war, a Morgan Gallop Poll conducted in May 1967, showed that 62% of the Australian population continued to support the nation's involvement in the conflict. Perhaps encouraged by the Morgan Poll, in October, new Prime Minister Harold Holt announced that Australia would increase its commitment to the war, with the addition of a third Infantry Battalion, and a tank squadron, bringing the number of troops on the ground to 1700.

The Government's decision to increase the number of Battalions in Vietnam to three presented the Army with a problem. To enable the existing Battalions to be rotated out of the war zone, and to allow them sufficient time to recuperate and retrain prior to redeployment to the war zone, an additional Infantry Battalion was required. As a result of this requirement the raising of the 9th Battalion Royal Australian Regiment (9 RAR) was ordered.

The new Battalion would be manned from ARA officers and soldiers drawn from resting Battalions, new recruit intakes from the Regular Army, and National Servicemen. To enable the Army rotation plan to be implemented it was imperative that 9 RAR was ready to deploy by December 1968. This requirement was to have a profound effect on the way the new Battalion would be trained. It also had a profound effect on the Bawden family.

History records that when the 9 RAR was raised at Keswick Barracks, Adelaide on the 13th of November 1967, the first man to arrive at the barracks was the Commanding Officer (CO), Lieutenant Colonel A.L. Morrison, MBE. However, this is not strictly correct. For while the CO may well have been the first man selected for the new Battalion, in fact the first member of the Battalion to actually arrive in location was Captain Mick Bawden.

When Mick received his posting order to 9 RAR in early October 1967, he had expected to remain as Adjutant 10 RSAR until the end of the year. However, this expectation received a shock when he was summoned to the Headquarters of Central Command at Keswick Barracks. On his arrival at the Headquarters, he was ushered into the office of a senior Central Command staff officer where his worst fears were confirmed. There had been a change in his posting. Mick's spirits plunged, only to be revived moments later when he was informed he was still going to 9 RAR, but a little sooner than he had expected. In fact, as of that moment his work at 10 RSAR was to cease, and forthwith he was now the Acting Adjutant of 9 RAR and he would commence work to raise the new Battalion. Mick was relieved, but he wondered at the suddenness of his new appointment, and why he had been selected for the job. A logical explanation was provided. The change in arrangements was purely expedient, an officer of appropriate rank was needed to commence raising the new Battalion, and as Mick was a captain, and already located in Adelaide, he was it.

With little idea as to how he was meant to accomplish such a feat, Mick made his exit from the Headquarters without asking the staff officer for further direction on the matter. He was, however, more than a little concerned as to what his next step would be. Mick Bawden:

"...Well, what does one do? How do you start raising a Battalion? Fortunately, there was plenty of advice and guidance available within the barracks, and so the mammoth task began..."

As it turned out the task was not as difficult as he had first feared. Under the guidance of several friends, he soon learned his main task was to indent for items of equipment that the new Battalion would require in order for it to begin to function. This list of requirements ranged from a variety of motor vehicles, to office furniture, and even pots and pans and other kitchen utensils. Feeling decidedly more confident Mick spent the next few weeks indenting for the new unit's equipment scale which slowly began to arrive at 9 RAR's temporary home at Keswick Barracks. Among the newly arrived vehicles was a brand-new HR Holden station wagon, and on the 13th

November Mick drove that vehicle to the Adelaide airport to meet the Battalion's CO.

Lieutenant Colonel Alan Lindsay Morrison, known throughout 9 RAR as "Alby", was a professional soldier who was widely acknowledged throughout infantry circles at that time as a man to watch for promotion. His reputation was founded on excellent man management skills, compassion, and a thorough knowledge and skill in all aspects of his chosen profession.

Born on the 15th of August 1927 to John and Eileen Morrison of Sydney, New South Wales, Alby Morrison was the couple's second of their three sons. He spent his early childhood in Sydney's inner western suburb Haberfield, but later the family moved to the seaside suburb of Bronte. He completed his education at Waverley College where he proved to be a keen student and an active participator in sports, particularly rugby union and body surfing at Bronte beach. He left school in 1944 and early the next year entered Royal Military College, Duntroon, from whence in December 1947, he graduated as an infantry officer.

Early the following year Morrison was posted to Japan to join the 66th Battalion, 34th Brigade, which was part of the British Commonwealth Occupation Force. At the end of World War Two, the Australian Government recognized that if the nation was to take a positive role in world affairs, it would need a regular army. However the Australian *Defence Act* severely limited the number of regular troops in peacetime, allowing only some garrison artillery units and a cadre staff to train the part-time militia. The Act was amended, and an "Interim Army" raised in order to meet Australia's international responsibilities. The 34th Brigade was the nucleus of the Interim Army and it was deployed as Australia's contribution to the British Commonwealth Occupation Force, while plans were enacted to enable the Australian Regular Army (ARA) to be raised.

The ARA officially came into being in September 1947, but it took time for the new army to be organized, and it was not until November 1948 that the restructure impacted on the 34th Brigade. For the 66th Battalion this resulted in a retitle to that of the 2nd Battalion, Royal Australian Regiment, and a return to Australia. Morrison returned to Australia with the Battalion, however, world affairs decreed that his stay in Australia was to be temporary.

In 1950 the Australian Government committed 3 RAR, as Australia's main land force deployed to the United Nation's forces in the Korean War. Keen to gain operational experience Morrison requested a transfer to 3 RAR and was soon posted to that unit as a Platoon Commander. The Battalion arrived in South Korea in late September 1950 as part of the 27th Commonwealth Brigade and took part in the United Nation's offensive into North Korea; and the subsequent withdrawal into South Korea that followed the Chinese offensive in the winter of 1950–51. For once Morrison's luck deserted him and he suffered a serious eye injury requiring his evacuation to hospital. After recovering, he worked in the British Commonwealth Occupation Force Headquarters in Japan and then the 28th Commonwealth Brigade's Headquarters until he returned to Australia in 1953. Morrison's work and enthusiasm during this time had been noted and he was appointed a Member of the Order of the British Empire for his "outstanding contribution to successful integration of all units" whilst a part of the staff headquarters in Korea.

Morrison was next posted to Cairns as the regular army adjutant to the 51st Battalion, Far North Queensland Regiment, a CMF unit. During that posting he met his future wife, Margaret, and in 1954 the couple married. They had two children: a son David[15] and a daughter Jenny. Aside from these domestic features Morrison's career continued to progress. He was posted as an instructor at Duntroon, and then later he attended the British Army Staff College in Surrey, England, as a student. Having successfully completed Staff College he spent the next 2 years on the military staff at Australia House in London. On his return to Australia, he was posted to 1 RAR (Pentropic) an experimental organization under the command of Colonel Sandy Pearson, first as the Operations Officer and later as the Battalion 2ic. From 1965, as a lieutenant colonel, he instructed at the Australian Army Staff College at Fort Queenscliff in Victoria. With such a wealth of regimental and staff experience he was an ideal choice for the position of CO of the Army's newest Infantry Battalion, 9 RAR. However, the appointment almost did not occur as Morrison somewhat ruefully recalled:

---

[15] David Morrison would follow in his father's footsteps as an Army officer and eventually appointment as Australia's Chief of Army.

"I had been posted in August 1967 to command 5 RAR and in October of that year the posting was changed; I was told that I was to raise and train 9 RAR for Vietnam. I was incensed. I rang the then Director of Infantry, Colonel David Thomson, and, I must say, I let fly and quite properly was told to calm down. I said, 'Why should I? I'll never get to Vietnam with 9 RAR'. He said, 'You'll be in Vietnam before 5 RAR gets there'. I said, 'But 9 RAR hasn't been raised'. He said, 'That's your problem'. I then felt quite humble having been so brutally outspoken..." [16]

New CO's can be extremely enthusiastic about their new command, and as a result unit officers are often cautious, even nervous, on meeting the "boss" for the first time. However, as Mick helped his new CO place his luggage in the staff car, any such feelings of insecurity he may have harboured were quickly swept aside, and the two men chatted amiably as they completed the journey from the airport back to Keswick Barracks.

The Adelaide press welcomed the new Battalion with a light-hearted article regarding the Battalion presence at Keswick Barracks. The headlined read: "NEW BATTALION ONLY 17 STRONG". Much was made of the fact that on the 16th of November 1967, the unit had only seven private soldiers. However, the new CO is quoted as responding, "Just you wait until we're up to our full strength..." The article also mentioned three South Australian officers who had already arrived at Keswick Barracks: Captain Bawden, Captain Presgrave and Second Lieutenant Bates.

Shortly after the CO had established himself in his Keswick Barracks office, he conducted a more formal meeting with his acting adjutant where he outlined his concept for the raising and training of the new Battalion. It was an impressive and challenging plan, aimed at enabling the Battalion's scheduled deployment to South Vietnam in November of 1968. However, in order to meet that deployment date, the Battalion had to be operationally ready by August 1968, a period of a little less than 9 months.

The CO's training directive had four key objectives which he explained in detail to Mick. The first of these was to assemble the Battalion's officers and

---

[16] Edited by Garth Pratten and Glyn Harper, <u>Still The Same Reflections on Active Service from Bardia to Baidoa</u>, (Army Doctrine Centre Headquarters Training Command, 1996) p 107.

men, weapons, stores and equipment at the Woodside army camp in the Adelaide Hills. This location was to be the Battalion's home once the current tenants 3 RAR, had deployed to Vietnam. The second objective was to conduct a rigorous individual training program for all ranks. Officers and men had to be physically fit as well as proficient in the use of their personal weapons and equipment. The third objective was to conduct collective training at Section (approximately ten men), Platoon (approximately 30 men), Company (approximately 100 men) and Battalion (approximately 800 men) level. This training was to be structured to present the nature of situations likely to be experienced in Vietnam. The fourth objective and by no means the least, was to develop a strong and binding 9 RAR spirit.

During the meeting the CO also addressed Mick's tenure as acting adjutant. He appreciated the work Mick was doing and announced his decision to confirm Mick as the adjutant. Years later, Morrison was to recall that his decision regarding Mick's appointment as adjutant was not well received:

"Mick was aghast, he wanted to lead soldiers and he prevailed on me to let him have a command. Finally, I agreed that he could lead the Mortar Platoon".[17]

In fact, there was a period of several weeks between Mick's appeal to be released from his administrative duties and the CO changing his mind. Eventually the Battalion secured the services of a senior captain, T.A. Gee who was appointed adjutant and Mick was able to focus his attention on the Mortar Platoon. However, during that interim period Acting Adjutant Captain Bawden had plenty to do.

From the moment the CO arrived in Adelaide, the tempo of work associated with the raising of the new unit dramatically increased. A small team of around 13 men had joined Mick in the management of the reception of newly marched-in officers and men, and in accounting and storing the ever-increasing amounts of stores and equipment. These men included the Quartermaster Captain Gerrans and the Regimental Quartermaster Sergeant WO2[18] Arthur Weaven. Both the human and the materiel assets of the

---

[17] Letter from Major General A.L. Morrison to Mick Bawden.
[18] Warrant Officer Class two

Battalion were first housed at Keswick Barracks until 3 RAR had deployed to South Vietnam. That milestone was reached in December 1967 and soon afterward those elements of 9 RAR who had arrived at Keswick Barracks began to relocate to their new home at Woodside.

During this period the ARA component and the stores and equipment of the new unit continued to arrive at a steady rate. The CO had been advised that he would be provided with a complete complement of officers, warrant officers and staff sergeants, 80% of his sergeants and 40% of his corporals. The situation regarding the sergeants and corporals was a further complication to an already complex plan to raise the Battalion. The additional sergeants and corporals required would have to be identified early in the raising process, from within the Battalion, and trained to enable the Battalion to continue to prepare for deployment.[19]

The 140 National Servicemen assigned to 9 RAR presented an even greater issue. They were not due to arrive until April 1968. The delay in the arrival of the National Servicemen presented the CO with an even greater complicating factor.

Under normal circumstances, prior to marching-in to a Battalion, the National Servicemen would have completed their Recruit Course at either Puckapunyal in Victoria, or Kapooka in New South Wales. Those destined for the infantry would then undertake their Corps training at the School of Infantry, which at that time was at Ingleburn in New South Wales. This meant that those National Servicemen destined for 9 RAR would not complete their Corps training until July 1968. Morrison knew that if he was to achieve his training objectives and deploy the Battalion to Vietnam by the due date, he simply did not have time to allow for this "normal" state of affairs to transpire. He asked for and was granted permission to adapt a radical training plan to meet his operational requirements. As a result, 9 RAR conducted Corps Training for its National Servicemen within unit lines at Woodside. Aside from the time saving aspect of this arrangement, it enabled the National Servicemen to be quickly integrated into Battalion life.

---

[19] Edited by Garth Pratten and Glen Harper, <u>Still The Same, Reflections on Active Service from Bardia to Baidoa (Army Doctrine Centre Headquarters Training Command, 1996)</u>.pp 107 – 108.

The integration of the National Servicemen into the Battalion was crucial, and the CO proudly recalled how his Battalion achieved this:

"I suppose one could imagine that there would be a 'them and us' attitude between the two, but this was never the case. National Servicemen marched into the unit just like regular soldiers. They received the same training. The only difference was that the National Servicemen had an obligation to serve for two years whereas the regular soldier was enlisted for a longer period. National Servicemen were in every part of the unit. In each Rifle Company I insisted on a balanced allocation between regulars and national servicemen and at no time could I tell the difference..."[20]

From early January 1968, so far as 9 RAR and its associated married families were concerned, all roads led to the Woodside Army Barracks. The barracks was established in 1927 and was then known as *Woodside Camp*. Located 27 kilometres (17 miles) east of Adelaide and consisting of 162 hectares (a little over 400 acres), the camp was initially used for the training of Militia units. Accommodation at that time was generally tented. However, with the outbreak of the Second World War single story barracks buildings were constructed with the capacity to accommodate up to four Infantry Battalions. At various stages of the war the 2/10th, 2/43rd and 2/48th Battalions of the Second Australian Imperial Force were accommodated at the camp. The base also continued to provide training facilities for Militia units and in 1942 temporary accommodation for elements of the United States Army's 32nd Infantry Division on its arrival in Australia. In 1949 the camp was converted into a refugee reception centre and could house up to 3000 people. The camp returned to military service in the early 1950s as a centre for training national servicemen. At the end of that national service program, it remained in operation as an Army facility, and prior to 9 RAR's tenure, at various times the camp had been home to 3 RAR and 4 RAR.

When the time came, the Bawdens left their new home in Klemzig and headed for a married quarter in Woodside's Lucknow Street. It was their third move in 2 years. Accommodation at Woodside was strictly ordered. Single men lived in basic barrack buildings that World War Two soldiers

---

[20] Opcit, p 118.

would probably have found familiar. Married couples occupied Defence Homes in the nearby enclave of Inverbrackie.

For the soldiers there was little time to worry about their living quarters for the training regime Alby Morrison established meant much of their time was spent away from Woodside, either on a course relative to their job, or on training exercises. It was different for the wives of the married men however, Lieutenant Colonel Morrison, hellbent on promoting Battalion unity and spirit, took an enlightened position to the importance of Army wives, and he later recalled this situation:

"I think it is incumbent on the unit to help families feel that they too, are part of the Battalion. Wives are good at achieving this unity by their willingness to help each other but they need encouragement and some support to undertake this important work. This happened in our case, led by my wife and the wives of the officers and sergeants. My experience has led me to devise this maxim: 'Look after the wives, and you can flog the men'."[21]

Mardi was swept up in the CO's scheme:

"Being with a Battalion and a founding member of a newly raised unit was a special honour, and in those heady days, preparing for service in Vietnam, our men were often away doing courses at Jungle Training Centre, Canungra, Shoalwater Bay and Cultana Training Area near Port Augusta in South Australia. The wives were busy settling into houses, tending children, digging gardens... we pretended to be busy".

It was during that settling in time, while Mick was still adjutant, that he became aware of a family situation regarding one of the newly marched-in men. Corporal Harry Musicka. Harry was a regular soldier aged 23 years and already a veteran of the Malayan Emergency. His brother, also a Regular Army man, had recently been critically wounded in Vietnam. On learning of this situation Mick approached Harry and suggested that under the circumstances his family had done enough for the nation. There would be, Mick argued, no shame if Harry was to accept a posting somewhere else in Australia. This suggestion, while well received, was flatly rejected. Harry saw deployment to Vietnam as part of his job as a professional soldier, he wanted to go. In the belief that he might be able to ensure Harry's safe return

---

[21] Opcit, p 114.

home, Mick proposed a compromise. As he was about to assume command of the Mortar Platoon, he suggested to Harry that he might like to join that Platoon. Under normal circumstances the Mortar Platoon fired their weapons from a firm base or defensive position, and thus was less likely to be exposed to direct enemy contact. In an evocative moment Harry agreed. Certain he had just achieved a good thing Mick followed this success by promising Harry's mother that he would look after her son.

The Mortar Platoon at that time, and possibly still is, one of the more complex Platoons within an Infantry Battalion. The Platoon was part of the Battalion's Support Company, in itself a complex organization, consisting of a Headquarters, the Mortar Platoon, a Signals Platoon, an Anti-Tank Platoon, an Assault Pioneer Platoon, and a Survey Platoon (tracker dogs).

The Mortar Platoon consisted of two officers, a captain and a lieutenant, and 39 Other Ranks. Its main armament during the Vietnam War era was six 81-millimetre mortars, but in theory the Platoon also had at its disposal five M60 General Purpose Machine Guns, plus the personal weapons of each member. In addition, the Platoon was well served with other equipment, including five ¾ ton vehicles (Land Rovers, that in Vietnam were often replaced by APCs), plus numerous radio sets.

The 81-millimetre mortar was a smooth-bore, muzzle-loading, high-angle-of-fire weapon used for long-range indirect fire support, across a Battalion's zone of influence. With a range of approximately 5650 metres, the mortar could fire high explosive, smoke and illumination rounds. Australian Battalions at the time had a complement of six mortars, employed in three sections of two mortars per section. Under normal circumstances each weapon was crewed by three soldiers, although in some situations five or six men might be assigned to each mortar. The weapon was capable of being man-packed, but its weight (35.3 kilo or 78 pounds) plus the need for additional soldiers to carry ammunition, made it preferable to move the weapons and ammunition by vehicle or helicopter. Supporting and managing the Mortar Sections required an additional structure within the Platoon, the Fire Control Centre Team and a team of Mortar Fire Controllers (MFC).

Each Rifle Company was assigned at least one MFC whose task it was to travel with the Company headquarters and call for and direct supporting fire from the Mortar Firing Line as required. To achieve this, the MFC needed to be a skilled navigator and wireless operator. Most MFC established a close working relationship with the Company to whom they were assigned, many being reluctant to work anywhere else.

The MFC calls for fire were directed by radio to the Fire Control Centre Team who ensured the details for each fire mission were quickly and accurately recorded and passed to the Mortar Firing Line as a fire control order. The 9 RAR Fire Control Centre Team generally consisted of the Platoon's two officers and eight other ranks including a Signaller and a Driver. This team was normally located close to the Mortar Firing Line.

Members of the 9 RAR Mortar Platoon were drawn from other RAR Battalions, some new enlistees and national servicemen. However, regardless of former skills and experience, for this complex organization to function, all of its members needed to be extremely well trained and confident in one another's abilities. As a result, for the first few months of the Battalion's existence members of the Platoon underwent a series of rigorous training courses. As the CO later recorded:

"Mick and his men spent almost three months at School of Infantry at Ingleburn in New South Wales learning about mortars. When they returned to Woodside, they showed what a fine team they were, one that was to prove very successful in South Vietnam ..."[22]

The Platoon was indeed a tightknit group when they returned to Woodside and when off-duty often played hard. Again, the CO recorded his impressions:

"They were a fine team in other ways. Their haunt off-duty in Adelaide was the Gresham Hotel...I never visited the place, but to this day I know the design and décor of the bar and surroundings – they were described to me by mortarmen as part of some heart-rending evidence that I heard in my Orderly Room. I hope the original members of the Mortar Platoon held a wake when the Gresham Hotel was demolished."[23]

Throughout their training Alby Morrison drove the Battalion hard. Basic sub-unit (up to Rifle Company strength) training was conducted in the Kuitpo

---

[22] Letter from Alby Morrison on the occasion of Mick's 40th birthday party.
[23] Opcit

State Forest (in the Mount Lofty Ranges), and the Humbug Scrub (north east of Adelaide). A brief pause in this program was called in late March while the soldiers prepared for an Inauguration Parade. The parade was conducted on the 29th of March, followed by a church service. The Guest of Honour for the parade was the Commander Central Command Brigadier S. J. Bleechmore CBE. Then with the pomp and ceremony of the parade over, and presumably with God's blessing, it was back to training for war.

Mick had not been present for the Inauguration Parade as he was in Ingleburn completing a Mortar Officer's course. By the time he returned to Woodside the Battalion was well on its way to achieving full strength. The senior officer appointments were now filled. The Company Commanders had been appointed, A Company - Major W. L. H. Smith; B Company – Major E. A. Chitham; C Company Major - L. J. Lewis; D Company – Major W. McDonald; Support Company – Major J.A. Sheldrick (who was also the Battalion Operations Officer); Administration Company – Major J. M. Stewart. The Battalion Second-in-Command (2ic) was Major D. B. Anstey.

Within days of the Inauguration Parade a series of training exercises at Battalion level were conducted at Cultana, a military training area approximately 370 kilometres north west of Adelaide, close to the Upper Spencer Gulf between Port Augusta and Whyalla. The first of these exercises held in April 1968, focused on infantry minor tactics and counter insurgency operations. Communications proved to be an issue during this exercise. Radio communications were greatly improved since the days of World War Two and even the Korean War, but had yet to approach the level of personal communications achieved for Allied forces deployed in Afghanistan. As a result, while 9 RAR trained, hand signals, known in the Army as "field signals" were the main form of communicating between individuals. This was fine in daylight, but clearly the method was severely limited in darkness. As the Battalion struggled with this issue the idea of using toy tin "clickers" was proposed and adopted with varying degrees of success. On one occasion during the exercise, the 2ic of C Company Captain Lew Tizard, a cultured Englishman who had migrated to Australia, was asked repeatedly where he was located and he finally replied haughtily, "I'm holding onto this bloody clicker, you cretin, can't you hear it?"

The Battalion returned to the area in July the same year for combined operations training, which involved the application of air support, armour (APCs), artillery, and of course the Battalion's own mortars. Other training, particularly "live fire" training was conducted at the large Murray Bridge Training area.

Aside from unit, sub-unit and individual training, the specialist Platoons including the Mortar Platoon continued their training. Mortar Platoon was for a time hampered by a lack of 81mm ammunition, but this was overcome through the use of 3-inch mortar ammunition. The 3-inch mortar was no longer in use in the Australian Army, but there remained stockpiles of 3-inch ammunition. This ammunition was slightly smaller than the 81mm projectiles and so it could be used in an 81mm mortar. There was some reduction in accuracy associated with this practise, but it enabled the Mortar Sections to conduct live fire practises: Mick recalls that innovative training with some pride:

"We were able to carry out diverge and converge firing practices with the line of six mortars. It worked pretty well we could observe our fall of shot out to say about 2000 metres, which is what we wanted and then do a convergence toward the target..."

Much of Mortar Platoon's live fire training was conducted at El Alamein training facility near Port Augusta, and then later at the then newly developed range complex at Murray Bridge. The Platoon also gained some Australia wide notoriety when it discovered an anomaly with the 81mm ammunition fuses. This fault with the fuses resulted in a significant number of "blinds" or failures to detonate when the 81mm mortars were fired. As Mick recalls:

"...I reported these defects to Major John Sheldrick who arranged for an Ammunition Technical Officer (ATO) to be sent from Gladstone to investigate the problem. This man, a Warrant Officer Class One, arrived at the mortar firing area or base plate position, and refused to believe that the rounds were faulty, and in fact said that we were not removing the safety pins before firing. Of course, this was not the case as we were very strict in our adherence to all safety procedures. So, I invited the ATO to observe some rounds being fired to see for himself. He then said that he wished to prepare and fire the rounds, I agreed that he could go ahead. Ten rounds were fired and only one exploded satisfactorily in the target area, much to

the dismay of the ATO. He then wished to go out into the impact area to inspect the unexploded rounds (known as blinds). The impact area was very stony and most of the rounds were laying on the surface, however the tailfins of two were visible and the ATO insisted on digging these two up and knocking the dirt off them with a spade before proceeding to examine them minutely. I might point out here that my training had expressly forbidden the touching of a blind let alone striking the thing with a shovel..."

The ATO survived, the issue was reported to the manufacturers and as a result 81mm fuses across the Army were withdrawn and replaced.

In addition to these home-based training activities the Battalion progressed to its pre-deployment training. As the John Schumann song "I was Only 19" states: *"We did Canungra and Shoalwater before we left"*, so it was for 9 RAR. All soldiers deploying to Vietnam, regardless of rank, Corps or trade were expected to attend pre-deployment training at Canungra's Jungle Training Centre (JTC)[24]. JTC had been originally established during World War Two to train Australian and American soldiers prior to their deployment to the South West Pacific theatre of the war. After the war, Canungra remained as an important training facility for troops deploying to Malaya and Borneo and later for the conflict in South Vietnam. In 1968 the JTC consisted of a Headquarters and four instructional wings – Battle Wing, Tactics Wing, Peace Administration Wing, and the Research and Development Wing[25].

During the Vietnam War, a major focus for Battle Wing was the Battle Efficiency Course which put the attending "students" through a series of field exercises: navigation, ambush, harbouring, countering vehicle ambushes, patrolling and shooting exercises such as sneaker and shooting galleries. The course also included the confidence course, rope training and a battle inoculation course. The instructional team for these courses were all veterans of at least one of the recent conflicts that had involved Australian troops. The training was exacting, and the instructors were unflinching in their desire to maintain the highest standards. Most soldiers who attended a Battle Wing

---

[24] Later renamed as the Land Warfare Centre.
[25] Booklet titled –A History of Kokoda Barracks Canungra 1942 – 2002, p 32.

course look back on the experience as a highlight of their careers. For example, Brigadier George Mansford AM (retired) recorded with pride his time as a Battle Wing student:

"The memories are still very clear of a Spartan, demanding life. Wet, exhausted, desperate for sleep, cold or hot, but never in between. The neverending barks of the instructors and our determination not to give in...One aspect is clear, for all masochists, Canungra was the home of soldiering and you wouldn't have missed it for quids."[26]

However not all attending units appreciated the instructors' methods. Some unit commanders felt their authority was being usurped by the Battle Wing instructors, and in one case, a doctor complained the course was too rough on his hands.[27]

9 RAR had few (if any) complaints. The CO 9 RAR fully appreciated the Battle Wing syllabus and the value Canungra training would have for his men. His positive attitude was noted by the Battle Wing Chief Instructor Lieutenant Colonel Ron Grey who recorded:

"Logically there was some resentment to Battle Wing assessing a subunit's basic military skills and readiness for war. Our job was to maintain standards regardless of background. The syllabus for all courses was approved by DMT. It was a requirement that reports on sub-units and units were submitted to DMT and Head of Corps. The support by units was generally good. An example of this was CO 9 RAR Alan Morrison, who provided excellent liaison and a good cadre but stood back and allowed us to get on with our job..."[28]

During the period May to July 1968 all of 9 RAR's companies rotated through Canungra's Battle Wing and its Battle Efficiency Course. For many of 9 RAR's soldiers, Canungra was their first encounter of a tropical jungle and most found it to be an educational and yet somewhat alarming experience. Mick's recollection of the jungle and Battle Wing is probably typical of many in the Battalion:

"Each Company was put through intensive training and fitness tests

---

[26] Opcit, p 36.
[27] Opcit p 40
[28] Opcit

before being finally tested in the "Wiangaree Walkabout". Support Company operated as a Rifle Company during its Canungra visit and we entered into the training with enthusiasm. Among the realistic training courses was the battle inoculation course which involved crawling under barbed wire entanglements whilst a Vickers Machine Gun fired overhead not from behind us, but from our front, while explosives were detonated alongside the hapless soldiers.

I shall never forget the sound of that machine gun firing as it didn't appear to be dangerous, in fact a totally different noise from in front of the muzzle compared with behind. Any soldier who has experienced the unpleasant sensation of being fired upon will know what I mean. It just doesn't seem as though those cracking noises could be harmful. Suffice to say that the Jungle Training Centre soon found any defects in the fitness of individuals as the program was extremely vigorous and even though it was located near the Gold Coast, it was very frosty in the mornings. It was often said that if you could endure Canungra, Vietnam will be easy. By the time we had completed the muscle toughening and confidence courses, the Company was certainly fit enough to take on the "Wiangaree Walkabout" with great confidence.

It was rather disconcerting upon arrival in the training area to be shown cages containing, among other things, a very large taipan snake and told with great delight by the instructor that its bite was almost always fatal. As if the snakes were not enough, there were plenty of "enemy" about and we went through various tests of our individual and collective reactions to situations that we could encounter later. I remember one night, while lying in ambush at the bottom of a deep gorge. I have never experienced a situation so dark, and crawling along a cord line to relieve those men in the ambush was very nerve racking, not knowing if the ground rose or dropped in front of you."[29]

Support Company completed its Canungra training successfully, but on spending their last night in the jungle, at first light the next morning the Company found it had one last exercise to complete. As Mick recalls:

---

[29] 9<u>th Battalion Royal Australian Regiment – Vietnam Tour of Duty 1968 – 1969 - On Active Service,</u> 9 RAR Association 1992, p 10.

"...the Company had to march out to the transport for movement from the exercise area back to Canungra. The march was very arduous and lasted through the morning, into the afternoon, to end at about 1500 hours when we finally reached the trucks. It was yet another test of fitness and the ability to keep going when every muscle in your body says, 'that's enough, let's stop'. I am sure most of the soldiers don't remember much about the truck trip back to Canungra as most slept..."

For the Battalion elements remaining in South Australia, having either completed Canungra or waiting their turn to do so, training continued unabated.

On the 4th of September the Battalion was airlifted in twelve Hercules aircraft flights to Rockhampton and from there in Caribou aircraft to Shoalwater Bay the scene for the final training exercises for units deploying to Vietnam. At Shoalwater Bay every aspect of a unit's conduct was examined and the exercise scenarios made as realistic as possible. Individuals who failed to meet the required standards of proficiency could find themselves transferred to a unit that was remaining in Australia, so these final exercises were approached with some tension. Fortunately for 9 RAR the exercise was completed to the satisfaction of the Directing Staff and the unit returned to Woodside certified ready to deploy.

Soon after the Battalion had returned to Woodside a Battalion parade was held, during which the unit was officially warned for overseas service. For the ill-informed this seems to be a superfluous activity for every member of the Battalion was under no illusion as to where the Battalion was bound. However, the parade and the warning had a particular purpose which was to provide any member of the unit with the opportunity to declare his objection to service in South Vietnam. The parading men were advised that any member with such an objection was at the conclusion of the parade, to seek an appointment with their Company Commander to register their objection. That done, the objecting member would be immediately posted out of the Battalion. This opportunity was provided to all, regular and national service soldiers alike. After the parade all members of the Battalion had their service book stamped "WARNED FOR OVERSEAS SERVICE". This warning and the opportunity to opt out gives the lie to anti-war supporters that soldiers, particularly National Servicemen were sent to Vietnam against their will[30].

The final realisation that their deployment to the war zone was imminent came on the 4th of October 1968 when the Battalion made a farewell march through Adelaide. They formed up in the city on the Torrens Training Depot parade ground, Mick Bawden's old stomping ground while he was with 10 RSAR, and then with a mounted police escort, the Battalion marched through the major streets of the city, past the Adelaide Town Hall where the salute was taken by reviewing officer Sir John Wilton KBE, CB. A photograph in the Battalion book, <u>9th Battalion Royal Australian Regiment, Vietnam Tour of Duty 1968 – 1969, On Active Service</u>, shows Support Company marching past the saluting dais. The John Schumann's song that so evocatively describes the 6th Battalion's farewell march might be applied to any of the Battalions that deployed to Vietnam:

> *"This clipping from the paper shows us young and strong and clean*
> *And there's me in me slouch hat with me SLR and greens…"*

Certainly the men of 9 RAR fitted that description to the tee. They were proud of bearing and not a little excited. Short weeks away, they would relieve 3 RAR and begin their own 12-month tour of duty in Vietnam.

---

[30] The media found this truth difficult to believe, and when 8 RAR was preparing to board *HMAS Sydney* for the voyage to Vietnam where they would relieve 9 RAR, reporters demanded access to any soldier being sent to Vietnam against his will. The CO of 8 RAR obtained permission from *Sydney's* captain for the reporters to board the ship to interview his troops. Further he declared that if any such soldier was discovered he would ensure that soldier would not sail with the Battalion, and that no punishment would follow. The reporters searched for hours but no objecting soldier was discovered. (Edited by Garth Pratten and Glyn Harper, <u>Still The Same Reflections on Active Service from Bardia to Baidoa</u> (Army Doctrine Centre Headquarters Training Command, 1996), p 119)

CHAPTER 6

Our brother's gone to Vietnam,
To fight there in the war
We didn't think we'd miss him much
He used to get us sore
But now we keenly wait for news,
Of all he's seen and done
His letters interest all of us,
He writes it's not all fun.[31]

Vietnam

"DUTY FIRST" THE PROUD MOTTO of the Royal Australian Regiment…while a few members of 9 RAR might have had misgivings about where they were to go, and what they were going to be asked to do, they were all determined to live up to this exacting dictum. As the time for their departure for the war drew closer there was pre-embarkation leave to be taken… a time when the members of the 9 RAR family lived life to the full. Many a young soldier determined to use his leave to sleep with his girlfriend before he deployed, others were too shy to try. There were others who spent their leave in a

---

[31] 5rar.asn.au/poems/our-brother-in-vietnam <u>Our Brother's Gone to Vietnam</u>, by Mrs M Everett, April 1967.

drunken haze, while many returned home to visit parents...perhaps for the last time. They all promised to write.

Mick and Mardi spent his final leave fulfilling a whirlwind of farewells to Mount Gambier based family and friends. On bidding so-long to his parents, his mother expressed her belief that he was born lucky and as a result she knew he would return...a comforting prediction. There was also a wedding to attend when Mick and Mardi's long term friend Sandy Haig married Helen Pick. Back in Adelaide they attended another nuptial ceremony this time when Harry Musicka the man Mick had persuaded to join the Mortar Platoon, married Kay, his childhood sweetheart and mother of their baby daughter Sandy. Mick, Mardi and the whole of the Mortar Platoon were invited to a dual ceremony...the wedding of the parents, and the christening of baby Sandy. Afterward the newly-weds were toasted and the baby's head well and truly dampened at a reception at the Oakbank Pub.

Those final days in Woodside were hectic indeed as the Battalion finalised its affairs. Mick had recently been appointed as a Justice of the Peace and his services in that capacity were in keen demand as soldiers arranged for Power of Attorney and other legal matters to cover their pending absence. Work parties were busy with equipment that had to be marked and packed ready for transport. Extra was packed...after all it was a long way to come back for something that was later found to be required.

As the day for final departure grew ever closer, many felt more and more aware of how precious their families were to them. Mardi recalls that time in their lives:

"I didn't have any anti-war feelings. I felt the boys were going to do a job, they were trained for it, and I could see they were excited and anticipating it. I was always confident that Mick would come home, but I didn't know about consequences. I think I believed if he wasn't shot or blown up everything would be fine.

It was a time when life was lived in the fast lane, crammed with every sensation and emotion extractable from living. One experienced a delirious appetite for fulfilment, because we simply didn't know what fate had in store for us.

I decided a pregnancy would be a good idea, it would give me something to look forward to, help to pass the time more quickly. I went to a doctor in Woodside, but he couldn't confirm my pregnancy until I was at six weeks, by which time Mick had left. How young and optimistic we all were...how very naïve."

The first 9 RAR group to depart Australia was the Advance Party. An advance party is a relatively small group of soldiers who go ahead of the main body of troops to prepare the way for their arrival. On the 4th of November 1968 the 9 RAR Advance Party of 150 officers and men left Adelaide on a QANTAS flight bound for South Vietnam. In commanded was Major J. Stewart, the Officer Commanding Administration Company. Other officers in this group included Major J.A. Sheldrick, the Battalion Operations Officer, Captain Rodney Curtis MC at the time the 2ic D Company, Captain Mick Bawden, the Officer Commanding Mortar Platoon, and a number of other officers, Non-Commissioned Officers and men from each of the Battalion's sub-units.

At the appointed hour the members of the Advance Party and their families, travelled by bus to the Adelaide airport for their last farewells. It was a sombre occasion, with the potential to deteriorate into a tearful, morale sapping, goodbye. However, the moment was saved when Anne Curtis, Rodney Curtis's wife, produced champagne from an ice filled plastic bucket, along with a variety of drinking vessels. As a result, at least some of the Advance Party was sent off in fine style. Even so as Mardi recalls the last farewells were gut wrenching:

"...the wine broke the tension and the boys left with fewer tears than there might have been...I was left with a feeling more like bewilderment...."

It was a lonely bus trip back to Woodside for the wives and families...the cost of duty was starting to bite.

The flight to South Vietnam required a brief stopover at Singapore and it was there the Advance Party experienced a minor piece of diplomatic theatre. Dress of the day for the 9 RAR men was polyester summer dress Number 2, consisting of slouch hat, polyester shirt and trousers with belt and black shoes. However, the Singapore Government did not support the war in Vietnam, and while it turned a blind eye to air traffic bound for that country, it insisted all military passengers were not in uniform. To meet this requirement the 9 RAR Advance Party members were required to be hatless and to don civilian shirts, providing a thin disguise as to their identity, and preserving "face" for their temporary hosts.

Diplomatic eccentricities were soon left behind and after a further 2-hour flight the 9 RAR Advance Party landed at the Tan Son Nhut airport in South Vietnam. At that time Tan Son Nhut airport was an important facility for both the U.S. Air Force and the Republic of Vietnam Air Force. Almost every conceivable type of aircraft operated from Tan Son Nhut: jet fighters, bombers, helicopters, transport aircraft, tiny Cessna light aircraft and large Boeing 707 passenger aircraft. It was reputed to be one of the busiest airports in the world with an aircraft take-off or landing occurring every minute.

For the newly arrived 9 RAR Advance Party, the heat, noise and activity was almost overwhelming. Shepherded into an empty aircraft bay and given a boxed meal to consume, they waited while local bureaucrats processed the necessary forms that countenanced their arrival in-country. It was a short wait, and they were quickly released to complete the journey to 1 Australian Task Force Base at Nui Dat. The final section of the journey was completed by air in a C123 aircraft. Mick recalls that flight with bemused amusement:

"The 'plane was a two-engine job, a poor man's Hercules, which for reasons I was never able to ascertain carried the Royal Thai Airforce markings. The passengers sat on the floor with a strap across the front of you to hold you down, rifles held between the knees. The Crew Chief in his pre-flight briefing told us there were only five parachutes on board. Should the plane get into trouble, he (the Crew Chief) had one parachute, the other three crew members had one each, which left one parachute for the passengers..."

No doubt the crew chief greeted all his newly arrived passengers with the same spiel.

The 9 RAR party was met at the tiny Nui Dat airfield by the CO of 3 RAR, Lieutenant Colonel Shelton, who with a twinkle in his eye, told the new arrivals how very pleased he was to see them. This was a standard greeting from the outgoing Battalion to the incoming Battalion, but in 3 RAR's case they had had an eventful tour and were particularly pleased to be going home. 3 RAR's first operation against the Viet Cong occurred in

January 1968, at the start of the Tet Offensive, which was a series of major communist attacks across South Vietnam, timed to coincide with the Lunar New Year (Tet). One of the cities penetrated by the attacking communists was Baria the provincial capital of Phuoc Tuy Province. Heavy fighting developed in the city and A Company 3 RAR was deployed to the city to assist hard pressed American and local forces. Overall, the Tet Offensive proved to be an expensive defeat for the communist forces. However, in America and Australia the attacks shook public confidence, fuelling anti-war sentiment, resulting in a public relations victory for the communists.

Subsequent operations undertaken by 3 RAR had seen the Battalion deploying in and out of Phuoc Tuy Province on mine clearing, counter mortar and rocket tasks as well as numerous reconnaissance-in-force operations. In May 1968, 3 RAR was heavily involved in the major battle of the Fire Support Bases, Coral and Balmoral. Over the period 26th to the 28th of May 1968, from a defensive position at Fire Support Base Balmoral, 3 RAR withstood two determined assaults by regimental sized units of the North Vietnamese Army. Throughout these and other operations during their tour, 3 RAR lost twenty-four men killed in action and ninety-three wounded in action. It is little wonder they looked forward to going home and so enthusiastically welcomed their relief.

Located in Phouc Tuy Province north of Baria the provincial capital, Nui Dat was the base for the First Australian Task Force (1ATF). At that time 1ATF consisted of approximately 4500 troops in a defensive perimeter around Luscombe Airfield. There were three Infantry Battalions (when 9 RAR Advance Party arrived this was 1 RAR, 3 RAR and 4 RAR), a Field Regiment including 161 Battery Royal New Zealand Artillery (16 RNZA) the battery which was to become 9 RAR's close support battery. There was also a squadron of Centurion tanks, a squadron of M113 Armoured Personnel Carriers, a Field Engineer Squadron, a Special Air Service (SAS) squadron, a reccie flight of Army Aviation and other supporting units. The whole base resembled a defended tent city. Permanent buildings were few and far between. Wherever the 9 RAR men looked they were confronted by large amounts of Marston Matting, a perforated steel mat designed for use as helicopter landing pads to prevent loose objects on the ground being thrown about by the helicopter down draft. However, all around Nui Dat, the mat was also employed as protection against rocket attack, and as an aid to movement in wet areas.

The accommodation, which was currently occupied by 3 RAR and which 9 RAR would soon inhabit, was set in a timbered area of the base. Suburbs of ageing canvas tents were nestled in the trees, each tent surrounded by sandbagged walls to provide a level of protection should an attack on the base take place. The 9 RAR Advance Party members were bunked in as far as possible with their 3 RAR opposite numbers. In Mick's case he was teamed up with the 3 RAR Mortar Platoon Commander, Captain Bluey Doyle. The two officers had met before and got on well.

There was a myriad of tasks to be undertaken by the Advance Party and dozens of issues to be checked and where necessary resolved before the handover of Battalions could be completed. Some of these tasks were administrative, others operational. Each representative section of 9 RAR were paired off with their opposite 3 RAR numbers. Mick's recollection of this period would have been common to the majority of the 9 RAR Advance Party:

"We only had two weeks before 3 RAR went home, and it was a matter of learn as much as you could from them in the short time available. They told us techniques peculiar to the terrain, the latest enemy tactics and methods of using some of the supporting weapons not previously seen by us. I was shown the 155mm self-propelled howitzer, a weapon we would use many times in support. It had a longer range than anything we had trained with and was computer controlled, and when used correctly, very accurate. I also took the opportunity to go in a 01 Cessna Bird Dog flight whilst an air strike on a suspected enemy position was carried out. This small aircraft was the most rudimentary flying machine I had ever seen. It had tandem seating, high wings thereby giving great visibility, and it could remain airborne for long periods of time. The air strike was controlled by the pilot of the 01 and he indicated the target by firing rockets with a white phosphorus war head. The rocket left a visible white smoke as well as an initial flash on detonation, providing an aiming point for the ground attack aircraft which orbited the target area.

The attack aircraft were F4 Phantoms and on that particular occasion they dropped 750lb bombs, and then strafed the area with cannon fire. After the attack the 01 circled the target for what seemed like hours while the pilot looked for signs of the enemy. My impressions of the air strike were heightened by the fact that in the humid air the shock waves of the explosions were actually visible as it spread rapidly out from the flash. This was something I'd not seen before..."

Mick was fortunate in his 3 RAR opposite number. Bluey Doyle was a little older than Mick and a very experienced mortar man. Besides sharing a tent, Mick accompanied Bluey and the 3 RAR mortars on several operations, observing their methods and procedures.

It was a policy at that time for major equipment items, such as trucks, APCs, and heavy weapons, such as field guns and mortars to be retained in-country and handed over to the incoming unit. These equipment items were only replaced if they became damaged beyond local repair. To enable "local repair", the Royal Australian Electrical and Mechanical Engineers had established the 101 Field Workshop a large facility capable of repairing anything from a wristwatch to a tank. The Workshop had a first class reputation for maintaining the Task Force equipment in an operational state. Even so, it was often a source of concern to incoming units that the equipment they were to inherit from the outgoing Battalion was in good condition. Mick was pleased to find that the 81mm mortars his Platoon was to receive from their 3 RAR brothers were in excellent condition. In addition, he found the mortar positions at the base were well sited and maintained.

During this time Mick led his first patrol in the war zone:

"...the patrol was mounted to give members of the 9 RAR Advance Party their first operational experience, and to allow 3 RAR some rest from their patrolling activities. I look back on that patrol as the culmination of all of my training. We laid an ambush in a dry rice field for the whole night watching a track that was frequently used by the Viet Cong to visit the village of Hoa Long. Mosquitoes made life difficult but except for two dogs, there was no activity in the ambush area. At first light we pulled in the mines and flares and returned to the Battalion area somewhat wiser and pleased that the first

patrol was over as it made one feel slightly less new to the operational world..."

While work was the primary focus of the Advance Party there was even time for a little sightseeing and Mick and his brother 9 RAR officer Rod Curtis decided to visit an ARVN Training camp that was situated close to Nui Dat:

"While we were at the Training Camp, Rod Curtis met this bloke McGee who had been in the Company Rod had been with in Borneo. Of course, we had to have a few drinks with him, and it turned out that McGee[32] was now stationed at Baria and he said to us 'why don't you come over have a meal, and stay the night?' I was a bit nervous about this and asked if we were allowed to go there, after all there were VC about and back in February, they had mounted a major attack at Baria. However, my concerns were ignored, and McGee and Curtis assured me everything would be fine.

So Rod and I jumped in our Land Rover and headed for Baria. It was a moonless, pitch dark night, and as we got close to where McGee lived, we found this barbed wire barrier across the road. Well, that wasn't going to deter us! We got out of our vehicle and shifted the thing out of the way. Then back into the vehicle and off we went again. I can only assume if the VC had been watching they were too amazed at our naivety to do anything about us.

McGee was a genial host. We had several more drinks and he had put on a barbeque for us. The meat was buffalo and as I received my helping the first thing I noticed was that prior to cooking the beast had not been skinned. There was this hairy hunk of hide covering one side of the meat, I thought it was bloody awful, but in retrospect it probably provided us with a unique kind of disposable plate.

Meanwhile back at Nui Dat there was general alarm and despondency. Two 9 RAR officers were missing and nobody knew where they were. Next morning when we arrived back at the base, we received a well-deserved ticking off and reminded we were in a war zone..."

Back in Australia on the 9th of November the Main Body of 9 RAR embarked on *HMAS Sydney* for the long sea voyage to Vietnam. There were many similarities with the departure of the Advance Party, with a mixture of

---

[32] Possibly WO1 G.F. McGee of the AATV.

excitement and sadness among the crowd of soldiers and their families at Adelaide's Outer Harbour.

The *Sydney* took 11 days to reach Vietnam. During the journey the Battalion celebrated its first birthday, and it became the first RAR Battalion to deploy before being presented with its regimental colours, an event that was addressed on the Battalion's return to Australia. On arrival at Vung Tau Harbour the *Sydney* anchored and the 9 RAR troops were ferried ashore in landing craft.

Trucks awaited them there for the road trip to the Task Force Base at Nui Dat. The convoy of vehicles to carry the troops was protected by a force mounted in APCs and commanded by Captain Mick Bawden.

With much justification Mick was particularly chuffed to be appointed OC Protection Force. After all, there were other more experienced officers in the Advance Party who might have been assigned the task. It was a huge responsibility, for it was not a task without risk. During the recent Tet Offensive communist forces had demonstrated their ability to strike deep into the Phuoc Tuy Province. Should a similar attack be repeated during the 9 RAR road move, Mick would be responsible for protecting around 700 of his 9 RAR comrades who were mounted on soft skinned vehicles and virtually unable to protect themselves. As Mick recalls:

"I had three M113 Armoured Personnel Carriers in which were mounted twenty-five soldiers for the job. My greatest concern was the possibility of the VC mining the road, closely followed by the fear of a sniper attack. There were a number of other possible scenarios that I had considered, but when it came right down to actually carrying out the job, I knew we would just have to wait and see what happened. The whole journey was about fifty miles, and involved crossing a bridge that had replaced one previously blown up by the enemy. The bridge was now guarded by Army of the Republic of Vietnam (ARVN) soldiers, but it was not unusual to see these guards asleep in hammocks as you went past...not a scene to fill you with confidence.

We had one anxious moment when a truck blew a tyre and until this could be replaced the whole convoy came to a halt. I recall being pretty tense..."

The road move to Nui Dat was completed without incident. Indeed, the journey took on an educational aspect for many in the Main Body, as the route took them through the city of Ba Ria. Bullet and rocket damaged buildings provided confirmation that they had arrived in a war zone.

With the convoy's human cargo safely delivered, the Protection Force made a return trip to the Vung Tau Harbour to escort a second convoy that carried the Battalion's stores and equipment that had been unloaded from the *Sydney*. Fortunately, that task too passed without incident.

The Advance Party, somewhat cockily, greeted the newly arrived and began to show them about. The little knowledge they had gained during the previous fortnight was trotted out at every opportunity, much to the chagrin of the rest of the Battalion. This situation was compounded by a particular administrative issue.

By the time the Main Body had arrived in country, the Advanced Party members had already qualified for their first campaign medal, the Australian Active Service Medal (AASM), awarded after one day in a war-like situation. The issue of eligibility for the AASM has been an issue for Australian Defence Force members since World War Two. During that conflict recruits from Tasmania who were required to travel to the mainland by ship were eligible for the medal, while those recruits who travelled the same distance by air were not. The burning issue of contention in that situation being that Japanese submarines were known to be operating in the seas around Australia, making sea travel " war-like" service. There were no Japanese aircraft in the Bass Strait area so therefore Australian air travel in the area did not entail the same risk and was therefore not counted as war-like. The AASM issue for 9 RAR did not assume this level of bureaucratic hair splitting, after all, following one day in Nui Dat the Main Body was on equal terms with their "veterans". However, early on in 9 RAR's tenure in Vietnam the Battalion newsletter titled "Sharp End Splinters" ran with the following article aimed at bringing the old soldiers of the Advance Party back into line:

"No real chronicle would be complete without a mark of respect and appreciation from the Main Body to our seasoned veterans, the Advance Party. How we love you! How we admire you, especially now you are wearing those great big medals. It must have been rugged sweating it out at

the swimming pool at Tan Son Nhut, braving the rigors of Saigon and enduring the services at its finest hotel..."[33]

3 RAR departed, their pleasure at being relieved was reinforced as the RAAF 9 Squadron helicopters showered the 9 RAR lines with leaflets welcoming the Battalion and reminding them *"...only 365 days to go."* At that moment it must have seemed like a lifetime away.

Over the next 12 months, 80% of the Battalion's time would be spent "outside the wire", that is time spent away from the relative safety of Nui Dat defences in the surrounding countryside and beyond. During that time the Battalion would undertake no fewer than twelve major operations. The nature of these operations included locating and destroying enemy forces, denying the enemy main force access to large installations, working closely with civilian authorities to isolate the enemy from the population, training local forces and protecting local communities.

It was to be a tiring and costly 12-month tour of duty.

---

[33] 9th Battalion Royal Australian Regiment Vietnam Tour of Duty 1968 – 1969, p 254.

CHAPTER 7

"We used every piece of information that we could find in order to get the feeling of what we were going into and I must say everyone in the Battalion felt the need to learn."[34]

A Learning Experience

THE CHANGEOVER OF BATTALIONS ACHIEVED, 9 RAR commenced to settle in and to familiarise itself with the new surroundings. A period of intense training followed for all companies, and as their CO, Alby , recalled the training that was greatly appreciated by all:

"All in all, we received some first class training when the unit arrived in South Vietnam and I was pleased and impressed at the thoroughness of the training offered us."[35]

During this training the Rifle Companies gained greater confidence in Mortar Platoon's ability to provide close support. Mick went on patrol with C Company to gain further experience in adjusting artillery and mortar fire in a close situation and was well pleased with the results his Platoon was able to achieve. In spite of this vote of confidence Mick had some personal doubts.

---

[34] Edited by Garth Pratten and Glen Harper, Still The Same, Reflections on Active Service from Bardia to Baidoa (Army Doctrine Centre Headquarters Training Command, 1996)., p 113.
[35] Opcit, p 113.

In November, in a letter to his brother-in-law, he revealed his struggle to come to terms with the war, and his concern for the future situations he knew he was sure to face:

"...I find it very easy to be that way (sentimental) I find myself missing Mardi and Byron just so much it hurts. They really are that precious to me...

...what a fascinating country this is, there is evidence of the war everywhere and the people appear to have learnt to live with it, after all they have had 24 years to learn to do just that. The towns are very battered and run down and this is obviously because people are not interested in beautification when the place could be destroyed by rockets or mortars the next day. I think that this is the most striking thing about the towns is their drab appearance. The country out from the towns is mostly jungle, but there are rubber plantations, rice growing areas and mountains as well. There is constant firing by artillery and mortars day and night, this of course is a little unnerving (to say the least) at first, however I am getting used to it, not of course when it's pointed our way. I don't suppose I'll ever get used to that.

There have been casualties here recently, but that again appears to be remote from you unless you are personally involved. Of course, we haven't mounted any major operations yet, but this will happen shortly, and one will then come face to face with all sorts of terrifying situations. I hope that I can handle myself properly, it is probably the thing that worries everyone, time alone will tell. I am sorry if I sound a little morbid but when I think of Mount Gambier and your happy safe situation, I feel that you are the only haven of sanity I can hang my hat on as it were. That sounds very confused I guess but I suppose I miss the Mount more than I care to admit and am essentially a country boy deep down. Life in the Mount I suppose was secure and had meaning and I believe a strong sense of right and wrong. I didn't adhere to that all of the time of course, but I do have a lot of reasons to be grateful for the well-ordered existence that you are still enjoying.

I have never seen so many aircraft in my whole life as you see here every day. They range from small helicopters to B52 heavy bombers which bomb the mountains near here as there are enemy camps located in them. There seems to be a constant stream of helicopters flying around and it is like flagging a taxi when you want to go somewhere by chopper. The accommodation is pretty good really, we live in tents which are protected by bags of sand 6 feet high all round them, this is for protection from rockets and mortars which the enemy use a lot. We have all Yank food, ham, turkey, pork, all frozen and pretty bloody awful really but then again one gets used to that too in the long run..."[36]

Mick was embarrassed by the tone of his letter and almost decided against sending it, however there was nothing unusual in the feelings he described, and the feelings were in fact just another cost of duty. Deployment is different from an exercise. On exercise a soldier and his or her family, experience separation and stress, however in the back of the minds of all involved is the comforting thought that an exercise is training. An operational deployment removes the "comfort" and replaces it with "uncertainty".

Thirty odd years later the Army Psychological Unit would describe the feelings expressed in Mick's letter as being typical of those experienced by a soldier early in a deployment...the stress at missing loved ones...cultural shock as the life at home is contrasted with the life of the locals...fear at letting one's mates down. Indeed, the soldier of today is encouraged to write home as the preferred means of addressing sensitive personal matters with loved ones, as it is considered committing one's thoughts to paper as the process allows a more rational, thoughtful and balanced communication[37]. Such feelings are yet another cost of duty.

9 RAR's first operation in Vietnam was code named Operation King Hit 1. This operation was purposely short, commencing on the 11th of December 1968 and ending the next day. Essentially it was a cordon and search operation focused on the village of Xa An Nhut, located south of Nui Dat on the road between the provincial capital Ba Ria and the district capital of Dat Do. The village was known to be a Viet Cong staging area and an important supply point for rice and other items required by the enemy. However, King Hit 1 was in reality a shakedown exercise, to introduce 9 RAR to the real thing.

For this operation it was decided that the Mortar Platoon would not be required, and that 9 RAR would limit its commitment to the Rifle

---

[36] Letter from Mick Bawden to Ken McPherson dated 21 November 1968.
[37] 1 Psychological Unit, Deployment Guide, printed July 2000.

Companies. The first stage of the operation was to establish a cordon around the village. After this had been successfully achieved the second phase, the search, commenced. King Hit 1 may have been a practice go, it was however a genuine operation. At some stage during the search phase, a Viet Cong (VC) soldier was discovered hiding in a large basket of rice. The enemy soldier attempted to resist and was shot and killed. During the remainder of the operation, over 1000 villagers were screened, and several VC suspects were detained.

Although short in duration King Hit 1 typified the Australian strategic approach to operations in South Vietnam. 1 ATF had determined that the war in Phuoc Tuy Province would be fought using classic counter insurgency techniques. This meant that generally Australian forces would engage the enemy in a series of contacts and small battles. When larger battles developed, for example at Fire Support Base Coral and Fire Support Base Balmoral, the Australians would employ the combined power of infantry, armour, artillery and aircraft to defeat the often numerically superior communist forces. The prime focus for 1 ATF was the security of the province's population, through the application of low intensity warfare.

With the Mortar Platoon effectively left out of battle, Mick was assigned temporary duty as a Liaison Officer to an American unit which was supporting a Vietnamese Regional Force unit based at the village of Long Dien. This village was close to where 9 RAR's cordon and search operation at the village of Xa An Nhut was taking place. His liaison task was to ensure an accidental clash between 9 RAR and the Americans or the Regional Forces was avoided.

Mick was met at the village by the US major commanding the local unit, and soon after his arrival the major took him on a familiarisation tour of the village and its surrounds. Mick's recollection of the liaison visit remains strong:

"The major had a roofless Jeep to which an angle iron structure had been welded to the front end. The structure had a kink in it so that it was set at head height, and its purpose was to defeat the Viet Cong practise of stringing a strand of wire across a roadway in an effort to decapitate the vehicle's driver. He called our rapid drive around his area of responsibility the "Rat

Patrol" and during our journey our speeding vehicle drew fire several times."

The visit provided Mick with a tough lesson as to the harshness of the war he had entered just a few short weeks previously. He was shocked to witness the Americans and their Regional Force comrades practise of summary arrest and imprisonment of members of the local population purely on suspicion of their contact with the enemy. After an attack or incident, the bodies of any dead Viet Cong would be displayed to enable locals to identify the dead, but the Americans would then arrest anyone who came to view or remove the bodies for burial. Mick was also shocked at the level of racism that existed among the American troops toward one another, for example their refusal to interact with soldiers of a different ethnicity. He was not unhappy to leave their company and return to 9 RAR.

Another harsh reality awaited Mick on his return to 9 RAR. The VC killed at Xa An Nhut, had been carried to an evacuation point by an M113 APC. The body had been placed in the space between the trim-vein and the hull of the vehicle. The trim-vein was designed to provide the vehicle with additional stability when crossing water obstacles. However, the trim-vein also provided a convenient space to carry some additional load, in this case the dead VC's body. Mick and the 2ic of A Company, Captain Dave Presgrave, viewed the body:

"The dead man was not a pretty sight. I remember Dave saying, 'well this is what we're here for,' and I replied, 'yes I suppose it is, but I don't like it very much.' He nodded, 'neither do I,' he said."

It was indeed a stark lesson in the cost of duty. The dead VC had paid the ultimate cost performing his duty. The two Australian officers were presented with a reminder that the business they were in dealt in death, and it might just as easily have been either of them that had paid a similar price to that of their dead enemy.

King Hit 1 was immediately followed by Operation King Hit 2. Like its predecessor, King Hit 2 was another shakedown operation, but with a change in focus away from cordon and search to Reconnaissance in Force. In addition, the operation was of considerably longer duration, commencing on the 12th of December and ending on Christmas Eve. King Hit 2 was conducted in the area known as Area of Operations (AO) Barossa, which was situated about 18 kilometres north of Nui Dat. 9 RAR's stated mission for this operation was to locate and destroy the enemy and his assets in the AO.

Lieutenant Colonel Morrison's plan was for B Company, mounted in APCs, to clear the road from Nui Dat to a Fire Support Base (FSB) known as FSB Avenger. The Company would then secure the FSB, whilst the majority of the Battalion, including Mortar Platoon, deployed by air to the FSB. Once the Battalion was consolidated in location, patrols would move out into the surrounding area. The patrols would be supported by the Battalion's mortars and if necessary, artillery and air assets. Designed as a final learning exercise for the new Battalion, King Hit 2 was to provide 9 RAR with some bitter lessons in the reality of war.

B Company were the recipients of the lesson, a harsh reminder that a cost of duty may well be injury. B Company's task was to clear Route 2, referred to locally as "Mine Alley". They were required to pay particular attention to the area from the village of Ap Ngai Giao and FSB Avenger. The Company was mounted in M113 APCs from A Squadron 3 Cavalry Regiment and supported by tanks from 4 Troop C Squadron 1 Armoured Regiment. At some stage of the journey an APC ran over a mine and an officer and a soldier were wounded but remained on duty. After this incident, B Company continued on to secure the FSB where they waited for the rest of the Battalion to arrive.[38]

Once the Battalion had consolidated at FSB Avenger a rigorous patrol program began. Intelligence reports suggested that the Battalion was likely to contact elements of the Chau Duc C41 District Company of the Viet Cong and to locate at least some of their base camps. This enemy unit was influencing the villages of Ap Ngai Giao, Xa Binh Ba and Ap Suoi Nghe to lay mines along Route 2.[39]

The Battalion had been provided additional support for the operation.

---

[38] Bruce Picken Fire Support Bases Vietnam, (Big Sky Publishing 2012) also 9 Battalion Royal Australian Regiment Vietnam Tour of Duty 1968 – 1969 Tour of Duty (9 RAR Association).
[39] Opcit

Under direct command of the Battalion were two Combat Engineer teams from 1 Field Squadron Royal Australian Engineers, this is to say that for all intent and purpose, these two teams were part of the Battalion for the period of the operation. In direct support of the Battalion were 161 Field Battery Royal New Zealand Artillery, 4 Troop C Squadron 1 Armoured Regiment, 3 Troop A Squadron 3 Cavalry Regiment and 161 (Independent) Reconnaissance Squadron. These elements were to provide priority of effort to the Battalion, but in theory, should a situation have developed elsewhere, and 9 RAR could temporarily afford to be without the support of these elements, they could have been redirected to provide temporary support to the new set of circumstances. In addition, the Battalion was supported by the RAAF's 9 Squadron, who flew Iroquois helicopters. This squadron was tasked to fly the main body of the Battalion to FSB Avenger. On completion of this task the Squadron's support ended and they then returned to their base for reassignment.[40]

For the patrolling phase of the operation, each Rifle Company was allotted its own AO, and within these territorial allocations they began to strenuously seek the local enemy forces. Success soon followed. A Company ambushed a party of 10 VC and whilst no bodies were found in the killing zone, many blood trails were later found and followed. In another ambush, B Company killed the second-in-command of the local VC Company, while D Company discovered a complex of VC camps which the 9 RAR Assault Pioneer Platoon destroyed with explosives.[41] During these contacts the Mortar Platoon provided invaluable fire support to the patrolling companies and it may be assumed that as a result further casualties were inflicted on the enemy.

Tragedy, however, was not far away. As Mick recalls:

"From the mortar position in the Fire Support Base we heard gunfire. Each type of weapon has a distinctive sound, and we were learning to tell sounds of our own weapons and that of the enemy's. On this occasion we judged the gunfire to be all Australian. The Support Company Commander, Major Sheldrick, was close by and I asked him what he thought was going

---

[40] Opcit
[41] Opcit

on. 'Mick,' he replied, 'that was a clash of friendly patrols, I hope to God we never hear another.' Tragically he was right. Two C Company patrols had clashed, each believing the other was VC. In the resulting exchange of fire, Private Ronald Gaffney was killed."

Duty had exacted its highest price. Ronald Gaffney was a National Serviceman from Mudgee in New South Wales. He volunteered for service in Vietnam and was posted to 9 RAR and allocated to 7 Section, 9 Platoon, C Company. Ronald had been in Vietnam for 34 days. He was 21 years of age and 9 RAR's first combat related death.

In spite of this tragedy King Hit 2 was acknowledged as a success, and on Christmas Eve the Battalion elements returned to Nui Dat, where they would remain until New Year's Day 1969. During this brief stand down period another tragic accident befell 9 RAR when a fire ravaged some of the tentage in D Company's lines, and 22-year-old Private Gary Archer was badly burned. Gary was evacuated to the US General Hospital in Tokyo where he died on the 4th of February 1969. Before being conscripted, Gary was a boot maker by trade. He was called up for National Service in 1968. Initially he was buried at Terendak in Malaysia, but following requests from his family, his remains were returned to Australia in 2016.

A subdued 9 RAR prepared for the next operation. The loss of two of their number so soon in the deployment was a shock, but it was also a sombre lesson that the performance of their duty in this place was going to involve bitter cost.

The hard fact, however, was that back in Australia the Battalion had trained for just this set of circumstances. Every member of the Battalion understood that once they were in the war zone casualties would occur. With their first casualties and the others that followed, good leadership and their training stood them in good stead. They grieved for their losses but got on with the task at hand. Aside from this situation in the war zone, the CO was mindful of the impact on the families of the Battalion's casualties:

"*The Vietnam War featured extensively in the press and the casualties were reported soon after they occurred. In our case this made our families very edgy. My wife, together with Army Welfare, took a leading role by calling on the families of our casualties. She found that difficult, but the bonding of families as part of the unit, was an important help when we were in Vietnam."* [42]

Indeed, for the 9 RAR wives at Woodside, life now assumed a lonelier more stressful path. Mardi and 2-year-old Byron remained at their Lucknow Street home where they faced a rather glum Christmas season. It had been somewhat of a hollow jest that while the Battalion had been in residence at Woodside, that the wives claimed they "pretended to be busy"…with their men gone and the news of casualties there was no such pretence. It was essential to be busy. Activity dispelled some of the loneliness and kept at bay some of the worry. Mardi threw herself into an assiduous round of social and domestic activities:

"I played tennis with the sergeants' wives; I went to yoga lessons. The colonel's wife taught us to play bridge. We needed to make friends and renew old acquaintances, since we had to spend the next twelve months together without our men.

I spent my private time drawing gum trees and writing letters to Mick. I wrote every day, and after my pregnancy was confirmed I used to include little drawings of my expanding waistline as a decoration to each letter.

Every Sunday I attended the Presbyterian Church in Woodside, and I gardened ferociously, rearranging the front garden by removing all the flower beds and making the front entirely lawn, which I mowed regularly…"

---

[42] Edited by Garth Pratten and Glen Harper, <u>Still The Same, Reflections on Active Service from Bardia to Baidoa (Army Doctrine Centre Headquarters Training Command, 1996)</u>. p 115

CHAPTER 8

If on one of these ops I'm KIA,
Shot full of metal out there in the "J";
I realize those, from this war, far away,
May pause briefly, and some may say;
What a tragedy he had to go that way.[43]

Operation GOODWOOD

WHILE 9 RAR HAD BEEN engaged on Operations King Hit 1 and 2, the other two 1 ATF Battalions, 1 RAR and 4/NZ RAR (ANZAC) had been engaged in the Battle of Hat Dich, code named Operation Goodwood. Since the 3rd of December 1968, these two Battalions supported by armour and artillery had been operating against suspected North Vietnamese and Viet Cong bases in the Hat Dich area, in western Phuoc Tuy, south-eastern Bien Hoa and south-western Long Khanh Provinces. It was feared the communist forces would attempt to conduct another offensive based on the season of Tet. Geographically the area was very rugged and included the hills of the Nui Thi Vai and Nui Dinh in the west of the Phuoc Tuy, and thick jungle that stretched north to the junction of Biên Hòa and Long Khánh Provinces. The whole area was known as the Hat Dich. In close proximity to Saigon and

---

[43] 5rar.asn.au/poems/soldiers-self-epitaph.htm A Soldier's Self-Epitaph.

important American and South Vietnamese bases, the Hat Dich was an important area for the Viet Cong.

As was the Australian practice, as soon as 1 RAR and 4/NZ RAR arrived in the area they began a sustained patrolling program throughout the Hat Dich district. Tracks and river systems were ambushed and as the operation progressed, a series of fire support bases were occupied. These operations were supported by American, South Vietnamese, and Thai forces operating in nearby areas as part of a division-sized action. Operation Goodwood was 1 RARs final operation before going home, and on New Year's Day 1969, that Battalion was withdrawn from the Operation, and replaced by 9 RAR.

On entering the AO, 9 RAR first occupied FSB Digger's Rest. It was immediately obvious that Operation Goodwood was no shakedown operation…this was the real thing. Digger's Rest was to be the Battalion's initial firm base for the operation, and as soon as the Battalion arrived there, Lieutenant Colonel Alby Morrison deployed a series of Company strength patrols across the AO. This patrolling activity continued throughout the month of January, and almost without exception, each day brought a series of contacts with small groups of Viet Cong. There would be on occasion, clashes with larger enemy groups of up to Platoon (around thirty people) and even Company strength (a hundred plus people). In addition, numerous bunker complexes and camps were discovered and destroyed.

It was at Digger's Rest that the Mortar Platoon established its firing position ready to provide fire support for the Battalion's patrols. Also in location was 161 Battery Royal New Zealand Artillery, the dedicated artillery fire support unit for the Battalion. The Battalion was also supported by a variety of air assets that could be called on as required. It was not long before all of these supporting elements were busily engaged. Mick recalls his time at Fire Support Base Digger's Rest with some distaste:

".. life in the FSB was a dirty, noisy business, with the incoming helicopters raising dust that covered everything. Guns and mortars fired large numbers of rounds, and in one case Mortar Platoon fired 328 rounds in one day. Everyone was tired and tense…"

As the tempo of the operation increased, so did the cost…duty was proving to be particularly demanding.

On the 5th of January at 1220 hours, 4 Platoon, B Company came in contact with a group of five Viet Cong. In the ensuing fire fight two of the Viet Cong were killed, but so was 4 Platoon's Platoon Sergeant, Jeffrey Duroux, killed by a bullet ricochet. Jeff was an Indigenous Australian, from Grafton New South Wales who had joined the Regular Army. A veteran of the Battle of Long Tan, his first tour of Vietnam had been with 6 RAR in 1966. On his return to Australia, he was promoted to the rank of sergeant and posted to 9 RAR as the Platoon Sergeant for 4 Platoon, B Company.[44]

At around the same time as the B Company contact, D Company discovered a Viet Cong base camp and in the resulting fire fight five members of the Company were wounded. Then at midday on the 6th of January, a section of 5 Platoon B Company was engaged by a claymore[45] like mine and small arms fire from a range of approximately 20 metres, killing one man instantly and wounding another five, one of whom would die of wounds the next day. Later, when the area where this ambush took place was being cleared, 9 RAR's Assault Pioneer Platoon discovered a complex bunker system containing a large cache of weapons and food.

The man killed was Private George Nagel. George was an Irishman, born in County Tipperary. In 1963, aged seventeen, he enlisted in the Irish Army and was allotted to the 12th Infantry Battalion. The following year he saw operational service as part of the Irish contingent with the United Nations Force in Cyprus. Following that deployment, he saw further overseas service again with the UN. However, in October 1966 George took a discharge from the Irish Army in favour of a new life in Australia. In August 1967 he enlisted in the Australian Regular Army and after basic training was allocated to 9 RAR and deployed to Vietnam as a member of 5 Platoon B Company.[46]

---

[44] rslvirtualwarmemorial.org.au
[45] The Claymore mine used by Australian and US Forces in Vietnam was a directional anti-personnel mine, it was a command-detonated and directional mine, meaning it could be aimed to cover a particular area of ground and fired by remote-control, shooting a pattern of metal balls at the enemy like a shotgun. The Claymore could also be used as a booby-trap fired by a trip wire. The lethal range of the mine was approximately100 metres in a 60 degree arc to the front of the device.
[46] freewebs.com

In this same action, Corporal Allan Graham was severely wounded. He was evacuated to the 1st Australian Field Hospital at Vung Tau, where he died of his wounds. Allan was a Regular Army soldier and at 22 years of age was already a veteran of the Malayan campaign where he had served with 4 RAR. Allan was transferred to 9 RAR on the new Battalion's raising. He was married and the couple had an infant son. Sadly, there was further tragedy to follow Allan's death, for on hearing the news of her husband's death Mrs Graham lost the will to live and soon died, leaving their infant son an orphan.[47]

Four days after this engagement, an intense fire fight developed when A Company discovered another large bunker system. The Company was fired on by heavy machine guns and one of the Platoons was pinned down. The Company Commander decided to conduct a flanking attack with his remaining two Platoons, supported by mortar and artillery fire.[48]

Prior to this attack, the Mortar Platoon had been in action providing fire on to targets that 9 RAR patrols had either seen or heard. However, this fire mission in support of the A Company attack had a more definite objective. Under the cover of combined mortar and artillery fire the remainder of A Company attacked with fixed bayonets. The battle continued for approximately 3 hours, with numerous calls being made for 9 RAR Mortar Platoon and 161st Battery RNZA for fire support. As evening approached, in the fading light the fighting drew to a close. A Company's attack was inconclusive and during the course of the engagement another Australian soldier had been killed. This was Private Thomas Meredith.[49]

Thomas Meredith a carpenter and joiner in civilian life in his hometown of Burwood New South Wales, was called up for National Service in February 1968, and posted to A Company, 9 RAR. War service and duty had had tragic consequences for the Meredith family. Thomas's father had been badly wounded during World War Two and died as a result of his war injuries, now his son Tom had also paid the supreme sacrifice.[50]

The following morning A Company with the additional support of

---

[47] sites.google.com/site/9rarsa/in-memoriam/graham-a-w
[48] awm.gov.au/cms_images
[49] 9th Battalion Royal Australian Regiment Vietnam Tour of Duty 1968 – 1969 (Published by the 9 RAR Association) pp 40 - 47.
[50] nashoaustralia.org.au/Honour20Roll

tanks, made another assault on the bunker system and found it abandoned.

Over the following days the Battalion's contacts continued, generally as short, savage fights, where survival for either side depended on shooting first. On the 13th of January, 8 Platoon of C Company 9 RAR made contact with two Viet Cong, killing one and capturing an AK47 and the pack from the other VC who fled the scene. Soon after that contact, B Company discovered an unoccupied camp and captured a variety of weapons and equipment including a 60 mm mortar and base plate. Then some hours later, A Company found a disused camp and bunker system, capturing a quantity of grenades and explosives. They also discovered eight bodies and it was concluded the dead had been killed during the battle that had taken place on the 10th of January.[51]

9 RAR's game of cat and mouse with the Viet Cong continued and late on the afternoon of the 16th of January, forty Viet Cong were sighted in a camp. The CO Alby Morrison ordered C Company to deploy by helicopter to a nearby area, there to set up an ambush to destroy any enemy attempting to flee the camp. He then engaged the enemy camp with artillery. Close to midnight approximately fifteen North Vietnamese soldiers carrying torches entered C Company's ambush killing ground. Five of these enemy soldiers were killed. At first light the next day, C Company entered the now abandoned enemy camp and discovered a number of enemy dead killed by artillery fire. Nothing else of note was discovered.[52]

During the afternoon of the 18th of January, 3 Platoon, A Company contacted another group of enemy and in the resulting action Private Reginald Phillips was fatally wounded and two of his comrades wounded. Reg was a 21-year-old National Serviceman from Murray Bridge in South Australia. In his short civilian life, he had been a mechanic. He was survived by his parents, two younger sisters, and his fiancée. [53]

The following morning, the situation in AO Wondai suddenly became more complex as all four of the Battalion's Rifle Companies and Support

---

[51] en.wikipedia.org/wiki/Battle_of_Hat_Dich
[52] 9th Battalion Royal Australian Regiment Vietnam Tour of Duty 1968 – 1969 (Published by the 9 RAR Association) pp 40 - 47
[53] sites.google.com/site/9rarsa/in-memoriam

Company were in heavy contact at the same time. The Mortar Platoon and 161 Battery engaged multiple and dispersed targets, the Mortar Platoon alone firing many hundreds of rounds in support of the patrols. During the course of the day, three more Australians were killed and five wounded when the Viet Cong fired Rocket Propelled Grenades into A Company's position. Those killed were Sergeant John Cock, Private Robert Key, and Private Arnold Sykes.

John Cock, was originally from Adelaide, a regular soldier he was 29 years of age and had been in Vietnam for 76 days. He was survived by his wife and parents.[54] Robert Key was from Melbourne, also a Regular Army soldier. He was 21 years old and had been in Vietnam for 64 days. Arnold Sykes was from Bunbury in Western Australia. He too was a Regular Army soldier and had been in Vietnam for 68 days. He was 25 years of age.[55]

B Company too suffered a fatal casualty on this day. Private Peter Smith was a member of Company Headquarters and following a successful ambush carried out by 6 Platoon, B Company, Peter had accompanied the Company Commander to visit the ambush site, when Peter was shot by a wounded Viet Cong, who was lying undiscovered in the jungle. Peter was a deeply religious man who was profoundly troubled by the prospect of taking human life, but in spite of his beliefs he was determined to perform his duty. He was 24 years old.[56]

That same day the Support Company suffered its first fatal casualty when Corporal Harry Musicka, a member of the Mortar Platoon, was accidently killed. Harry was born in Melbourne; the family had later moved to South Australia and in 1965 he was called up for National Service. On completing his obligation, Harry opted to sign on as a regular soldier and was posted to 9 RAR. Soon after his arrival at the Battalion his brother had been seriously wounded in Vietnam and as a result Mick had tried to talk Harry out of deployment to Vietnam. That recommendation had been rejected and by way of compromise Harry had agreed to a posting to the Mortar Platoon. Mick's

---

[54] Opcit
[55] vietnamroll.gov.au/VeteranDetails.aspx?VeteranId=1260582
[56] 9rarsa.com.au/wordpress/wp-content/-Roll-call-November-2011 p 4, article written by Michael Hauser a year 10 student at Sydney Boys High School.

well intended thought was that Harry would have been employed on the Mortar Line. However, Harry had instead become a Mortar Fire Controller, where his job was to move with patrols beyond the wire, where the danger was even more acute. At the time of his death, he was working with a patrol from the Battalion's Anti-Armour Platoon. He had been in Vietnam 68 days and was survived by his wife Kaye and 14-week-old baby daughter Sandy.[57]

The Mortar Platoon was devastated. It seemed so unfair that Harry Musicka of all people should be killed. He was a legend within the Platoon, most of them had been to his wedding and baby Sandy's christening. They had of course been saddened by the other deaths in the Battalion, but Harry's death shook them to the core. Mick still grieves this loss:

"The patrol Harry was working with were in a tense spot, and in the heat of the moment Harry was mistaken for an enemy soldier and shot. It was just so terribly sad and affected everyone in the Platoon. The impact is still with us today..."

Mick sent a message to the Battalion's rear headquarters back at Woodside, for Mardi to visit Kaye Musicka who at that time was living with Harry's family in suburban Adelaide. Mardi recalls a most difficult moment:

"I was 24 and hadn't confronted death before, besides I was 3 months pregnant and this was an exceptionally stressful situation I found myself in. I don't know how others coped in similar circumstances, but I found that I was overcome with a cool steadiness, detachment even... I performed the task in awe of the situation, as an onlooker, and not until it was done did the enormity of the meeting hit me and I wept. I cried for the cold, silent, angry mother, and I cried for Harry's warm, young, pale wife and their innocent child..."

In Vietnam the price of duty continued to rise. Late on the day after Harry Musicka's death, 10 Platoon, D Company contacted an enemy group and during this fire fight Private Bruce Plane was killed. Bruce was from Ardrossan in South Australia and in 1968 he was called up for National Service. He arrived in Vietnam as a reinforcement, and when 9 RAR had

---

[57] sites.google.com/site/9rarsa/in-memoriam, also 9th Battalion Royal Australian Regiment Vietnam Tour of Duty 1968 – 1969 (Published by the 9 RAR Association) pp 40 - 47

deployed on Operation Goodwood, he had remained at Nui Dat with the Reinforcement Holding Platoon. However, following the casualties suffered by D Company on the 5th of January, Bruce was called forward as a replacement. He had been in Vietnam 35 days.[58]

Intelligence reports and the general pattern of enemy activity seemed to suggest that the enemy was planning an attack against the township of Long Thanh. In an effort to counter this possibility, on the 29th of January 9 RAR was directed to extend its operations westward and to establish Fire Support Base Jenny. FSB Jenny would enable mortar and artillery support to be better provided to the patrolling Rifle Companies in the extended AO.

In establishing FSB Jenny, the defences at FSB Digger's Rest had to be dismantled and moved to the new FSB location. During the work to remove the stores a trip flare was accidently ignited, starting a grass fire. The fire burned for some hours, hindering the withdrawal process and by mid-afternoon it was clear not all of the stores would be moved before dark. The CO directed that the remaining stores were to be destroyed in situ to ensure the VC did not access them. To manage this task a Rear Party was established consisting of a Rifle Platoon, the Assault Pioneer Platoon, and a section of mortars. Mick was placed in command of this party and as he recalls:

"The rest of the Battalion and the artillery battery had left for the new fire support base, leaving around about seventy of us in the old base, and we set ourselves up in the field battery gun pits. There was talk of a North Vietnamese Regiment being at large in the area and I felt rather tense and exposed. And not without some cause, for that night while I was using a starlight scope to take a look at the surrounding area, I could see Viet Cong running along the trail. Then after I got over that shock one of the flares we had set up on the remaining wire was initiated. We were not attacked but it was a very stressful night.

The next morning the plan was for the Assault Pioneer Platoon, under their Platoon Commander Lieutenant Graham Dugdale, to position explosives on the veritable mountain of stuff to be destroyed, wire, misfired mortar bombs, artillery shells and so on, and then at the appointed hour to

---

[58] sites.google.com/site/9rarsa/in-memoriam

blow the lot up. The explosives were positioned and as the moment for the demolition drew near most of the rear party embarked in helicopters and flew to FSB Jenny. The last helicopter waited for Doug to light the fuse and then in an orderly fashion, he was expected to embark on the aircraft and fly away before the explosion occurred. Doug initiated the charge and made his way hurriedly to the waiting aircraft. However, before the helicopter could become airborne the demolition charges exploded in a flash of light and a deafening roar. The helicopter crew chief watched in horror as from the depths of the explosion a star picket flew through the air like a spear, barely missing the aircraft."

When the Rear Party alighted at FSB Jenny there were angry recriminations and Mick and Doug were on the receiving end of a severe ticking off.

FSB Jenny was far cleaner and a much more pleasant place than FSB Digger's Rest. FSB Jenny was located adjacent to the Mekong Delta and close to Route 15 which was the main road from Vung Tau to Saigon. Perhaps the most welcoming aspect of the FSB was the existence of some shade, an aspect of life that had been absent at FSB Digger's Rest. There was, however, one unwelcome factor, lying benignly in the soft earth was an unexploded 8-inch artillery round. During their occupation of FSB Jenny, 9 RAR chose to leave this projectile undisturbed.

The reported Viet Cong attack on Long Thanh failed to materialise, and after a time the majority of 9 RAR Rifle Companies returned to their original area of operations. However, the Mortar Platoon and the New Zealand artillery battery remained at FSB Jenny. For the Mortar Platoon, aside from providing fire support missions, they were also called on to fire on Viet Cong parties who were attempting to use boats to traverse the nearby waterways as they attempted to infiltrate the area. Mick recalls:

"An MFC had called in a fire mission on some boats and we decided to use proximity fuses[59] in mortar bombs which should have caused the bombs to detonate while in the air over the boats or sampans we were targeting. Now I'd never used proximity fuse before and I didn't know that if you fired

---

[59] A proximity fuse is a fuse that detonates the bomb automatically when the distance to the target becomes smaller than a predetermined value.

two mortar tubes together, that while the bomb was in flight the electronic device in the fuse could become confused by the nearness of the other projectile. If this happened the bomb would detonate. This is exactly what happened to us. Two tubes fired together and the next second there was one hell of a bang. Fortunately, the bombs had reached a height of about two hundred feet before they exploded, so luckily no one was hurt, but it certainly frightened us.

Of course, the solution was when using these fuses, to fire one tube at a time. However, we were getting bloody tired and I was worried that weariness combined with the tension and excitement of firing a mission, mistakes could be made and next time we might not be so lucky. So we stopped using proximity fuse..."

During their occupation at FSB Jenny, 9 RAR began to employ two Bell 47 Sioux helicopters in a combined reconnaissance and fire support control role. One aircraft would operate at low level, a little above tree height, and the other at a higher altitude. The Intelligence Officer (IO) Captain John Rayward was generally in the low flying aircraft and Mortar Platoon Commander Mick Bawden in the higher aircraft. The IO reported enemy sightings, and Mick controlled the fire support on to the target. It proved to be a successful arrangement.

Operation Goodwood still had a sting in its tail. Back in AO Wondai D Company found a bunker system occupied by a Platoon sized enemy force. A heavy fire fight developed, the enemy engaging D Company with small arms and RPG fire. D Company responded calling in mortar, artillery, air strikes and a helicopter light fire team. The battle lasted for over 5 hours, and six Australians were wounded. To evacuate the wounded a Dustoff helicopter was called for, but the enemy fire was so great that the helicopter pilot had to delay the mission until the enemy fire could be supressed. During this delay one of the wounded Lance Corporal Malcolm McConachy died. Malcolm was a Regular Army soldier, originally from Mount Isa, Queensland. He was 21 years of age.

Then on the 14th of February C Company contacted an enemy group who rapidly withdrew into the jungle. As the Company followed the fleeing enemy, they were engaged by machine gun, RPG and small arms fire. The

Company called for mortar, artillery support and a Light Fire Team helicopter. However, as the Company manoeuvred, five Australians were wounded including Lance Corporal Peter Chant. A Dustoff helicopter was called, but before it arrived Peter died of his wounds. Peter was originally from Rose Park in South Australia. He had joined the Regular Army in 1967 and after his initial training was posted to 9 RAR. He had become engaged to be married just prior to the Battalion's departure for Vietnam. He was 29 years of age.

9 RAR's part in Operation Goodwood ended on the 16th of February when the Battalion reassigned to a new operation. As Mick recalls:

"Goodwood was a hell of an operation for the Battalion, we lost a lot of men, but we handed out punishment too. In addition to the success the Rifle Companies achieved, between the Mortar Platoon and the New Zealand artillery battery with whom we shared the Fire Support Base, we fired thousands of rounds in support of our patrols."

Indeed, in terms of impact on the enemy Goodwood was highly successful. 9 RAR's constant patrolling, and the continued operations of 1 RAR and 4 RAR/NZ and the other supporting elements, had a significant impact on North Vietnamese and Viet Cong operations in the area. Their movement through Hat Dich had become a dangerous undertaking and their resupply system for weapons, ammunition and food had been severely disrupted. As a result, they were forced to find other routes and supply sources away from the patrolling Australians. That success had been at the cost of 13 members of the Battalion, killed in action, and the wounding of numerous others. In spite of this cost the members of 9 RAR maintained a steely resolve to perform their duty… back in Australia the bereaved families wondered if the loss of their loved ones was worth it.

CHAPTER 9

As a way to start the day, it's not much fun
A gentle nudge, a whispered word - "Stand-To!"
A short nap since your two hours on the gun
Just once you'd like to sleep the whole night through.[60]

A New Operation

THE BATTALION'S NEXT OPERATION WAS code named Federal. The mission for the new operation was to protect the major logistic support base at Long Binh against an anticipated renewed communist offensive for the 1969 celebration of the Lunar New Year or Tet. For this operation 9 RAR was deployed to AO Arunda.

The topography of AO Arunda was very different from AO Wondai, in that Arunda was characterised by open rice paddy, grassland and low yet dominant hillocks that were covered with secondary jungle growth. Secondary jungle growth occurs after the original growth has been disturbed, either by natural causes such as a storm or fire, or by man. Often the original growth remains on the jungle floor and new or secondary growth develops over and through this. The result is an almost impenetrable mass of vegetation.

---

[60] lachlanirvine.tripod.com/poetry/id19 Morning Stand To

Prior to the Battalion's move to AO Arunda, a new FSB area had been selected and named FSB Kerry. Mick was appointed to command an Advance Party to where FSB Kerry would be established. He was to plan the layout of the fire support base, and when the Battalion and its supporting elements arrived, he was to allocate them to specific areas. For the move to the new FSB the Advance Party was provided with a troop of APCs. There was a very tight schedule to achieve this, for later in the day the remainder of the Battalion would arrive at the new location by helicopter.

The Advance Party reached the site for the new FSB without incident, and on arrival Mick discovered one of the APC crewmen was popular singer, now National Serviceman, Normie Rowe. As a singer Rowe had quickly risen to national fame to become Australia's 1968 King of Pop. He had a number of big hits including "Que sera sera" and "It Aint Necessarily So". He was called up in February 1968 and after basic training was allocated to the Armoured Corps. He served in Vietnam with A Squadron 3 Cavalry Regiment. However, on the 17th of February 1969 Mick and Normie had no time to discuss popular music.

As Mick recalls, his initial inspection of the Battalion's new base filled him with concern:

"The area was as bare as a baby's bum, no grass, no trees anywhere near. I soon realised that at some stage the place had been used as a range by the Americans or maybe one of our own Battalions on a previous tour. There was unexploded ordnance all over the place, particularly anti-personnel mines. I couldn't pick the things up, but I tried to mark all of them so they could be easily seen. I was still worrying about how I could achieve this task when I heard the sound of approaching helicopters. It was C Company and as soon as they landed the Company Commander Major Laurie Lewis asked, 'Where do you want us, Mick?' I directed them to their area and before long the other companies and Battalion Headquarters arrived. Luckily no one was blown up. That place became Fire Support Base Kerry and we stayed there for two or three weeks over the Tet period."

Some war historians have a slightly different opinion regarding Fire Support Base Kerry describing the location as occupying spectacular views of the surrounding countryside, overlooking converging routes to Saigon. It was also noted that because of its proximity to these routes and the congestion of friendly forces in the area, there were often long delays in obtaining clearance to conduct fire missions. Operational Federal is also described in some publications as being less intensive, and limited to ambushing and patrolling, with none of the Australian fire support bases subjected to attack. However, in spite of these descriptions the operation was active enough for those who actually took part. As Mick recalls:

"The Viet Cong and North Vietnamese Army probed the position and buggered us around, particularly at night. So far as the Mortar Platoon was concerned, we did a lot of fire missions from there

I was particularly proud of the Mortar Platoon. During Operation Federal the Platoon had fired a total of 11,000 rounds, a reflection of the confidence the Rifle Companies had in our accuracy. The base plate crews under Corporals Geoff Rice, Gary Mallison and Bluey Moore were outstanding. MFC Sergeants Smiley Jenkins, Con Connellan, John Vautin and Corporal Norm Wolf were a credit to their training and their relationships with their respective Rifle Companies was excellent. The Mortar Command Post staff Corporal Bill Awcock, Signaller Dave Benford and Driver John Crawford were great to work with..."

Even though the number of contacts were less numerous than the previous operation, patrolling from Fire Support Base Kerry was just as stressful. C Company had the most notable successes at this time…on the 23rd of February the Company attacked and captured a bunker system, confirming that the enemy had an active presence in the AO. Then the next day a C Company ambush killed five Viet Cong and captured another. For those working within the FSB there was more good news of another kind as Mick recalls:

"Great news on 5 March, we were permitted to remove our shirts during the day! There is nothing worse than sleeves rolled down and a dirty shirt..."

This decree would be enough to make the OH&S conscious Army of today turn grey with fear as visions of sunburn and resulting skin cancer flash before their eyes. Not to mention the horror of malaria at the thought of the mosquitoes being provided with all that exposed skin to feast on. However, there is no doubt the relief offered by allowing the removal of shirts lessened, to a degree, the stress and fatigue the soldiers were suffering.

Stress and fatigue were contributing factors in the tragic death of Private Grantly Scales. On the night of the 6th of March, Grantly strayed outside the perimeter. Because of enemy probing activities 9 RAR sentries had been directed to assume all night-time movement outside the perimeter to be enemy. Grantly's movement was detected, a sentry fired and Grantly was killed. Grantly was a National Serviceman from Glandore in South Australia. He was 22 years of age.[61]

In addition to the Battalion's deaths, the cost was rising for the living... they were now exhausted. This is hardly surprising when one considers the situation faced by a soldier on patrol in the Vietnam bush. The Australian War Memorial provides a broad insight into the conditions faced:

"Each soldier carried an individual load of around 50 kilograms including, in the dry season, up to eight litres of water per man. They lived on combat rations for lengthy periods, receiving re-supplies of fresh food and water on average only once every five days. Movement on operations was generally continuous but often painstakingly slow for an average of seven and a half hours each day and frequently accompanied by the threat of enemy action or detonating enemy mines and booby traps. The resulting physical and mental fatigue was exacerbated by the need for continuous alertness and the manning of ambush positions by night. In these conditions the fitness of soldiers was no guarantee against illness and injury: skin disorders, heat rashes, infected cuts and abrasions, insect and reptile bites were frequent, along with sprains and strains, heat made necessary by the special circumstances of having to defend a fixed base and at the same time subdue trouble spots and seek out the enemy in his bases. The helicopter enabled the rapid transfer of units between areas, from one kind of operation to another, from defence to offence, from village to rainforest. The ability of units to respond to such pressures had much to do with the health and fitness of the men, and the relatively short tours of duty combined with the high quality and availability of medical backup. But a year of this was more than enough; troops were simply worn out..."[62]

---

[61] nashoaustralia.org.au also Vietnam Killed in Action amvif.com
[62] VOLUNTARY GUIDES BACKGROUNDER Number 05 Issue #4 - Part 2 of 2 January 2010 Vietnam War 1962-1975, awm.gov.au

On the 10th of March, 9 RAR was withdrawn from the operation[63] and returned to Nui Dat for well-earned rest. They had been in the field almost continuously for 99 days.[64] As Mick recalls the Battalion had a procedure they followed on arrival at Nui Dat:

"When we came back from an operation, the idea was you'd go to the range and use up all the ammunition you carried. You'd be issued with new ammunition before you went out again. After firing the ammunition down range, if you were due for leave, you might get a couple of days Recreation Leave in-country. After six months in-country you were entitled to one week's leave in a country of your choice. I think after Operation Federal, most of us got down to Vung Tau, and a visit to the beach for a swim and to let off steam with a few beers. We were bloody tired and the 12 days off was very welcome."

Some have since described Vung Tau as a rather unattractive beach resort with a suburb of dubious comfort providers living around and within it. Others report the resort as being a beautiful haven, where Australian, American, South Vietnamese soldiers and it was rumoured, even members of the Viet Cong and North Vietnamese Army, were able to spend at least a few days rest in-country. If indeed the enemy soldiers were present, both sides ignored the other in an unofficial treaty that maintained a relative peaceful situation compared with the combat areas they were resting from.

For 9 RAR their rest and recreation were over too soon, and on the 2nd of April 1969 the Battalion again returned to the field. That same day Mick had an interview with Alby Morrison who advised him that he would soon be changing jobs. Mick was to move to D Company as the Company 2ic, and Captain Peter Macaulay would take over the Mortar Platoon. Mick remembers receiving this direction with some emotion:

"I received this news with mixed feelings as the Mortar Platoon had been a big part of my life and its members were a very professional and dedicated team. Having formed the Platoon from Day 1 in Woodside, it was understandable that my attachment was strong."

In the meantime, it was business as usual and Mick deployed on Operation Overland with his beloved Mortars.

---

[63] AWM Collection/U53504.
[64] This time includes Operations King Hit 1 and King Hit 2.

CHAPTER 10

"The men were in a permanent state of exhaustion. They were in a shaft, plunging daily from one level of fatigue to the next, and the squad leaders kept pleading for a break. "They're tired, Lieutenant. They're so tired that half of 'em are half asleep on patrol. They've got to get some slack." But there was no slack..."[65]

No Rest

OPERATION OVERLAND WAS A RECONNAISSANCE in Force in AO Goulburn. The new AO was situated on the border of Bein Hoa-Long Khanh and Phouc Tuy Provinces, and was characterised by numerous streams, hills with steep spur lines, and large stands of open forest. To the north rubber plantations managed by the Michelin Rubber Company, provided another major feature. The AO was an important communist base and transit area, and the Battalion was under no illusion that this operation was one of high risk.

A Reconnaissance in Force operation was typified by aggressive action by a large force for the purpose of discovering the position and strength of the enemy. 9 RAR adopted the proven tactic of dividing the AO into individual Company areas of operation within which the Rifle Companies actively

---

[65] Phillip Caputo, <u>A Rumour of War</u>, (Owl Books) P 138.

sought the enemy. By the 3rd of April A, B, and D Companies had contacts with the enemy with varying degrees of success. On the 6th of April C Company discovered a huge bunker complex with some 98 individual bays including a hospital facility. The system was painstakingly destroyed by the Assault Pioneer Platoon. The next day, as the demolition work continued, a small group of the enemy returned to the complex, but they were driven off in a short sharp engagement.

Over the next 3 days there were several heavy contacts. On the 7th of April a contact involving A Company, resulted in the death of Private Barry George from Rylstone, New South Wales. Barry had been called up for National Service and had arrived in Vietnam in February 1969.[66] He was 22 years of age.

The next day there was a heavy contact involving D Company. One of the Company's Platoons was trapped by enemy fire and was forced to withdraw covered by mortar and artillery fire. During this engagement Private Trevor Black was killed. Trevor was from Bowen in Queensland. A National Serviceman, he was 22 years of age. He was the son of a World War Two veteran who had fought at the Siege of Tobruk.[67] Duty never ceases in its demands.

The 8th of April was particularly busy for the Mortar Platoon as they fired in support of contacts throughout the day. Mick worked for 9 hours straight in the Command Post, and the Platoon fired a record (to that date) total of 768 rounds for the day. The next day was little different with the Platoon firing in support of A, B, and C Company contacts and an A Company assault on a base camp. Mick recorded that up to that point in the Battalion's tour the Platoon had fired a total of 14,350 rounds.

Operation Overland ended on the 10th of April when 5 RAR relieved 9 RAR at Fire Support Base Kerry and assumed responsibility for AO Arunda. 4 RAR continued operating in the adjoining AO Belconnen south of Route 1. 9 RAR now commenced Operation Overlander and for this operation the Battalion was redeployed into AO Picton. Overlander was another Reconnaissance in Force, and a continuation of the efforts to protect the US

---

[66] nashoaustralia.org.au also Vietnam Killed in Action amvif.com
[67] Opcit

bases in the Long Binh, Bien Hoa area.[68] The Battalion's mission for Operation Overlander was to deny the enemy his source of food and resupply, by preventing enemy supply parties moving through the area and by locating and destroying caches and bunkers. The enemy main force was thought not to be in the area. AO Picton included parts of the Long Thanh district and the Long Le district. These areas included well populated villages, and a major waterway, and were bordered on the east by the jungles of the Hat Dich. To commence the operation A and C Companies moved to their allotted areas on foot. B and D Companies moved in to AO Picton by APC.

Having moved into the area B and C Company were tasked to set night ambushes to the approaches to the village of Thai Theu. Aggressive patrolling by all companies across the AO followed and on the credit side of the ledger numerous enemy assets were uncovered and destroyed. On the debit side of the ledger, in a contact on the 12th of April, Private Lyall McPherson of B Company was fatally wounded. Lyall was originally from Northham in Western Australia and prior to his call up in February 1968 he had been a sign writer.

Operation Overlander ended on the 15th of April and the next day 9 RAR deployed on another Reconnaissance in Force mission, this one closer to Nui Dat. In a case of "while the cat was away the mice will play," the local enemy had taken advantage of the situation that saw the majority of 1 ATF elements engaged on operations elsewhere and become more active.

The new operation titled Operation Surfside was designed to reassert 1 ATF dominance in the area, to trap the enemy, and then to ambush him as he moved to avoid the Australian forces. The overall strategy was to keep the enemy moving and uncertain as to where the Australians were. 9 RAR's responsibility in this operation was in AO Glenelg, a generally flat area, with large expanses of paddy fields, swaths of secondary forest, swamps and sand dunes. Most of the AO was within the Dat Do district, but it included some of the Xuyen Moc district too.

The majority of 9 RAR redeployed from AO Picton to AO Glenelg, by helicopter. This move involved a deception plan which saw the helicopters

---

[68] 5rar.asn.au/ops/fedover1 Also 9th Battalion Royal Australian Regiment Vietnam Tour of Duty 1968 – 1969 (Published by the 9 RAR Association) pp 58 - 61.

land briefly at Nui Dat before taking off again to deliver A, B, D, and Support Companies elements to unsecured Landing Zones, close to suspected enemy locations. Battalion Headquarters, Mortar Platoon, and 161 Field Battery RNZA, deployed into the area by road, protected by tanks from 4 Troop 1 Armoured Regiment and APCs from 3 Cavalry Regiment. This group established Fire Support Base Mardi.

Throughout the various operations they conducted during the months of March and April, to ensure his Battalion had the best fire support available, Lieutenant Colonel Alby Morrison had no qualms in establishing new fire support bases in various locations across an AO. The establishing of FSB Mardi is an example of his methods in manoeuvring his Battalion. As a result of the CO's tactics, 9 RAR became very adept at constructing new fire support bases. Swift action was essential, for the Viet Cong often attacked these bases as soon as they were occupied. As soon as the APCs and engineer equipment arrived in location, work would commence at a feverish pace. Command Posts, weapon pits and gun and mortar positions were excavated. Helicopters would fly in defence stores, such as barbed wire, timber and corrugated iron. Generally, all being well, a new fire support base could be established to a defendable condition in a matter of hours, further development of the base would then occur over the following days. The privilege of naming each new FSB was shared around the Battalion and generally resulted in a family member's name or the title of a home town. When Mick's turn to name a base arrived, he immediately chose his wife's name.[69] FSB Mardi was situated in a rice paddy with 3 rivers fringing its perimeter. The base area was 3200 metres from the coast, 2800 metres south of Route 23 and 18.2 kilometres south-east of Nui Dat.[70] Having been successfully inserted into their Landing Zones, A, B, and D Companies immediately established blocking positions in the south west of the area. Early the next day C Company, supported by tanks, began to search the area with the idea of pushing the enemy forces on to the Australian blocking positions.

---

[69] Many years later when asked how she felt about having a fire support base named after her, the question drew an amused "How about that".
[70] books.google.com.au/books?Fire+support+Base+Mardi&source

At FSB Mardi these activities drew a violent response from the enemy and on the night of the 16th of April, 11 Platoon, D Company, was heavily attacked but the enemy were repelled. The Mortar Platoon fired at a report of movement near the FSB perimeter, but no enemy casualties were recorded. Since the 23rd of March the Platoon had now fired an additional 4000 rounds, further testament to the hectic nature of 9 RAR operations.

Explosive incidents, or at least the potential for these, were a characteristic of life in Vietnam. On the 19th of April while delivering ammunition to the Field Battery, an APC hit a mine. The incident occurred about 500 metres out from FSB Mardi. The vehicle was blown over on to its side by the blast, and three men were injured and were evacuated. However, as Mick recalls the episode did not end there:

"The Kiwi gunners were unloading boxes of ammunition out of the back of the APC. These boxes were bound by hoop iron, strips of metal that held the boxes together. One of their number was using an axe to strike the metal bands off the boxes when the inevitable happened. A spark generated from the force of metal on metal, ignited a box. We all took cover for fear the fire would explode the shells, but fortunately nothing blew up, however the fire was impressive..."[71]

The Kiwis tended toward a love hate relationship with 9 RAR. As one 161 Field Battery officer recorded of the Battalion:

"One minute they could be crushingly arrogant and the next superbly generous..."[72]

The Kiwis were also amazed at the youth of the Australian soldiers, compared with their own men who on average were older, and more physically mature. As one Kiwi depreciatingly observed:

"...They certainly could not carry the loads our soldiers could carry..."[73]

The Australians had a different perspective on loads and strength. They carried only what they required. In 9 RAR's opinion a huge pack, full of all manner of generally useless items, was quite simply unnecessary.

---

[71] Mick Bawden 2018.
[72] Ian McGibbon, <u>New Zealanders' Vietnam War: A History of Combat, Commitment and Controversy,</u> (Exisle Publicity 2010) <u>p 218.</u>
[73] Opcit

The Kiwis were, however, impressed with the professionalism of the young Australians they supported and saw them as: *"very effective fighting soldiers"*. [74]

There was of course a degree of rivalry between the two allied contingents, most of it friendly. However, for all that most 9 RAR diggers had great respect for the Kiwi gunners. As Barney Bigwood, co-author of the book 'We Were the Reos: Australian Infantry Reinforcements in Vietnam' recalled:

"...The guns of the Kiwis worked closely with all companies of the Battalion. There were Forward Observers (FOs) embedded with every Rifle Company living, fighting and suffering every painstaking step of every operation..."[75]

On the 21st of April the Mortar Platoon was again active. Mick had accompanied an 9 RAR river patrol along the Song Rai River to the river mouth. During the patrol several mortar missions were fired at groups of Viet Cong attempting to navigate the rivers in sampans. As a result of the mortar bombs detonating in the water numerous fish were stunned and floated to the surface. Eager 9 RAR riflemen collected the fish and that night there was welcome relief from hard rations as they dined on fresh fish.

At a later stage in 9 RAR's tour, fresh fish was again the bi-product of a potentially dangerous issue that confronted all Allied forces in Vietnam. A series of incidents involving an American made hand grenade had led to the discovery that a particular variety of grenade fuse was faulty. The fault caused the grenade to prematurely explode with great potential for the soldier throwing the grenade to be killed or injured. As a result, that particular batch of grenade fuses, were withdrawn from service. A check was made of 9 RAR stocks of grenade fuses and it was found the Battalion had quite a number of them. The grenades were immediately withdrawn from the soldiers, and the decision made to quickly destroy them. Mick as a qualified demolition officer was detailed to destroy the faulty items and he recalls the task with some amusement:

---

[74] Opcit
[75] Richard "Barney" Bigwood and Andrew Bigwood, We Were The Reos: Australian Infantry Reinforcements in Vietnam, (Xlibris Corporation, 23 May 2011).p 206.

"I decided the best way to get rid of the things was to place them in sandbags with a slab of C4 explosive and a suitably long fuse, and blow them up in the river. So I took the things down to the mouth of the nearby Song Rai River, right where it flows into the South China Sea. D Company was in location down there, so I went to their OC and told him what I was going to do. Then of course when the demolition took place all these fish came to the surface. Well D Company were most excited, and they got one of their aluminium assault boats with an outboard motor and one of them took me out to gather fish. I saw this big fish lying on its back with its gills opened and I thought…I'll have you. However, it was so bloody heavy that when I leaned out of the boat and tried to pull it into the boat, I fell in. To add insult to injury, the fellow on the outboard yelled out, "Croc! Look out, boss it's coming for you!" There wasn't of course but I just about flew back into the boat…"

Over the next week, beyond the precincts of FSB Mardi, the Battalion discovered several enemy camps and numerous caches of weapons, food and equipment, all of which were destroyed. On the 23rd of April the Battalion returned to Nui Dat for a rest. The cost of duty had not risen in terms of lives, but in terms of stress and weariness the Battalion was paying a significant price.

For Mick, a constant source of support at this time was Mardi's letters, now decorated with a rather more pronounced drawing of her waistline. However, back in Australia, duty had compelled Mardi to an important decision. With an active toddler running around the house and the birth of their second child drawing ever nearer, she recalls it was time to leave their house in Inverbrackie and return to Mount Gambier to the care and support of her family:

"…I had gone home to have both my babies, but with Amanda I didn't go home to Mount Gambier until the last trimester. My mother was always a wonderful support while Mick was in Vietnam, and I had the additional support of Sandy and Helen Haig. Sandy had been the Best Man at our wedding and as Amanda's birth grew closer, he assumed the role of "surrogate father".

There were changes in Vietnam too…

CHAPTER 11

"The trouble was that from an Australian point of view, the American military authorities in Vietnam did not comprehend the 'Hearts and minds' battle."[76]

Pacification

A PROFESSIONAL ARMY RARELY STOPS training, and whenever the Battalion returned to Nui Dat a series of courses were conducted to prepare for the next operation, and to qualify soldiers for promotion or new appointments. At the completion of Operation Overlander, the Mortar Platoon conducted a mortar course to train not only some new National Servicemen replacements, but also its new Commander Peter Macaulay. At the end of that course Mick officially moved to his new job as 2ic D Company, a bittersweet moment.

In addition to these changes, Mick addressed what he saw as a lacking in his personal life. He had been raised as an Anglican, but had never been christened, an oversight that was addressed on the 27th of April when he and fellow officer and friend David Presgrave were baptised. A fortnight later the

---

[76] Edited by Garth Pratten and Glen Harper, Still The Same, Reflections on Active Service from Bardia to Baidoa (Army Doctrine Centre Headquarters Training Command, 1996). p 117.

two friends were confirmed as Anglicans by Archbishop Strong, the Primate of Australia who was visiting 1ATF at that time.

Mid-1969 heralded an adjustment in 9 RAR's approach to the war. Instead of focusing on the destruction of enemy forces, the Battalion's next operation focused on a process the Americans termed "pacification".

Pacification sought to remove the enemy's ability to influence the local population through fear, reprisals, threats, acts of terrorism and even popular political appeal. To achieve this, Government and western forces needed to drive the enemy guerrilla forces out of the area; remain in the area after driving the enemy away; train territorial forces in counter insurgency warfare so that they could carry out operations against any enemy attempting to re-enter the area; and restructure the local police force to ensure any members of the force who might have been influenced by the enemy, were weeded out. Once the population were able to feel secure and free from the threat of enemy retaliation, Government civic action programs were to be implemented to demonstrate the Government could deliver programs that would ensure future prosperity. The catch phrase for this strategy was "winning the hearts and minds of the people" and on the 8th of May, 9 RAR commenced its part in Pacification in Operation Reynella.

Operation Reynella was designed to assist the population to achieve security and to protect land clearance operations in the AO. For this operation the Battalion's area of responsibility was AO Aldgate. Located in the southern extremity of Phuoc Tuy Province, AO Aldgate included the districts of Long Dein and Dat Do and FSB Horseshoe. The topography of the area was characterised by well populated villages, paddy fields and included the Long Hai hills, a major Viet Cong haven.

For 9 RAR the mission for Operation Reynella was three-fold. First to keep the enemy moving, next to better develop village defences, and thirdly to inspire confidence in the South Vietnamese Government's cause. The operation commenced on the 8th of May when Battalion Headquarters, C Company, the Mortar Platoon and the New Zealand Field Battery moved to Fire Support Base Horseshoe. The remainder of the Battalion deployed to allocated areas within the new AO.

FSB Horseshoe was 1 ATF's only permanent fire support base. Located on a circular hill around 8 kilometres to the south east of Nui Dat and just to the north of the village of Dat Do, the base provided an extensive view of the surrounding countryside. It was first constructed and occupied in 1967 as part of a defensive plan that included the Dat Do to the sea barrier minefield. The minefield, the brainchild of Brigadier Stuart Graham, had been a spectacular failure as it had been provided insufficient protection, and as a result the Viet Cong were able to remove large quantities of the mines and re-employ them against the Australians. In spite of this failure, FSB Horseshoe had been retained, and for Operation Reynella the Horseshoe was a ready-made position for 9 RAR Headquarters and its fire support elements to occupy. C Company's allotted task was to improve the training of the local 2/48 ARVN Battalion. However, a short time after occupying the Horseshoe, Lieutenant Colonel Alby Morrison, became dissatisfied with the FSB location, believing the Horseshoe position provided insufficient artillery cover for his Battalion in the AO. To alleviate this situation he chose a new, centrally located fire support base position. The new base was named "Thrust", and on the 11th of May the CO moved his headquarters and his fire support elements to the new location.

At this time Mick had assumed his new appointment in D Company, however events transpired resulting in his temporary return to the Mortar Platoon. Peter Macaulay, Mick's replacement at Mortar Platoon, was completing an educational course and was due to sit for examinations. To ensure Macaulay had the best opportunity to pass his exams he remained in Nui Dat for this operation and Mick was temporarily seconded back to his old position, deploying with them to the Horseshoe and then to FSB Thrust. The CO was almost certainly pleased to have Mick with him during this time, as the two had developed an excellent working relationship. This was made evident on the 15th of May when at least a Company of the D445 Viet Cong Battalion occupied the village of Dat Do. Alby Morrison took his forward headquarters team, including Mick and John Rayward the 9 RAR Intelligence Officer, into Dat Do to visit the Provincial Chief's headquarters. As Mick recalls the Provincial Chief was less than co-operative

'Alby kept saying to the Chief "they're in the village, the VC are in the village." However, the only response the Chief would make to Alby was "My

men will kill." Alby wanted D Company and the 4 RAR/NZ W Company who were attached to us at the time, to do a sweep through the village and clean the VC up, but the Chief would have none of it and kept on insisting "My men will kill.' In the meantime, I was talking on the radio to a forward air controller and he told me he could see a group of VC setting up a machinegun at a particular grid reference. Without worrying about the Provincial Chief, I got on to the Mortar Platoon and ordered five rounds fire for effect. It was perfect the mortars got the lot. For me that was a euphoric moment, something I'd not achieved before and never achieved again, a moment when all our training just clicked, and we produced the perfect result.

The Chief was still resisting all efforts by Alby to release his troops to clean the VC up, and he only relented the next morning after the VC had successfully withdrawn from the village.'

The rest of the Battalion had been far from idle, occupying ambush and blocking positions between FSB Thrust and to the north of the Dinh Co Monastery. It was during one of these operations on the 9th of May that a tragic accident occurred claiming the life of Second Lieutenant Geoffrey Locke. Whilst Geoffrey was checking his men, a member of his Platoon saw movement and opened fire, and Geoffrey was killed. Originally from Tasmania, he was a Regular Army officer. He was 22 years of age.[77]

Mines, mainly of the M16 variety lifted from the failed Dat Do to Sea minefield, were almost the Viet Cong's weapon of choice at this time. On the 11th of May one of these insidious weapons took the life of Private Robert Yule of B Company. Robert was a regular soldier from New South Wales. He was aged 20 years.[78]

Alby Morrison was incensed by this death held the local villagers responsible:

"Immediately I had the local people rounded up and through an interpreter I told them what they had done, and I cautioned them that if any such incident occurred again, I would fill in their well. I even said that if anyone was caught laying mines they would be shot. The District Chief was

---

[77] vwma.org.au/explore/people/654437
[78] vwma.org.au/explore/people/654695

not very pleased about this nor was his American adviser, but I made it quite clear to them it was my soldiers who could be maimed or killed, and such incidents had to stop."[79]

It was a fine display of loyalty to his men, but sadly ineffectual so far as local enemy soldiers and sympathisers were concerned. The war and the employment of mines continued unabated.

With 9 RAR firmly ensconced in the area, the Viet Cong began to drift across the region seeking resupply and on the evening of the 20th of May, 2 Platoon, A Company ambushed a party of ten Viet Cong, killing three and wounding several others. Then on the 25th of May while protecting a group of Engineers involved in a land clearance operation Private Paul Reidy was killed in another mine incident. Paul was from Bendigo in Victoria. A salesman in civilian life, he had been called up for National Service in May 1968 and posted to D Company, 9 RAR. He was 22 years of age.[80]

On the 26th of May, Mick celebrated his 30th birthday, however at Dat Do there was hardly time to celebrate such a milestone. Back in Nui Dat the quartermaster sergeant had noted the occasion, and in the resupply flight that day, he included a frozen can of beer as a birthday present. It was a nice thought, but when Mick opened the beer can it exploded into a fountain of froth. It was a disappointing conclusion to a stressful day, but at least an exploding beer can lacked a lethal impact.

Not so the mines the VC lifted from the failed mine field barrier. Each mine incident had the potential to result in fatalities, or at the very least serious injury. The impact of these incidents on the Battalion cannot be over-estimated. Stress levels rose and morale fell as men considered the fact that their next step could detonate a mine that might kill them and their mates. The price of duty was being nakedly displayed in front of them, and instead of willingly performing their duty, it now took a great effort of will to continue to do so.

On the 30th of May in another mine incident four men were wounded, and

---

[79] Edited by Garth Pratten and Glen Harper, Still The Same, Reflections on Active Service from Bardia to Baidoa (Army Doctrine Centre Headquarters Training Command, 1996).. p 118.
[80] vwma.org.au/public/

in another on the 31st of May a further seven were wounded, some seriously. Then just after midnight on the 6th of June FSB Thrust was subject to enemy mortar attack. Over thirty 82-millimetre rounds were fired into the base, killing Corporal Brennan and wounding seven others.

David Brennan was a regular soldier from Bathurst, New South Wales, and had been with 9 RAR since its raising. His father, also a veteran, never recovered from the loss.[81] Duty had claimed a double payment.

Mick was in the base when the attack took place and well remembers the attack:

'The VC mortar men were bloody good. My blokes and I were trying to work out where they were firing from, but it was obvious they were firing at our mortar flashes but more particularly at the New Zealand Field Battery gun flashes. I stopped our mortars firing, but I couldn't convince the Battery Commander to have his guns cease fire. This was annoying because it was a setup, fake news if you like. The VC had made some kind of show out in the AO and as a result our patrols had called for fire support, but the VC melted away and the gun flashes that lit up the night sky above Fire Support Base Thrust, gave the VC mortar men the perfect point of aim.

We were fortunate with the wounded as the Battalion doctor was visiting the base from Nui Dat. Sadly there was nothing he could do for Corporal Brennan. The good doctor was seated on the toilet when the mortar attack commenced, and initially he thought the explosions of the enemy mortar rounds was our guns firing out at the enemy. There was a degree of disorganization when the attack commenced but Captain Rob Curtis, whose job I was about to take at D Company, did a wonderful job pulling the defence of the base together. I was desperate to establish the calibre of the mortar the VC were firing at us, and I was rushing about in the dark trying to find a tail fin from one of the rounds. Eventually I found one, but I couldn't see well enough to tell if it was either a 60-millimetre, or an 82-millimetre. In the end I took it over to one of our 81-millimetre weapons and tried to fit the tail fin into it. It didn't fit so I had my answer they were firing 82-millimetre bombs at us.

One of our patrols found the VC base plate position the next day, it was

---

[81] vwma.org.au/explore/people/654231

over a kilometre away from Fire Support Base Thrust... a demonstration of our enemy's skill.

I noted in my diary that as we left the Horseshoe the Mortar Platoon had fired 20,000 rounds since commencing our tour..."

On the 10th of June 1969, Mick officially assumed his new position of 2ic D Company but if he had hoped for an easy transition he was to be mistaken. Mick Bawden:

"D Company was still at Dat Do and it was a bloody awful situation. The Company was protecting Engineers who were working in and around the town, and there had been a couple of nasty mine incidents. There were more mines all over the place, and the men were tired, and morale was low. To make matters worse on either the first or second night I was there, the OC fell ill and had to be evacuated. As 2ic this had an immediate impact for me. I'd only been with the Company ten minutes and suddenly I was the OC! No sooner had I assumed command than the VC re-entered Dat Do through a temple complex and we were ordered to confront them. It was night, and we had all our claymore mines out, but I was being pressured by Battalion to move against the VC. I called a quick Orders Group and picked Lieutenant Steve Rowe's Platoon to be the point Platoon for our advance to contact. He was less than thrilled and reminded me about the deployed claymores. My solution was I thought simple, fire them off! However, there was still some procrastination from my young officers and I too was beginning to think the whole idea was bad.

In the end we stood fast and did nothing, and in retrospect that was a very good thing. For everywhere you went in Dat Do the VC had tunnels. We would have had no idea what we were facing, or where they would come from next.

We stayed there for a few more days. We had this D8 Bulldozer that we used to go through the area, with the blade in the ground about a foot, and pushed all the mines out of the way. Then on 15 June D Company of 5 RAR relieved us, they arrived in APCs and their Commander was Major Murray Blake. I met him on his arrival and gave him a briefing on the area. I was very frank with my comments and told him it was a bastard of a place and that we hadn't done that well, losing a few blokes and that our morale was *suffering. I also told him I wouldn't go anywhere in the area without the bulldozer going forward first, and even then you had to be careful, for the VC would come in after we had cleared an area and sow more mines. He was pretty confident and said he could see we were tired, but that he and his men would fix things.*

A few minutes later we mounted the carriers that had brought them in and gratefully left them to it. A short time later we heard them on the radio, 'This is 4 Delta, Contact Mine, wait out'.

In one of the vagaries of war confusion reigned. 4 Delta was our call sign too, and 9 RAR Headquarters listening into the radio traffic became confused and thought that it was us who had hit a mine and kept asking if we were okay. We were fine but D Company 5 RAR had been very badly knocked about".

It transpired that 12 Platoon 5 RAR detonated a mine killing two soldiers and wounding twenty-five others, one of whom died from his wounds that night. About half of the wounded were so seriously injured that they required repatriation back to Australia. A single mine had sprayed shrapnel at around 2 metres high over a radius of 35 metres. Almost certainly the mine had been laid by the locals who reportedly had been given information regarding the 5 RAR deployment plans by an informant at District Headquarters[82]. Perhaps if Mick's advice regarding use of the bulldozer had been taken the result may have been different.

Murray Blake's observation regarding the battle weariness of the 9 RAR troops could certainly be applied to Mick. Fatigue and stress had taken its toll, but when the mail failed to deliver letters from Mardi, his morale hit rock bottom. Mail has long provided an important link for the deployed soldier with his loved ones at home, and for Mick that contact with Mardi was a lifeline.

Indeed, the lack of mail became a major issue for troops deployed to the Vietnam conflict when postmen in Australia decided to adopt an anti-war stance and refused to deliver mail sent home by servicemen in Vietnam. That strike action resulted in an unofficial campaign calling on soldiers returning

---

[82] LTCOL Fred Fairhead (RTD), A Duty Done, rarasa.org.au/

home to "punch a postie".[83] Fortunately the posties' action was short-lived and in any case it was not the reason Mardi's letters were failing to reach Mick. As he fretted and imagined all manner of reasons for the break in communication with Mardi, other forces decided to intervene.

On hearing that their former Platoon Commander was down in the dumps, some members of the Mortar Platoon decided to cheer him up. Masquerading as a person more used to speaking and writing Vietnamese than English, they composed the following letter:

Us at Fire Bass Frust
Dear Mick,
We heared you didn't get no letter today. Pleez don't cry we writ yu wun. Is ther anything yu want, Mr Taylor says he will git it four yu. Mr Taylor says cum back as his education in slippin (Ratshit). Tar for the greens.

John John cries himself to sleep thinkin of you. Sgt Keys has not punched anywun for 3 days. Yu see things are not the same without yu. Do yu like being a Admin King (Hail Ceaser) Mr Taylor says yu are only a Admin Prince (hail Brutus). Mr Lunny sends his love.

Cum back we all miss yu
AQ Cell Staff
FCC Staff[84]

It helped…a little, and fortunately Mardi's letters eventually caught up with him.

As Mardi recalls, she had her own issues with the mail:

"*The first letters I received from Mick complained that he thought I wasn't writing to him and how desperate he was to hear from me. There was a plaintive and repetitive plea in the letters I received…"Have you stopped loving me?" My letters finally caught up with him and he was happy. However, at my end I would go ten days without any mail and then plop - 10 letters filled the mailbox…"*

---

[83] awm.gov.au/collection/C333388
[84] 9th Battalion Royal Australian Regiment Vietnam Tour of Duty 1968 – 1969 (Published by the 9 RAR Association).

By the time 9 RAR had returned to Nui Dat to rest and regroup, Mick was almost back to his old self.

On the 23rd of June there was exciting and welcome news from home. Mardi had given birth to a daughter Amanda, mother and baby were both well and the father wet the baby's head with a few brown ales in the Officers' Mess. He was yet to be eligible for Rest and Recreation leave and it would be almost 6 weeks before he would attain that status and have the opportunity to meet his daughter…another cost of duty. In the meantime, the war continued to grind onward.

Back in Australia, life for the 9 RAR families was becoming even more difficult. Every day an internal and underlying fear of what might be happening to their sons or husbands defeated any attempt to maintain any real normalcy. There was so little contact with their loved ones, no phone calls, e-mail and the Internet had yet to be invented, so the best that could be hoped for was an infrequent letter. On the other hand, the media knew much more than they did about what was happening to their men, and the men and women of the press had no compunction in communicating that knowledge to the general public. The nature of what was reported provided a very negative even horrific view of the situation, and as a result public support for the war was beginning to wane

In January 1968, 11 months before 9 RAR had arrived in country the communist forces had launched a major offensive to coincide with the celebration of Tet, the Vietnamese New Year. Whilst spectacular in the number of widely spread attacks the communists managed to mount, the Tet Offensive was a military and political defeat for the communists. However, inaccurate media reports caused widespread belief in America and Australia, that the Allies had lost control of the country and that the communists were winning. Coupled to this were reports of atrocities committed by Allied forces. A widely published photograph taken in Saigon during the Tet Offensive, of a South Vietnamese general carrying out a summary execution of a Viet Cong prisoner, further shocked the American and Australian public. However, for many civilians any pretext for supporting the war ended when American troops murdered over 347 civilians at the village of My Lai. Indeed, some Australians began to question if Australian soldiers might well be doing the same sort of thing. Public support for the war began to dwindle and by the middle of 9 RAR's tour the war had become electorally unpopular for politicians and others in influential positions. Both sides of Government had begun to publicly express anti-war sentiments, many to call for a withdrawal of Australian troops from the conflict. While many families of deployed servicemen and women would have welcomed the return of Australian forces, the change in political discourse added to the stress they were already experiencing.

Within the 9 RAR family most remained fiercely loyal to their deployed men, but some began to wonder if the sacrifice and pain was worth it. In Mount Gambier Mardi was supported through this time by her family and friends, sustenance she accepted with gratitude. Mardi Bawden:

"I made precious friends of dear people who accepted me with kinder and a husband in absentia. Sandy and Helen Haig had a little flat just down the road in Lake Terrace opposite the hospital. I used to go there when I felt a little low and they cheered me up with gin and tonic and enormous Spanish olives..."

In spite of growing public opposition the war dragged on. On the 29th of June the Battalion commenced Operation Matthew. This operation was a Reconnaissance in Force and the Battalion's mission was to locate and destroy a major enemy logistic unit, 84 Rear Services Group which was thought to be operating in Phouc Tuy Province. Intelligence reports stated that this unit operated in small groups between the Hat Dich and May Tao base areas, supplying enemy units by establishing caches of supplies and also through collaborating villages.

9 RAR would operate in an area of operations titled "Tom Thumb". AO Tom Thumb was a largely unpopulated area situated to the east of Route 2 and the Courtenay Rubber Estate, and to the north of Nui Dat. Movement through the area was challenging as B52 airstrikes had cratered the landscape and torn up trees and undergrowth. In addition to these difficulties the AO was a bad malarial area. Throughout the war Australian troops were required to take anti-malarial prophylaxis most commonly the drugs Paludrine and Dapsoneto to combat this disease. Soldiers were required to take the drug at least daily, although sometimes twice daily was the requirement. Generally,

this prevention regime was successful, however, there were some cases of adverse reactions to the drug Dapsone.[85]

Deployment into AO Tom Thumb was by road and air, with Battalion Headquarters, and fire support elements moving by road to Fire Support Base Flinders. A, B, and D Company were air lifted first to the fire support base but then to Landing Zones within the AO from where they commenced operations. C Company remained with 4/48 ARVN Battalion on a separate operation.

Conditions at FSB Flinders were less than ideal. Sited in a swampy jungle clearing, the base was plagued by atrocious conditions. As vehicles moved across the area the swampy ground was turned into a glutinous mess that stuck to vehicles, weapons and men. The Battalion was supported on this operation by a section of B Battery United States Artillery, and elements of 161 Field Battery RNZA as well as the Battalion's Mortar Platoon. The fire support base was located 23 kilometres north east of Nui Dat, and 7000 metres south east of the Xa Cam area and 6500 metres east of Route 2. The concept of operations in the early stages of Operation Matthew was for one Rifle Company to conduct patrols to find the enemy base locations, and to flush the Viet Cong into ambushes set by the other two Rifle Companies.

Contact with the enemy was almost immediate. B Company had established a patrol base and at 0800 hours on the 30th of June, two sentries on a listening post detected movement and returned to the Company position. As a clearing patrol was being organized the enemy fired into the base fatally wounding Private Gordon Sorrensen. Before his call up in July 1968 Gordon was a plant operator at Gympie in Queensland. He was 24 years of age.[86]

After this contact, Alby Morrison became dissatisfied with the method of operation he had employed. He believed the Battalion's tactics should have produced more contacts and he was advised this was probably because the Intelligence information, on which his concept of operation was based, was either faulty or out of date. He therefore decided to change his concept to enable all Companies to carry out Reconnaissance in Force operations within allocated areas. This adjustment soon provided results.

---

[85] aihw.gov.au/getmedia/
[86] vwma.org.au/public/

On the 2nd of July, D Company sighted two enemy, but because of the limited visibility they were unable to engage them. However, shortly after this sighting the Company found several significant caches of weapons and equipment that included an anti-aircraft gun.

The next day C Company re-joined the Battalion, and the following day deployed some 10 kilometres to the east to search for a possible enemy camp. No trace of the enemy camp was found and on the 8th of July C Company commenced to patrol to the west. The Battalion was now fully engaged in a search of the AO, but on the 9th of July, the enemy found them.

At approximately 0800 hours 10 Platoon, D Company was moving from an overnight ambush position, when it was fired on by automatic weapons and RPGs. Lance Corporal Richard Abraham was killed, and another man seriously wounded. Richard was originally from Whyalla in South Australia and prior to his call up for National Service in February 1968, he had completed an apprenticeship as a professional photographer. He was 22 years of age.[87]

D Company was again in contact on the 12th of July, when 11 Platoon discovered an enemy position. One of the sections was following up a sighting of some enemy soldiers when a Section Commander, Corporal Bruno Adamczyk and his Forward Scout, Private Paul Edwards, found a part of a bunker system. The two Australians threw a hand grenade into the bunker entrance. The enemy responded with small arms and RPG fire killing both men.

Bruno Adamczyk was born in Germany, immigrating to Australia with his parents when he was 3 years old. He had joined the Regular Army and had previously seen active service with 4 RAR in Borneo. He was survived by his wife and two daughters. He was 22 years of age.[88]

Paul Edwards was another regular soldier. He had arrived in Vietnam in September 1968 and joined 1 RAR as a reinforcement. When 1 RAR went home in February 1969, he was transferred to 9 RAR to complete his tour. He was survived by his wife Paula and daughter Bronwyn. He was 23 years of age.[89]

---

[87] vwma.org.au/explore/people/497080
[88] vwma.org.au/public
[89] vwma.org.au/explore/people/654315

The part of the bunker system into which Bruno Adamczyk and Paul Edwards had thrown the grenade was a minute section of an extensive system of tunnels and bunkers that could accommodate a considerable force. D Company was obliged to manoeuvre supported by artillery fire, and a Light Fire Team[90] in order to secure a position so that the bodies of the two Australians could be recovered, and a sharp battle ensued. During that battle the enemy withdrew.

It was in the aftermath of a battle such as this, that the 2ic of a Rifle Company performed one of his most important yet tragic tasks…the evacuation of those who had been killed in action. For Mick this became almost a sacred trust, to honour the dead and to care for emotions of the living. Mick Bawden:

"You had to try very hard to recover the bodies of our blokes who had been killed, and to get them away as quickly as possible. Certainly, you didn't want to keep a body overnight unless you absolutely had to. Having a body in the position was a real morale killer. It was bad enough losing the men, but if they were just left in-place, the other soldiers started to think that the next one could be him. The helicopters would come in and we would place the bodies on board the aircraft with as much dignity as we could manage…"

This was not the end of their responsibility to the dead, for once the deceased was evacuated from the battlefield, and the body was delivered to the mortuary where it was prepared for repatriation back to Australia, the corpse had to be formally identified by someone who had known the dead soldier well. This could be, as Mick recalls, a harrowing experience for those called upon to identify a dead comrade:

"The process was supervised by an American Notary Public at Vung Tau. Two people were generally detailed for the task. The two would be taken individually into the mortuary and briefed on what was to happen in order to identify the corpse, and then, again individually, taken in to view the body.

The body was frozen on a slab, at this stage, it had not been cleaned and in some cases was badly disfigured. The notary would ask, "Do you recognise this cadaver?" If the answer was positive the notary would then

---

[90] Helicopter gunships.

say, "How do you know it is who you say?" The corpse would have some identifying features...facial features, hair colour. The notary would then produce several documents which required signature. The procedure was then repeated with the other Australian identifier. It was not a pleasant experience".

Mick was unaware at that time that once the identification was completed, the American morticians then (as far as was possible) skilfully reconstructed the features of the corpse hiding the damage inflicted upon it. The purpose of the restoration was to make the dead more presentable to the grieving families should they have wished to view the body on its repatriation. The problem with this practise, as Mick was later to discover to his cost, was the morticians did their work too well. Thus, if a soldier had died in an explosion or from a gunshot, no evidence of this remained, often confusing the bereaved as to how their loved one had died.

Operation Matthew ended on the 17th of July and 9 RAR moved directly on to Operation Hat Dich in AO Porphrey. There had been an increase in enemy activity in the AO and Intelligence reports suggested that enemy attacks against the villages of Long Thanh and Binh Son were planned. AO Porphrey was directly west of AO Tom Thumb and the Battalion quickly extended its operations in that direction to conduct another Reconnaissance in Force. 9 RAR's mission was to locate and destroy enemy main force elements believed to be in the area.

The operation commenced with the Battalion deploying by air to Fire Support Base Dampier where 9 RAR Headquarters, its mortar elements, and the attached artillery battery established themselves. From there the Rifle Companies deployed on foot, B Company moved directly north, while D Company moved west and then south. These two companies were to search for enemy installations and infiltration routes. A Company deployed by air to establish an ambush in the north of the AO, while C Company patrolled to the west.

On day one of the operation A Company had two contacts that resulted in three enemy being killed. The next day, the 19th of July, C Company became involved in a heavy contact and Private Raymond Kermode was killed. Raymond was called up for National Service in February 1966 and had signed on for further service in the Regular Army. Originally from Brisbane, in civilian life he had been a tailor's cutter. He was 21 years of age.[91]

The operation continued and on the 24th of July A Company came across a bunker system and in the ensuing contact Private Ray Moore was killed. A Regular Army soldier, Ray was originally from Mt Evelyn, in Victoria. He was 23 years of age.[92]

Two days later B Company had a similar contact, but the enemy withdrew. All of the bunker systems discovered during this operation were destroyed.

In comparison with the other three companies, D Company had a relatively quiet week. They had no contacts with the enemy and found no enemy installations. This is not, however, to suggest the Company had an easy time of it. Co author of the book 'We Were the Reos: Australian Infantry Reinforcements in Vietnam', Barney Bigwood was a member of D Company and he recorded the physical and mental trials of Operation Hat Dich:

'The stress did not diminish. The requirement to be ever vigilant kept the adrenalin levels on constant high which had a damaging psychological effect on all involved...Being the middle of the wet season also wore down the diggers physically after lugging their 50 kilo loads of ammunition, rations and weapons through the raw dense jungle, through fast running streams and up and down muddy river banks..."

The operation concluded on the 31st of July, and perhaps as a reward for fruitless hard work, D Company was the first to be picked up by C47 Chinook helicopters and flown back to Nui Dat. At every level the cost of duty was continuing to rise.

---

[91] vwma.org.au/public/
[92] 9rarsa.com.au/in-memoriam/

Mount Gambier junior baseball team 1950.
Mick Bawden is seated on the ground holding the bats.

Mardi McPherson aged 16

The Officers of the 10th Battalion Royal South Australia Regiment 1966

Mardi and Amanda Bawden

Captain Mick Bawden Mortar Platoon Commander South Vietnam

The two Bawden children (Byron and Amanda) in PNG playing in wheelbarrow filled with water as a makeshift paddle pool.

9 RAR Mortar Platoon in action South Vietnam

Escorting the in-coming Commanding Officer of the 2nd Battalion The Pacific Island Regiment, Lieutenant Colonel Jeffrey, on the Battalion's welcoming parade in 1974.

Farmer Mick

*Mick and Mardi Bawden attending the
ANZAC Day ceremony at Portland in 2000.*

CHAPTER 12

"Stay a while, that we may end the sooner."[93]

The Beginning of the End

AFTER ANOTHER BRIEF RESPITE 9 RAR returned to the field. The next operation, Operation Neppabunna, was a combined Pacification and Reconnaissance in Force operation which was conducted in three separate areas of operation. The first AO, code named "Umberatana", extended toward Route 44, south to the coast and north east to a point just short of the village of Xuyen Moc. The second AO, code named, Gammon was located to the east of AO Umberatana, and the third AO, Burr some 25 kilometres south east of Nui Dat. All three areas of operation were notorious for mines infestation and during the course of the operation a great number of mines were located and destroyed. The ground, particularly in AO Umberatana was wet and boggy making it difficult to establish effective fire support bases, and at various times over the period of this operation, 9 RAR was provided fire support from FSB Serle and from FSB Wells. A distinguishing feature of FSB Serle was a 3-hole golf course established by 161 Battery RNZA.

Operation Neppabunna commenced on the 15th of August when C and D Companies deployed into AO Umberatana by road to commence

---

[93] G. Herbert, Outlandish Proverbs.

Reconnaissance in Force operations. Two days later D Company met with success. Patrolling near a river they fired on an enemy boat killing six Viet Cong. The situation made it impossible for the enemy dead to be retrieved from the river, and for the next several days the bodies of the dead enemy floated back and forth with the tidal surge in the river. This unfortunate situation gave rise to a moment of macabre suggestion. Throughout the war the Americans were obsessed with the number of enemy killed, and they pursued a policy known as "body count". As Mick recalls the floating VC dead presented D Company with a unique opportunity:

"…there was a suggestion made that we should keep counting the floating bodies as they went past each time the tide changed. It certainly would have made our body count score impressive!"

The D Company success was followed up on the 26th of August when a C Company ambush killed one Viet Cong and wounded two others. Tragically that same day there were several civilian fatalities caused by the much-feared anti-personnel mines. Four children found a mine and accidently detonated it killing all of them. It was an event that scarred the memories of the whole Battalion and further heightened the general awareness of the mine danger.

It was as this stage of his tour that Mick became eligible for Rest and Recreation leave. After 6 months in-country, a soldier was entitled to one week of leave in a country of his choice. Many young and single men chose to spend their leave in exotic destinations, such as Japan or Hong Kong, but most married men tended to elect to go home to visit their families. For Mick there was never any doubt where he would spend his leave, and he eagerly arranged transportation back to South Australia where Mardi, Byron and the newly arrived baby Amanda waited. Mardi remembers the day he came home as though it was yesterday:

"My brother picked him up from the airport in Melbourne and drove him home to his three-year-old son, the new babe and me. We hadn't seen him for nine months – he didn't know who to hold first! I think I won, Byron was hobbled by his knickers and Amanda was asleep in her pink rosiness…"

Mick thrived on the attention he received but it was all so temporary. Mardi was shocked at what the war had done to her man, but was determined to look after him:

'Five days of bliss. My young man with curly brown hair, flirty eyes and a wonderful sense of humour was back, but he was so thin and pale. We feasted on each other's company and I fed him wholesome food, but after the hard rations he was used to, my cooking was enough to give him diarrhoea.

I shared him with his parents, my family and our friends but it was all so brief and too soon the day of parting came..."

Others who saw Mick during his leave were privately shocked by his appearance, commenting he was haggard, grey and drawn. It was a glimpse of the cost that duty was exacting on all involved in the Vietnam War. A week later he was back in the jungle, and in many ways, it felt as though he had never been away.

September arrived and as 9 RAR cautiously carried out its mission, the stress and tension levels within the Battalion continued to rise. Then on the 7th of September in a contact involving A Company, Private Brian Rennie was fatally wounded. Brian was a Scot and inevitably had been nick named "Jock". He had arrived in Vietnam as a reinforcement, and had already seen service with 1 RAR and 4 RAR prior to transfer to 9 RAR to complete his tour. He was 21 years of age.[94]

C Company had another successful contact on the 10th of September in which they killed three Viet Cong. It was the final contact the Battalion experienced for that operation. 9 RAR's part in the operation ended on 15 September when they were relieved by 5 RAR.

On the 19th of September Mick received more news from home, but this time the news was not good. His father had passed away, and the CO, Alby Morrison, immediately arranged for Mick to go home on compassionate leave. Mick recalls with deep appreciation the care Alby Morrison extended to him:

'We were out in the bush when I got the news about my father. I was filthy, my uniform torn and grotty. Time was critical, I had to be extracted from the bush, rushed back to Nui Dat and packed and ready for the flight home in a matter of hours. The CO arranged for his batman to have a clean set of the CO's own uniform to be ready for me when I got back to Nui Dat, so all I had to do was shower and dress. I asked him if I could keep the

---

[94] Opcit

badges of his rank too, but he said we'd better not. Then he said an extraordinary thing to me: 'Mick under these circumstances I will understand if you don't come back here'. I replied that I would be back, and he said he hoped I would, but then he repeated he would understand if I did not...'

A helicopter picked Mick up out of the bush and flew him back to Nui Dat and from there he caught a Caribou flight back to the airport at Tan Son Nhut. An Air France flight took him to Manila then Air Philippines flew him to Sydney. The now defunct Ansett Airline delivered him to Adelaide and from there he caught a light aircraft to Mount Gambier, arriving half an hour before the funeral commenced. That day is deeply etched in Mick's memory:

'It was freezing cold; I was extremely tired, and I recall being totally bewildered by everything that was going on. I don't remember anything about the service, all I recall is standing at the head of my father's grave and saluting. People said to me afterward they thought I looked terribly lonely and I was.

I had a few days at home with Mardi and the kids before I went back to Sydney where I waited another two days before I could catch a flight back to Vietnam..."

No doubt when Alby Morrison had hinted to Mick that he might consider remaining home, the CO was alluding to the fact that 9 RAR was nearing the end of its tour; and perhaps he was offering Mick the certainty of survival as opposed to the chance of being maimed or killed should he return to Vietnam. Indeed, survival was the problem now for all the members of 9 RAR. A few more weeks and they would be on their way home...all any of them had to do was to stay alive.

9 RAR's next operation incorporated all of the battle-hardened skills the Battalion had gained during its previous 9 months in Vietnam. Titled Operation Jack, the area of operation, code named "Stuart", was all too familiar to the Battalion as it had operated in the area in January during Operation Goodwood. The Battalion's missions for Operation Jack included protection of land clearance operations, Reconnaissance in Force, search for a missing SAS soldier, patrolling, ambushing, and as this was the last scheduled operation for the Battalion, perhaps their most important mission was surviving.

For D Company the operation commenced on the 30th of September with an air insertion into the north of the AO. Major Hearn, the Officer Commanding the Company, was unavailable and for the duration of the operation Mick was Acting Company Commander. It was as he recalls another stressful time:

"I remember the receding sound of the helicopter rotors giving way to a silence that was total and forbidding. Suddenly there was the sharp sound, very like a rifle shot, and the hair at the back of my neck stood up in expectation of enemy activity... it was only a falling tree branch. Nevertheless the sound reinforced to me the fact that essentially, we were now on our own. There were no other friendly forces in our area to directly support us should we need help. However, it was reassuring to know that our radio links with the artillery and our Battalion's own mortars could provide us with close fire support if requested. Aside from this strength we could also call on the many and varied kinds of air support from both Australian and American sources.

We were, however, in a vulnerable position. Our insertion into the area might have been a surprise to the enemy, but if they were close by, they would have noted the location of the landing zone and could well respond with mortar fire or some other kind of attack. Our first task was to get away from the landing zone."

Once away from the landing zone the Company's real task began:

"The Company commenced to move on a pre-arranged bearing towards an area where we were to establish a night ambush. We had scouts out in front of a leading Platoon searching for any sight, sign or sound of the enemy. This part of the AO was heavy jungle and progress was slow. The Scouts working with secateurs[95] in one hand and an M16 in the other, cut the way through the jungle, and all the while on guard for the enemy. It was hard work for all of us, with our weapons and heavy packs, but I was always in awe of the scouts and the responsibility they almost always willingly accepted.

When we moved through the jungle, it was nothing like what one sees in American war films. Our main form of communication was by hand signal

---

[95] Secateurs were found to be more effective and less tiring to use than a machete or jungle knife.

and only when this means could not be used, did we converse in whispers. Company headquarters moved behind the leading Platoon. My main task was checking our navigation, marking off on my map every time we covered 100 metres. In this task I was assisted by my batman and runner who were counting paces.

Eventually we reached a suitable place to harbour for the night. This was close enough to the ambush site, but far enough away from it not to disturb any enemy who might be in the area. I indicated the areas to be occupied by the ambush parties and then there was time for a quick meal, and to arrange for patrolling tasks for the next day. Then the ambush parties moved off.

I don't think I ever had a peaceful night in the jungle. There were always hordes of mosquitoes and the multitudes of screeching cicadas. Aside from these attractions of the night, it was Alby Morrison's practice to talk by radio to each of the Rifle Company Commanders at about 1900 hours each night. That night when my turn came, he advised me that we were to prepare a landing zone in the morning, so that we could receive a helicopter and a change of orders. There were no other details.

The next morning after stand down I gathered the Platoon Commanders to advise them of the change of plans, giving them what little information I had regarding my radio conversation with the CO. I had checked the map and I had noted an area that might provide a suitable landing zone about 500 metres away, and after we had breakfasted, we moved off to that area to establish and secure the landing zone.

The map proved to be correct. The area we had selected was tall kunai grass and so we set up all round security, contacted Battalion Headquarters to send the helicopter and settled back to wait for its arrival.

After about thirty minutes the helicopter arrived and delivered the Battalion Intelligence Officer, and a Vietnamese gentleman. After greeting the newcomers, I moved the Company to a new harbour position in some nearby rainforest where we would receive our new orders.

In the new harbour the Intelligence Officer explained that we were to be led to a known enemy base camp by the Vietnamese fellow he had brought with him. This fellow had recently surrendered under the Vietnamese Government's "Chieu Hoi" or "open arms plan". This plan was designed to *encourage Viet Cong members to defect to the Government side. However, while I understood the concept, I did not like the look of this particular Chieu Hoi. He was a rather sickly individual who smoked Salem cigarettes incessantly and had a consumptive sounding cough. To add to my concern he spoke no English, luckily, we had an interpreter attached to the Company, and through him we learned the Chieu Hoi knew of a Viet Cong camp, about one and a half days' march from our present location. The Intelligence Officer then explained that the destruction of this camp was our new mission. I have to say I had plenty of misgivings about this new task, and I believe with some justification, found it difficult to forget that until recently our apparently friendly Chieu Hoi had been a VC.*

After the Chieu Hoi gave us a general direction in which we should travel, I gave the necessary orders and the Company moved off. We followed that direction for the rest of the day, stopped for an uneventful night and then resumed the march the next day. By midday there was no sign of the enemy camp and I was becoming increasingly concerned. I can remember asking the interpreter to find out from the Chieu Hoi, how far we still had to go, and being told there was yet another half day to go. We continued on until we were forced again to stop for the night with still no sign of a camp.

That night in my talk with the CO, I voiced my unease as to the reliability of the Chieu Hoi's directions. He told me to continue searching for half the next day and if there was still no sign of the camp, we should evacuate the Vietnamese and the Intelligence Officer and revert to our previous mission.

The next morning our Chieu Hoi became increasingly nervous and I warned the point platoon of this. Shortly after the scouts indicated that they had come to a washing point on a creek, and the Chieu Hoi announced the camp was very close. We proceeded extremely carefully.

Then just as Company Headquarters was crossing the creek behind the point Platoon, a burst of fire sent us to the ground, and we heard a shout from up ahead of "Contact!" The Platoon Commander was quickly on the radio and he told me the scouts had killed a Viet Cong who was walking toward them carrying his AK47 rifle by the barrel on his shoulder. The Viet Cong was obviously not expecting any trouble, and it appeared that he was going to the creek to wash. I passed this information on to Battalion Headquarters and then we continued to advance.

Our Chieu Hoi was by now shaking with fear and he kept saying "Vee Cee... Vee Cee" and indicating that he would go no further. He chose a very large tree, parked himself behind it and refused to move any further.

The point Platoon meanwhile had sent back the hand signal indicating an enemy camp was in sight. I went forward to the Platoon Commander in order to decide what our next action should be.

From the Platoon's headquarters I could just make out through the undergrowth what appeared to be a raised machinegun emplacement with what may have been an embankment leading up to it. I had never seen this sort of construction before as most Viet Cong camps were low to the ground and difficult to spot. Our immediate problem was that we had lost the element of surprise when we had killed the lone Viet Cong. However, rather than simply entering the camp I decided we should engage the area with artillery and an airstrike before we went any further.

We had to pull back to the other side of the creek we had just crossed, before we could safely hit the place with artillery. Once the Company was safely out of the way, the artillery observer who always travelled with us, radioed the Field Battery with his fire mission. This was commenced with a ranging round, which fell some distance away from the target. The forward observer then adjusted the fire onto the target. Once he was satisfied, he ordered "5 rounds fire for effect at my command". I warned the Platoons by radio, and after being assured that all had taken what cover they could, I gave the go ahead to the Forward Observer. Thirty rounds[96] of 105 mm high explosive commenced to fall in the camp area. The forward observer asked if we should have more and I agreed so he called "Repeat" on his radio. This was shortly followed by another 30 rounds being impacted onto the target.

I decided against an air strike as we would have had to move even further away to be safe. So I ordered one of the Platoons to move to the camp site followed by Company Headquarters, then the other two Platoons followed on. Once the point Platoon was in a position where they could again see the

---

[96] Five rounds from each of the field guns in the battery resulted in 30 rounds of artillery hitting the target.

camp fortifications, the Platoon Commander asked if the Platoon might fire an M72 rocket at the machinegun emplacement. Now the Company had been carrying about thirty of these M72 Light Antitank weapons for the whole of our time in Vietnam and we had never fired one of the things, so I readily agreed with the request. We all waited expectantly. However, we were to be disappointed for the weapon misfired, it was useless.

We then began to manoeuvre to secure the camp. There was no sign of the enemy and I informed Battalion Headquarters that we had occupied the place without resistance. Once we had formed a defensive perimeter, we set about conducting a detailed search of the camp before we took any action to destroy it.

The camp was the largest and most strongly built that I had seen. It was about 150 metres square, with machinegun emplacements on all four corners all connected by a trench system. There were ten large underground dugouts and a barbed wire cage, benches made of logs indicating outdoor class areas and there was a dry well in the centre of the camp. The artillery had collapsed a number of structures but had not done a great deal of damage. We were very fortunate that it was not necessary to fight our way into those fortifications.

I sent back a detailed report to the Commanding Officer and he ordered that a landing zone be prepared so that we could receive explosives and an engineer team who would destroy the camp. Preparing the landing zone proved very difficult and the only way we could complete the task was by having two chain saws delivered by helicopter in order to cut down the larger trees in the area.

The next morning after the delivery of the chain saws our work parties began to clear trees from the area we needed for the landing zone. During this time the Intelligence Officer made a detailed sketch of the camp fortifications and layout. He felt that it had been an indoctrination centre for new recruits and the man we had shot was probably one of the caretakers for the facility. The other members of the caretaking party would have left hurriedly when the artillery started falling on the camp.

The Engineer team were the first to use our new landing zone and they immediately began to assess the amount of explosive they would require to *destroy the camp. The Engineers were followed by a steady stream of interested visitors, including the Task Force Commander who commented the destruction of the camp, which was clearly a major enemy asset, would be a major blow to the Viet Cong.*

Over the next two days the Company ensured the security of the area and assisted the Engineers preparing the camp for demolition. The CO visited us each day, bringing with him in the helicopter hot meals for all and daily mail from home. So when the Engineers finally announced they were ready to destroy the camp, we were rather sad to leave.

The Engineers had used some 500 lb of explosive and they had decided on a 15-minute safety fuse for initiation. I left one of the Platoons to secure the Engineers and I moved the remainder of the Company away in an easterly direction for about 300 metres where we set up a harbour to wait for the security Platoon and the Engineers to catch up with us. They found us with about five minutes left before the expected explosions. However, at the appointed time there was no earth-shattering bang, nothing but the sounds of birds and insects. Somehow the explosives had failed to detonate.

For safety we had to wait 30 minutes before the Engineers and the security Platoon could return to the camp to check what had happened to the charges. On their return they had to be especially vigilant because there was the possibility the Viet Cong had returned and tampered with the charges. However, all was well and after correcting whatever fault had occurred, the Engineers and the Platoon returned to the harbour. This time there was a most satisfying explosion. I informed Battalion Headquarters that the camp had been destroyed. The Engineers went back to check that the job had been done properly and that no explosives remained for the Viet Cong to use. We then moved on toward an open area so that our extra people, including our Chieu Hoi, could be evacuated by helicopter."

D Company now resumed its original mission of Reconnaissance in Force which it continued until the second week in October when it assumed responsibility for night defence positions (NDP) for an American Engineering Company engaged in land clearing operations.

While D Company had been blowing up the enemy camp the rest of the Battalion had been far from idle. Across the whole of the AO there were numerous contacts, including one on the 3rd of October in which A Company soldier Private Kevin Prior was killed. Kevin was from Rockhampton in Queensland. He had been called up for National Service in May 1968. He was 22 years of age.[97]

On the 15th of October, D Company commenced its work with an American engineer unit engaged on land clearing operations. The purpose of the land clearing operations was to expose the landscape so that the enemy's movement could be observed. Some land clearing operations focused on the sides of roadways, other around defensive positions and villages. The actual clearing operation was conducted from a Night Defence Position (NDP) from where each day, formations of bulldozers left to clear the surrounding jungle. The American units employed on land clearing generally held around 28 bulldozers of varying sizes, but most times 20 of these large vehicles were employed on the land clearance work, while the other eight vehicles were either kept as a repair pool[98], or were actually being repaired. The larger bulldozers were equipped with the now controversial item known as a Rome Plough, or "stinger blade". This was a large knife-like item that was capable of removing large trees. Controversy arose over the large areas of jungle that were left desolate by the employment of this item of equipment, with conservationists claiming the use of the Rome Plough caused untold ecological damage. To the soldiers on the ground though, it was a pretty handy bit of kit.

Security for the NDP and during the actual clearance work was provided by an Infantry Company, in this case D Company, directly supported by a troop of APCs, and with indirect fire support provided by artillery and mortars from a nearby fire support base. Depending on the time of year, conditions within a NDP could resemble a dust bowl, or a swamp, the tracked vehicles churning the ground into either dust or mud. This now was D Company's lot and as Mick recalls:

"The Americans carrying out the land clearance work were a mixture of

---

[97] 9rarsa.com.au/in-memoriam/
[98] A repair pool consists of a number of serviceable items held at readiness in the event an issued item becomes damaged. The repair pool maybe drawn on to cover the damaged item.

civilian contractors and military the whole lot commanded by a US Army captain. Their job was to knock down trees and flatten the land around villages and defensive positions. The Yank engineers doing this work were armed, but given their single defensive tactic, which they called 'the mad minute', they certainly needed our additional protection. If threatened they would circle their bulldozers and rapid fire a magazine full of whatever weapon they had to hand. It might be a pistol, an M16, or a shotgun, regardless, all weapons were rapidly fired outwards. One bulldozer driver I spoke to was very proud of this method of defence. However, if the VC were half smart, they would have done something to set the mad minute off, and then moved in and fixed the Yanks up well and truly. In retrospect I suppose that is what we were there to prevent.

Night-time was the worst of the task as that was when the Yanks repaired their dozers. They would be up all night, floodlights glaring, welders flashing and hammers clanking on metal. They seemed happy enough, but it stressed the hell out of us. The day light was better and for much of the daylight hours we just hung around hoping not to get shot at.

Overall, the Yanks were nice enough blokes, but they had a propensity toward smoking dope. They thought I was a general because of my three pips of the rank of captain on my shoulders. Clearly, they thought the three pips were stars, so therefore I was a three-star general. They seemed disappointed when they found out the truth.

Among the various types of earth moving equipment the Yanks employed was a truck which was used to carry all their tools and equipment. Normally they would detail someone to drive this vehicle to wherever they needed it, but when they couldn't drive the truck, for whatever reason, they would tow it behind a bulldozer. Eventually they towed too hard and pulled the front axle off the truck. The US Army captain in charge of the engineers called a halt, and insisted an attempt was made to recover the truck. They did this by putting a chain onto the truck bumper bar and hitching it up to a bulldozer. Of course, they pulled the bumper bar off too. So the US captain announced the truck could not be recovered and that we were to destroy it.

Now part of the protection force with us was a troop of our APCs *commanded by a bloke from Penola[99], Captain Ray De Vere. Ray had won a Military Cross at the Battle of Binh Ba[100], anyway I said to Ray, do your blokes want some target practise shooting this truck up? He replied that they would, but first he wanted to take all the tools out of it. I checked with the Yank captain and he saw no problem with this, so Ray and his blokes unloaded the truck into one of their APCs. There were all kinds of stuff, welders, cutting tools, spanners and so on, enough to fill the back of the APC. Then once they had loaded up their ill-gotten gains, they shot the hell out of the truck."*

While D Company was engaged in the protection of the American engineers, the rest of the Battalion was experiencing almost daily contacts with the enemy. On the 10th of October B Company had a particularly successful contact in which several Viet Cong were killed and a large bunker system destroyed. On the 20th of October B Company had another two contacts which resulted in several more enemy dead. As a result of one of these contacts, Lieutenant Peter Cosgrove of B Company was awarded a Military Cross. After Vietnam, Peter Cosgrove continued his military career rising to the rank of lieutenant general. In 2000 he was appointed as Chief of the Defence Force, finally retiring from the Army in 2004. In 2014 he was appointed as Australia's Governor General.

A Company also experienced considerable success on the 24th of October when the Company ambushed a large group of the enemy killing many of them. Two days later A Company was again involved in a savage encounter in which Private John Holloway was killed. John was originally from Surrey Hills in Melbourne. He was a carpenter when called up for National Service in October 1968. He was 23 years of age.[101]

As D Company continued its protection duties it seemed they would be lucky and spared serious casualties, but then on the 27th of October their luck ran out. It was an extremely hot and humid day, and the Company was taking a rest in some thick jungle alongside a very large and deep bomb crater.

---

[99] A town to the north of Mount Gambier in South Australia.
[100] Captain Ray De Vere was awarded the Military Cross for his services in Vietnam with B Squadron, 3 Cavalry Regiment, including heroic and determined action at the Battle of Binh Ba.
[101] 9rarsa.com.au/in-memoriam/

Sentries had been posted with claymore mines positioned to cover likely enemy approaches. Finally, the threatening clouds and stifling humidity produced what they had long promised, a severe thunderstorm. Torrential rain cascaded down, and the soldiers took advantage of the downpour to trap water in their hutchies to fill their water bottles. At this time Private Bernd Bender, Bernie to his mates, was on sentry duty. His sentry post was a few metres to the front of one of the Company's M60 machinegun positions. Deployed to his immediate front was a claymore mine. The idea was that should the sentry detect the enemy, he could fire the claymore mine and then make his way back to the Company position covered by the M60. As the storm broke Bernd asked permission to be able to fill his water bottles too. Permission was granted, on the proviso that he brought the claymore mine back with him to a point where it could be covered from the machinegun position. This was a reasonable precaution as the Viet Cong had been known to reposition unattended claymore mines to point back toward the troops who laid them. Thus, when alarmed the unsuspecting soldier would fire the mine, only to find himself a victim of the mine's deadly contents.

Perhaps Bernd was in too much of a hurry to get his water bottles filled. Or maybe for a few minutes he just became careless. In either event he failed to disarm the claymore mine before carrying it back. At that moment the power of the thunderstorm increased dramatically. Lightning danced across the trees and thunderclaps erupted with deafening ferocity. As Bernd made his way toward the machinegun position a lightning strike detonated the mine and he was killed.

As one witness stated:

"the explosion took a terrible toll on Bernie's body, making the recovery a task that would never leave the minds of those who had to bring him in..."[102]

The major part of that recovery task was undertaken by Acting Platoon Commander of 10 Platoon Sergeant Mick Credlin, and the Acting Company Commander Mick Bawden:

"When the explosion took place, I had immediately run to the scene. It was a terrible sight and Mick Credlin and I started to retrieve portions of

---

[102] Richard "Barney" Bigwood and Andrew Bigwood, We Were The Reos: Australian Infantry Reinforcements in Vietnam, (Xlibris Corporation, 23 May 2011).

Bernd's body that had fallen into the bomb crater, there may have been others helping, but I can only remember Mick Credlin, he had been a policeman before joining the army, a hell of a good man.

All the while I could feel the eyes of 10 Platoon, Bernd's mates, watching me as I searched the crater and brought bits of body back to a central point. I felt they were waiting for me to pass the job on to them. I was determined to keep going, but the shock of the incident and of the catastrophic nature of Bernd's injuries left me feeling pretty ill.

Mick Credlin must have seen I was having trouble and he came over to me and asked if I was okay. I told him I was, but only just, to which he responded: 'Keep swallowing, sir, don't let them see you throw'. Somehow, I managed. However, as it was now dark, the storm was continuing, and poor Bender was dead, we had no option but to postpone the Dustoff to remove his body until the morning. 10 Platoon maintained an all-night vigil over the body and the next morning one of them drew my attention to a portion of Bernd's body Mick Credlin and I had missed in the rain. It was retrieved and placed with the body..."

The nature of this particular death and the ghastly task of retrieving the dismembered parts of the body, has never left Mick's memory. Bernd Bender was originally from Wangaratta in Victoria. He was 21 years of age.[103]

Three days later, Operation Jack concluded and the Battalion returned to Nui Dat to begin preparation for their return home. However, Fate had retained two final throws of the dice that would impact on 9 RAR. The cost of their duty would continue to rise.

---

[103] Opcit

CHAPTER 13

"So just because the ranks look thin, there's never an empty space,
Because when we lose a Digger, his memories take his place"[104]

Waiting for the Ferry

AFTER TWELVE OPERATIONS THE BATTALION was more than ready to make the journey home. The main focus shifted to final administrative tasks and the handover to 8 RAR who were soon to arrive in-country. However, one of the administrative tasks to face D Company had little to do with the return home, or the arrival of 8 RAR. Mick was now the Officer Commanding D Company, but he was to discover this new appointment had responsibilities he had never dreamed of:

"D Company had at various times kept other pets, a large snake that had been captured during an operation and brought back to Nui Dat, and a monkey that developed a fondness for alcohol. However, the most obvious of these pets, or 'mascots' as some members of the Company liked to term them, was Private Grunt.

Private Grunt was a rather large pig who, when he was considerably smaller, had surrendered to us during one of our operations and he quickly became a part of the scenery of D Company lines. He was keen on eating left

---

[104] Mal Lyons, Memories of ANZACs, 5rar.asn.au/poems/anzacs.htm

over food and rotting jungle fruit. His table manners left a bit to be desired, but he was a faithful fellow and followed several of the soldiers around like a pet dog. However, his grunting made his existence obvious and I was pretty sure the powers that be would not approve of his presence.

To avoid Private Grunt's discovery, his handlers began to hide him in a weapon pit with a duckboard placed on the top of the pit to prevent his escape. I was never confident this means of restraining a fully grown pig would work. However, for a time I was agreeably surprised as Grunt remained in his quarters, then at the worst possible moment, the pig made a successful bid for freedom.

It happened when several high-ranking officers were visiting our lines. I can't recall now exactly who all of the visitors were. It may have been that the Chief of the General Staff was one of them, certainly the Task Force Commander was there, as was our CO Alby Morrison. I was guiding the visitors around the Company lines and they were stopping to talk to soldiers who stood by their beds waiting for the visit to end. The tent flaps were all rolled back for coolness and easy access, and this enabled me to cast furtive glances through the tents for any sign of Private Grunt and I was heartily relieved when there was neither sight nor sound of him. I started to relax, but at that very moment Private Grunt came through the tent lines in a very casual manner. Grunting happily, he followed the visitors into the tent they had just entered, and totally ignoring their rank, pushed past them before going on his way to find one of his human mates.

To their credit the visitors made no comment as Private Grunt made his exit. However, as they moved on to the next tent, the CO said to me in an aside: 'Get rid of the pig'. He was obviously not happy.

The Diggers knew their pet's time had come, and I was elected to send Private Grunt to meet his maker. I undertook to implement the execution with my 9mm pistol, and after the unhappy deed was performed, Grunt's body was prepared for edibility by the Company cooks. However, there was no interest shown whatsoever by D Company Diggers in partaking of the feast, as they refused to eat a 'good mate'. I am not sure what happened to the meat after that, perhaps it was eaten by another Company."

While Operation Jack was 9 RAR's last scheduled operation, the Battalion was still required to carry out operational tasks in the area immediately surrounding the Task Force position at Nui Dat. This area was known as the TAOR or Tactical Area of Responsibility, and it was frequently and aggressively patrolled to reduce the risk of enemy attack on the Task Force base. There were also other outside the wire tasks to be carried out including provision of security for land clearing operations and laying ambush on suspected enemy infiltration routes.

These final operational tasks were particularly tense as every 9 RAR soldier contemplated the homeward journey, which was scheduled for the 25th of November 1969. The general feeling was that it would be tragic indeed to fall in the final short weeks of the deployment. That tragedy came to pass on the 5th of November for Lance Corporal Martin Bink.

Martin Bink was a member of 9 RAR's Anti-Tank Platoon and the Platoon had been tasked to provide security for a land clearing team at a point around 16 kilometres to the south of Nui Dat. During the land clearing a bulldozer ran over a land mine. The mine exploded and Martin who was standing nearby, was killed. Martin was originally from the Netherlands and he had arrived in Australia with his parents as a boy. A regular soldier, he had arrived in Vietnam on the 9th of November 1968. He was 25 years of age.[105]

Martin's death had a profound effect on the Battalion. It seemed so unfair to die so close to the end of the deployment. However, an event was soon to take place take would shock the Battalion to its very core. On the night of the 23rd of November, Second Lieutenant Robert Convey was murdered by Private Peter Denzil Allen. Both men were members of B Company 9 RAR.

The night of the murder, a number of B Company soldiers were involved in a noisy party in the tent lines. They were drinking heavily and at around 2300 hours Lieutenant Convey had told the party to stop drinking and go to bed. This request was ignored and about 45 minutes later Lieutenant Convey returned and ordered the men to go to bed. This time he was obeyed. However, the order appears to have incensed Private Allen, he was drunk and had admitted to a strong dislike of Lieutenant Convey. Allen waited until he thought Convey was asleep, then using the sandbag protective wall around

---

[105] Opcit

Convey's tent as protection, he armed a grenade, reached over the sandbag wall and placed the grenade next to Convey's bed. Convey was killed instantly and Allen ran back to his own tent and went to bed.

The explosion had woken Lance Corporal Bennett who shared a tent with Allen. He heard the sound of running feet and then he saw Allen enter the tent, undress and go to bed. After that it did not take long for suspicion to fall on Allen, and after initially denying any involvement in the crime, he confessed, and was immediately placed under close arrest.[106]

Mick has an additional reason to remember the occasion:

"D Company was detailed to provide the guard for Allen. He was held in an 11 x 11 tent and we had a section of men guard him through the rest of the night until the MPs came and took him away. It was a shit of a job and the blokes hated doing it.

At three o'clock in the morning each of the Battalion's companies held a parade, and all of the hand grenades were withdrawn."

Weeks later Private Allen was tried by general court-martial, found guilty and sentenced to life imprisonment with hard labour. He served 10 years and 8 months of this sentence much of it in Risdon Prison in Tasmania.

Allen's victim, Second Lieutenant Convey, was born in England and migrated to Australia with his parents. He had joined the Regular Army and was selected for officer training. On gaining his commission he was posted to 9 RAR. According to his father his son had lived for the Army. He was 22 years of age.[107]

The morning after the murder, a deeply shocked Alby Morrison decided to limit his Battalion's access to alcoholic beverages by sending most of the Rifle Companies out to patrol the TAOR. It was a strategy that was not without risk:

"D Company went out into the bush where we ran into a very large and hostile bunker system. One of our blokes was shot in the arse and we immediately radioed to Battalion Headquarters "Contact standby Dustoff". However no sooner had we got this message away, the main radio aerial was

---

[106] Australian Army Legal Corps, Justice in Arms: Military Lawyers in the Australian Army's First Hundred Years, Angus and Robertson, p xcviii.
[107] 9rarsa.com.au/in-memoriam/

shot off and suddenly we really were on our own. We couldn't call for mortars or artillery support, in fact for a while we couldn't talk to anyone outside of the Company. Back at Battalion Headquarters our sudden lack of communication was greeted with dismay. They had received our initial transmission for the contact and the Dustoff, and then nothing. Their worry was that we had been overwhelmed by a superior force, so they gave our internal radio frequency to all of the aircraft flying in our area. This was the frequency of our internal radio network, which was the means Company headquarters used to talk to the Platoons. It wasn't long before one of the aircraft flying nearby called us and I was able to tell them what had happened. I asked the pilot to take a look at the bunker system we had hit and tell me what he could see. Moments later he was back on the radio to advise me it was the biggest bunker system he had ever seen.

It was immediately clear to me that we had to pull back. Even if ultimately, we were told to go back to destroy the bunker system, we would still have to pull back before we could hit it with artillery and an air strike. So I radioed the Platoon Commander of the Platoon that was in contact with the enemy and told him to get out of there. He was reluctant at first, but after I explained the need to call in artillery and air support he agreed. Then the aircraft we were talking to relayed a call from the CO. Alby explained that he would not expose us to any more danger and he was arranging for the Company to be air lifted out of the area. We were to find a landing zone and he would send helicopters to pick us up.

Finding a suitable landing zone was no easy matter, but I picked out a likely looking spot from the map, which was about two kilometres away from us. So, after briefing the Platoon Commanders we headed off, only to run into a forest of bamboo...we just couldn't seem to get through the stuff. The CO was getting anxious and kept sending messages demanding to know our progress. Finally, he asked if he should send the helicopters anyway and I agreed to this.

We were still struggling to make headway through the bamboo, and we heard the helicopters arrive and they just flew around and around the landing zone waiting for us to appear. Finally, the CO called again to say the helicopters would have to return to base for fuel, and we were still trying to reach the landing zone. We heard them fly away and almost as soon as we could no longer hear them, one of the Platoons radioed in that they were on the landing zone.

Luckily the helicopters were able to turn back and in a moment of madness I decided to play a practical joke on the airmen. I got the Platoon Commanders together and told them what we were going to do. Now our normal procedure when we were to receive a helicopter into our area was to throw a smoke grenade, of any colour, out into the landing zone. The helicopter pilot would then radio to the troops on the ground the colour of the smoke he could see. If he correctly identified the colour, he knew it was our troops who had thrown the smoke grenade and not the enemy. My plan was when the lead helicopter pilot requested smoke, that the whole lot of us on the ground would throw smoke onto the landing zone...after all, this was going to be the last time we'd have to do it.

Well, the joke worked really well...we could hear the pilots reporting green, yellow, orange, all kinds of coloured smoke, but they had their little joke too. I knew the pilot of the lead helicopter, a chap called Rex Budd, he dropped off a new radio aerial for us, but before we could get on his aircraft, he took off again, and I was left shouting into the radio, "Come back, you bastard!'

Unfortunately, all of this nonsense was being transmitted over the radio and Battalion Headquarters was monitoring the conversations. Next minute the CO radioed a curt message to my signaller, "Tell your Sunray[108] from me, that this is no time for levity!"

In retrospect the joke and the silly banter was a bit unfair on Alby. He had a lot to cope with at the time: the murder and our contact with the bunker system, and I imagine the last thing he needed was a bunch of idiots mucking around in the bush. He apologised later for being cranky, and I to him for our foolishness. I was at a Battalion reunion recently and the fellow who was my signaller back then was there too, and he reminded me of the CO's message."

Karma has a way of responding to tricksters and when smoke grenades are involved the "joke" can often be extremely vicious.

---

[108] Sunray was the radio term used to identify a Commander.

D Company returned to Nui Dat and began to make final preparation for their journey home. However, Lieutenant Convey's murder had left a feeling of unease within the Battalion, particularly among the officers and senior non-commissioned officers. On arrival in Vietnam 9 RAR followed an established practice with regard to the consumption of alcohol, and each Company set up its own wet canteen, or "boozer". These were places where the soldiers could enjoy a beer and relax after the stress of an operation. Some of the companies, including D Company had also established an "officers' and senior non-commissioned officers' boozer". This segregation had nothing to do with snobbery but in fact enabled the junior ranks to relax without the continued close scrutiny of their more senior leaders. It was to this establishment that Mick led his Platoon Commanders and their Platoon Sergeants for a well-earned beer, following their brush with the bunker system. As Mick recalls:

"No sooner had we gathered together that we heard the unmistakable sound of a grenade arming itself prior to detonation. We all froze in terror... was this to be another case of "fragging"? However instead of a devastating explosion the soft pop of a smoke grenade was heard and in an instant the boozer began to fill with smoke."

According to some witnesses, one of the Platoon Commanders assumed the culprit was one of his own men, and he decided to award punishment based on his suspicions. The suspect was ordered to clean boots while seated outside the Company boozer. The punishment fell flat when the suspect's mates all got their boots and joined him in his cleaning task[109]. Mick described this "joke" as a "mongrel act" but years later at a Battalion reunion he learned more detail:

"At the time I never found out who had thrown the damned thing. Then years later at a Battalion reunion I was standing next to this fellow, who shall remain nameless, and the subject of the smoke grenade came up. He looked a bit sheepish and said, 'It might have been me.' I said, 'It might have been you what?' He hung his head and replied: 'It might have been me who threw the smoke grenade.' I just looked at him... in that moment I was

---

[109] Richard "Barney" Bigwood and Andrew Bigwood, We Were The Reos: Australian Infantry Reinforcements in Vietnam, (Xlibris Corporation, 23 May 2011).

recalling the absolute terror I felt when I heard the grenade preparing to detonate. When I could finally respond, all I could say was: 'You bastard'..."

There were other acts of exuberance or perhaps stupidity in those final days at Nui Dat. Vehicles were stolen by those intent on making a last visit to the flesh pots of Vung Tau. In spite of Alby's best efforts, some officers and soldiers drank too much and many a miscreant found himself on a charge and fronting the CO's Orderly Room procedures. Finally, the long-awaited day arrived and on the 28th of November the members of the Battalion climbed aboard the trucks for the journey to Vung Tau Harbour where *HMAS Sydney* waited to take them home.

Chapter 14

"Listen to the breeze at night,
And as it whispers his name with a sigh,
Remember the precious times you shared,
And his memory will never die."[110]

The Welcome Home

ON ARRIVAL IN VUNG TAU Harbour *HMAS Sydney* delivered the Main Body of 8 RAR, the relieving Battalion for 9 RAR. The handover process, now virtually seamless, swung into action. However, this time the newbees 8 RAR, were particularly glad to be on dry land, for during the old aircraft carrier's passage of the South China Sea they had sailed through a typhoon. Tales of massive waves and mass seasickness were told to the outgoing 9 RAR men who hardly listened, they were just glad to be going home. There was a general feeling of euphoria among the outgoing men, a little like a family going on holiday, however one important person could only watch and wave from the wharf...the Commanding Officer Lieutenant Colonel Alby Morrison. The CO was to remain in Vietnam for Private Allen's court-martial and as events transpired, he would not return to Australia until late January 1970... another cost of duty. It had been a hard tour for the

---

[110] Robert Kearney, Echoes of Remembrance, 5rar.asn.au/poems/remembrance

CO, and he had the sympathy of most of his Battalion including Mick Bawden:

"During the tour his Battalion had lost 35 men killed and another 150 wounded, then there was the murder and several other stupid acts in those last couple of days. It was more than most people could manage, but Alby seemed to take it in his stride. However, it was easy to see he needed extra time in Vietnam like Custer needed more Indians. I was disappointed and saddened he wasn't coming home with us...

Aside from this there were mutterings around various headquarters and in the other Battalions regarding us. Some referred to us as the 'Death Battalion' and hinted that the rush we had experienced in preparing for our deployment was the reason why our casualty rate was so high. It was unpleasant and hard to take..."

Indeed, in some Regular Army circles 9 RAR was seen as being different from its sister Battalions. That *difference* attracted covert criticism that attributed 9 RAR's casualty rate to the speed in which the Battalion had been raised, the use of unconventional training methods, and the number of National Servicemen posted to the unit. Some of the criticism may be attributed to inter Battalion rivalry, but most of the derogatory remarks including reference to 9 RAR as "The Death Battalion" were quite simply insidious and ill-informed, made by people who should have known better. Not all members of 9 RAR were aware of these disparaging comments, but for those who were it was extremely hurtful, an unnecessary cost of their duty.

The embarkation went smoothly. Most of the Battalion officers attended a farewell reception given by the Task Force Commander, while the soldiers took up residence in their respective areas of the Vung Tau Ferry, In the early days of Australia's involvement in the war the task of swapping Battalions over, took 2 or 3 days to achieve. However, by 1969 the Navy was well practiced in embarking and disembarking troops and equipment, and 8 RAR and 9 RAR exchanged places in a matter of hours. Once the exchange of Battalions was complete the *Sydney* and its escorting Destroyer *HMAS Duchess* weighed anchor and accompanied by the cheers of the 9 RAR personnel, headed for home.

For the first 2 days of the journey it was smooth sailing, but on the third day the *Sydney* and the *Duchess* ran into the same typhoon that had marred their journey to Vietnam with 8 RAR. It was a fearful experience. D Company soldier Barney Bigwood recalled in his book "We Were REOs" that the long queues for the mess decks suddenly diminished as seasickness took its toll on the Battalion. Barney was able to boast that he was not affected by the conditions, he ate well and was able to observe the effects of the elements on *Sydney* and *Duchess*, this was a boast he shared with Mick Bawden:

"The waves were enormous, two landing craft were lost off the Sydney, there was plenty of sea sickness but oddly enough the crook ones did not include me. I had dinner alone in the wardroom, which was described as the "joint" by the steward who served the food. As I recall there were no other diners from the officers of 9 RAR."

As the *Sydney* battled her way through the mountainous South China seas the 9 RAR soldiers were unaware that they were in fact receiving the best of the post operational debriefing arrangements the Government and the Army were to make available. It was a sad feature of the Vietnam War that neither the Government, nor the Army, had any effective policy in place to enable returning veterans to be de-briefed and eased back into a nation at peace. Inadvertently those veterans who were returned to Australia on the *Sydney* were provided with around 10 days of opportunity to at least reflect on their 12 months in the war zone with their mates. Conversely, those who were repatriated by air transport generally experienced a lonely and detached return that allowed no time for them to unwind. Indeed, some of these men and women arrived home before their immediate family could be advised. RAEME Craftsman Edward Bevans recalled his experience:

"…They flew you home. You got off the plane, went through this big customs' shed and out a door and that was it – there was I standing on the other side of the road looking for a cab. It was surreal. In the morning I was in the bush in Vietnam and that night I was standing outside a big shed looking around for a cab in Sydney…

…I caught a plane home to Perth and caught an airport bus into town intending to catch the 353 bus home to Balga. I was walking up William

Street to where the bus used to start its run, and I shit you not, there was my mother and brother John waiting to catch the bus. She freaked out when she saw me standing in front of her. Like Tom Hanks in a B grade movie, I can tell you. So I shouted us a cab home…"[111]

However, regardless of the mode of transport, or whether or not they took part in a Welcome Home parade, once the veterans were back in Australia they were simply expected to return to normality and to get on with their lives. It was a cost of duty many of them had failed to foresee.

For 9 RAR even with the typhoon, the voyage home assumed the atmosphere of a tourist cruise…well almost anyway. There were no duties for the soldiers to perform, some spent their time sunbathing on the old aircraft carrier's massive flight deck, others read or simply sat with their mates and chatted. However, that was where the tourist dream ended. The *Sydney* was an old ship, designed and built for World War Two service in the North Atlantic, and it was totally unsuited to employment in the tropics. Accommodation for the crew and its human cargo of soldiers was abysmal, overcrowded and with scant ventilation. Add to this access to alcohol was strictly controlled. The soldiers were limited to one large can of beer, per man, per day. Those drinkers with an eye for business no doubt came to arrangements with non-drinkers, purloining the non-drinkers can, perhaps for some small monetary consideration.

As they approached Perth, the holiday atmosphere was further dinted when Customs officers boarded the *Sydney* demanding excise to be paid on the various items the Diggers had acquired in Vietnam. As Barney Bigwood recalls it was only the threat to throw the TV sets and other items overboard that brought the Customs men to their senses.[112]

Having demonstrated his superiority as a sailor during the typhoon, Mick enjoyed the more peaceful aspects of the journey. He noted the beauty of the Sunda Straits and enjoyed the brief call at Fremantle to disembark the Western Australian members of the Battalion. Then as the *Sydney* crossed the

---

[111] With Skill and Fighting – Craftsmen of the Australian Army 1942 – 2014, pp 88, 89 (Copyright Publishing Company Pty Ltd 2014) by Max Carmichael with Frank Benfield and Kerin Joyce.
[112] Richard "Barney" Bigwood and Andrew Bigwood, We Were The Reos: Australian Infantry Reinforcements in Vietnam, (Xlibris Corporation 23 May 2011) p 209.

Great Australian Bight the rough weather returned, and once again Mick was one of a few who was not debilitated by seasickness:

"The waves as we crossed the Bight were enormous, and as I was one of the only officers not constantly going for the big spit, I accompanied the Captain on "Captain's rounds". We went through every part of the vessel preceded by a bugler."

"Captain's Rounds" is a special inspection of the entire ship, performed by the Commanding Officer of a Naval vessel. Traditionally this inspection is carried out on a Friday, or prior to entering a foreign port. The *Sydney* docked at Adelaide's Outer Harbour on the 9th of December 1969, a Tuesday, so perhaps the captain considered Adelaide to be a foreign port. *Sydney's* Commanding Officer at the time was Captain Clarke RAN, one of the Navy's characters of the post Second World War period. Clarke was well loved by his ship's company for they could see his primary focus was their wellbeing. He was also a keen sportsman, captaining the ship's volley-ball team and organizing tournaments during the repetitive passages to and from Vietnam. As one member of his crew recalled, the captain was extremely competitive and was not above changing the ship's course so that the sun's glare was in the eyes of the opposing team.[113] Clarke's choice of Mick to accompany him on his rounds may well have been because Mick had not succumbed to seasickness. However, it is also possible that the captain recognised a kindred spirit in the young Army officer.

Popular folk lore suggests that Vietnam veterans were all denied welcome home ceremonies on their return. This is not correct. While those who returned by aircraft as individuals or small groups, generally received little or no official reception, larger groups such as an Infantry Battalion who returned home on the *Sydney* were in fact greeted by dignitaries and afforded a parade. As a result, as the *Sydney* made her way toward Adelaide, 9 RAR spent the final day of the journey preparing for their welcome home parade. Best jungle green uniforms were ironed, boots and brass buffed to a high sheen, and their SLRs retrieved from the ship's armoury. Immediately after disembarking the Battalion boarded buses and were driven to Torrens Parade Ground for their Welcome Home march. There they were joined by 9 RAR

---

[113] hmassydney.com/library/sydney3/intheirownwords account by Jim Dickson

soldiers who had returned home early. The Battalion then formed up in their companies. The band struck up the Battalion's marching tune of "Pass Me By" and the Battalion stepped off to march proudly along the city streets.

The reception the Battalion received from the Adelaide public was generally very good. Mick leading D Company was unaware of any protests or insults being hurled at the marching troops, and from his perspective he believes the Battalion was greeted with happy enthusiasm. A photograph of him at the head of D Company as they marched past the Adelaide City Hall graced the front page of the January 1970 edition of *Army the Soldier's Newspaper*. Forty-nine years later he would make the following comment on Facebook regarding the photograph:

"I had the privilege to lead some of the bravest young men on operations in a most difficult environment. I will always remember them."

However other members of the Battalion recall a different story and tales of being called "baby killers" and murderers are exampled. Certainly, in the time 9 RAR had been away, Australian participation in the war had become much less popular, and a growing protest movement had become most evident. For a movement that included many of the nation's most educated citizens among its ranks, the protestors demonstrated a remarkable lack of knowledge regarding the democracy they so fervently claimed to support.

In a democracy, the armed forces are a tool of Government to be employed when Government policies cannot be advanced by civil means. As a result, the armed forces cannot simply decide to involve themselves in a conflict and must be ordered to deploy by the elected government. Once the Government makes such an order it is the duty of the members of the armed forces to obey and to carry out their duties. Inexplicably many Australians who involved themselves in the anti-war movement were either ignorant of this fact or chose to overlook it. Instead, they chose to blame the soldiers for the nation's involvement in the Vietnam War. It was harsh treatment, a bitter cost, for the men and women who had simply done their duty. In the years that followed that cost would be greatly magnified and complicated by the nature of their wartime experiences.

CHAPTER 15

"Australia, speak!
Is this the country I went forth to save?
Do you remember my name,
Or is my memory lost in your surging echoes,
And your voice, my voice, silent evermore?
Waken and speak to me,
For the dawn, all unregarded,
Fades...."[114]

Normal Life

AT THE END OF THE "Welcome Home" march, South Australian members of the Battalion were reunited with their families, while the members based in the eastern states returned to the *Sydney* to complete their journey home. A period of war service leave awaited them all, then for the Regular Army members reassignment that in theory at least gave them a rest from being at the sharp end. On the other hand, many of the Battalion's National Servicemen had completed their obligation and many of those men eagerly awaited their discharge. In either event the Army and the Government expected the returning veterans to get on with their normal lives. For many

---

[114] Frank Wilmot, Echoes.

this expectation would prove difficult to achieve. In the months and years that followed a lack of Government and public support impacted negatively on many veterans.

The veterans who opted to leave the Army on their return home tended to suffer the worst of this situation. Cut off from their mates with whom they had shared the experience of war, ignored by Government and in many instances vilified by the public, many of these veterans found it difficult to re-assimilate into Australian society. Those veterans who continued to serve in the military tended to fair better. They lived and worked with people who had often shared their experiences, generally understood the issues the veteran faced, and with whom they could talk.

By the year 2000, the Australian Defence Force was beginning to address the issue of returning veterans for life after deployment. In 1969 this was hardly the case. A circular that attempted to address the issue through humour, was distributed to the families of returning veterans. The circular suggested the returning veteran would be prone to seize women off the street, be likely to engage in excessive drinking, be mesmerised by blonde hair and blue eyes, sleep with his boots on and so on. While this rubbish was meant to alert family members to possible changes in the returning veteran, it in fact demonstrated a complete lack of the Government's awareness of the problem, and of the Army's dismissive attitude to its responsibilities. The circular concluded:

"*...the Viet Cong could not shatter his composure, but civilisation just might. His rehabilitation is up to you his family and friends. Thank you and good luck.*"[115]

This was a rather clumsy effort at avoiding a particular duty…the duty of care. The duty and the cost of this avoidance was being handballed back to the veterans and their families.

Mick chose to continue his Army service; he was not, however, to remain with 9 RAR. In early 1970 on his return from leave, he was posted to Richmond as a Ground Liaison officer with a RAAF C130 Transport squadron.

---

[115] 9th Battalion Royal Australian Regiment Vietnam Tour of Duty 1968 – 1969 (Published by the 9 RAR Association).

To some, the move from the position of Company Commander to that of a Ground Liaison Officer (GLO) would seem to be a retrograde step. However, a brief examination of the Army/RAAF relationship will demonstrate that particularly at that time, a GLO was a very important factor in ensuring the two Services maintained a workable relationship.

For much of the Vietnam War, senior Army and RAAF officers struggled to understand one another with regard to the employment of helicopters. As a result, it had taken considerable effort on behalf of those involved in the war zone to develop procedures and practices that were satisfactory to both Services. However, these sharp end solutions were tenuous, requiring careful management. On the Army's side, the appointment of experienced and tactful officers as GLOs was essential. A GLO had to be able to guarantee the troops on the ground were effectively supported while at the same time ensuring the aircraft and their crews were employed efficiently and realistically. With Mick's recent combat experience and his reputation for perceptive relationships with his peers and seniors, he was an ideal choice for such a position. There was, however, a problem. His new place of work was at RAAF Base Richmond and when the family started to look for suitable housing, they found there was none available.

Rented apartments and hotel rooms were not an acceptable solution for a family that included two small children. To add to the stress, Mick's new job continued to require him to be absent from the family for extended periods. It was a situation Mardi found very difficult to endure. Mardi Bawden:

*"Immediately after Vietnam when we had had two beautiful months of leave together. A little family getting to know each other over again. We stayed at the 'Dinner House' a small house on a property Blinx (*Mick's father) *had purchased on the outskirts of Mount Gambier. The house got its name when Mick was in Vietnam and Blinx took his grandson Byron to the farm. There they lit the wood stove in the house and cooked lamb chops for their lunch. Thereafter Byron referred to the house as 'The Dinner House', it was so cute that it stuck.*

Then Mick was posted to Richmond as GLO with the RAAF. When Mick left for Richmond, I had packed up the Inverbrackie house, sent all our furniture to storage, and then moved to Mount Gambier to stay with my mother there to wait for Mick to say he had a house. However, there was no accommodation available for us, not even a house to buy. I was furious... I don't think I had ever been so angry..."

The cost of duty was rapidly approaching a point where their marriage was under threat, and Mardi indicated to Mick that if he felt unable to raise the situation with his superiors, she would. She was not bluffing:

"...I was hopping mad and I wrote this amazing letter putting all my angst on paper and telling what I thought of the powers that be who would have us separated yet again for an unknown length of time..."

Thoroughly alarmed, Mick contacted Bruce Ridland the officer in command of the Mount Gambier CMF unit, warning him of Mardi's anger and asked if Bruce might speak to her. Bruce agreed and telephoned Mardi asking to hear what she had written. Bruce Ridland, a fairly unflappable character, no doubt listened sympathetically, he probably even congratulated Mardi on the letter, but then he would have quietly explained that the letter should not be sent. In the meantime Mick had spoken with his CO who in turn raised the problem with a higher authority.

The Army had a solution...Captain Bawden would be reassigned to a vacant GLO position with a helicopter squadron at RAAF Base Fairbairn in Canberra, where housing for his family was readily available. Mardi's letter, henceforth referred to as "Mardi's Ministerial"[116]-was never sent, and in a relatively short time the Bawden family was reunited in a brand-new house in Kinsella Street in the Canberra suburb of Higgins. Mick would still be required to spend considerable time away from home, but at least Mardi and the children would have a decent house to live in. However, in shades of their earlier Adelaide housing experience the new house was on a bare dirt block on which they were encouraged to create a garden. The situation drew a sardonic comment from Mardi:

"...at least Canberra made a limited number of free plants to get the garden established..."

Everyone appeared to be happy, and yet the Bawdens were not destined to remain long in their Canberra residence. Perhaps Mick's demands for better housing may have displeased those who managed Army officer careers and

---

[116] A Ministerial is a written representation to a Government minister.

in a fit of pique they decided to move him on. Or perhaps the same people realised Mick's talents would be better employed elsewhere. Either way, late in 1970 he was again reposted, this time to 2 Recruit Training Battalion (2 RTB) at Puckapunyal, Victoria.

The Puckapunyal Military Area was typical of many Australian military training areas. In the winter it could be extremely cold, and in the summer damn hot. The general area is characterised by low scrub with a series of rocky hills and ridges the two highest being Mount Puckapunyal at some 413 metres, and Mount Kappe at around 384 metres. The training area provided a great place to learn basic field craft skills such as navigation, and the hills and ridges were sufficiently rugged for testing route marches to be undertaken. The area was first used by the Army as a mobilisation and training area during World War I, and then in the early 1920s, as an ordnance store and rifle range. In 1939, the area was formally established as "Puckapunyal Camp" and throughout World War Two used to train units of the Second Australian Imperial Force, Militia units, and the US Army's 41st Infantry Division. During the war the Camp was increased in size with the acquisition of an additional 5,700 hectares (14,000 acres). After the war in 1949, the 1st Armoured Regiment was raised and based at Puckapunyal. In the 1950s, during the first National Service scheme, the Camp housed the 3rd National Service Training Brigade, and at the end of that scheme, the Camp continued to house the 1^{st}Armoured Regiment and to facilitate Militia and school cadet training.

In 1964 with the reintroduction of National Service, Puckapunyal became the destination for National Servicemen conscripted from states and territories other than Queensland and New South Wales, National Servicemen from these two states trained at either Kapooka, or Singleton. The training program at these facilities was the same. The conscripts, referred to as "Drafted Recruits Undergoing Training" or "DRUTs", were allocated to training companies, each with a strength of around 300. Training was exacting and tough with the conscripts rising at 5.30 am to shower, dress, make their beds, and clean their boots and weapons all prior to breakfast. The next 15 hours of the day were filled with parade ground drill, weapon lessons, bayonet fighting practise, target shooting, and physical fitness training. They were taught that they were now part of a larger entity, to rely on their mates for support, and the importance of camaraderie. Some were traumatised by the experience, but most, almost in spite of themselves, enjoyed it and took pride in their achievements. On graduation they were allocated to a Corps and disbursed across the country to various Army schools to complete training specific to that Corps. Some eventually deployed to Vietnam.

Puckapunyal and 2 RTB was in many ways an exciting destination for a DRUT, however for some Regular Army officers and men, a posting to 2 RTB was viewed with misgiving. The Battalion was the recipient of a self-imposed, unofficial and unfortunate title… "The Legion of the Damned". For some reason the Battalion had gained the reputation as the place where Regular Army members who had committed some kind of professional faux pas, were sent. The title was ill-deserved and detracted from the reputations of the many 2 RTB's officers and NCO staff who were highly experienced soldiers, and who provided extremely valuable work.

Mick had some sympathy with those who revelled in the Battalion's unofficial title. In later times he would jokingly claim it was because of "Mardi's Ministerial" that he was sent to 2 RTB, and that Puckapunyal was the place they sent you when you had a troublesome wife. In fact, the real reason for the posting was much different.

In their efforts to prepare young officers for promotion, the Army career managers endeavoured to provide their charges with a raft of military experiences. Mick's previous postings had provided him with regimental and operational experience, now a period in an instructional position would see him well placed for promotion. His new appointment was that of a Company Commander, and once again he was in charge of troops. While he was not to lead them in battle, he felt rewarded by his work; instructional tasks that would prepare them for the next step in their military careers. He thoroughly enjoyed the 2 RTB posting and recalls that time of his career with affection:

"There were four companies and each intake around 300 DRUTs were allocated to each Company. The training schedules were well established and repeated every intake, so all the staff had to do was follow the syllabus.

I found the process very satisfying and speaking to parents after the

March Out Parade, the general feedback I received was recognition of the positive effect the training that these young men had gone through, had had on them.

We won 'Champion Company' a couple of times and I was proud of our Platoon Commanders and instructors."

Domestically, the Puckapunyal posting was a much more acceptable one for Mick and his family. Adequate housing was available, and they took up residence at Derna Court Puckapunyal Base. They quickly settled into a steady routine. Mick would leave for work each morning, and most times at least, return home each night. Mardi soon established a comfortable and welcoming home environment. They enjoyed the social life offered by the well run and active Officers' Mess, although one aspect of the Mess activities did not sit too well with Mardi. 2 RTB conducted regular boxing competitions and the Mess Committee ensured these events coincided with formal Mess dinners, the pugilistic efforts of the competing soldiers providing a form of after dinner entertainment. Mardi Bawden:

"...the boxing nights when we had front row seats dressed in formal evening wear, getting splattered with the blood of the contestants... ugh."

Generally though, life at Puckapunyal offered the combined advantages of living in a town, with the beauty of living in the country. The base itself had a few facilities, from where the family's basic requirements could be purchased, and the township of Seymour, only minutes away, was able to offer most other household needs. Should the need arise to visit a big city, Melbourne was just a couple of hours down the highway. Life could once again be described as "good".

There was even time for a little mischievous fun. Mick purchased a motorbike on which he startled sleeping conscripts by attempting to ride the machine through their barracks. The bike was also used in numerous crazed night-time dashes from the Officers' Mess to the top of nearby "Tit Hill". This almost treeless feature lay to the immediate north of the Base, the summit had at some time been crowned with a stone obelisk giving the feature the appearance of an erect nipple on a breast. World War Two soldiers who once graced the same training area, had named the feature "Nellie's Nipple" but in 2 RTBs time the more generalised name "Tit Hill" had been adopted. Somehow Mick and the variety of passengers that he persuaded to join him on those wild motorbike rides, survived.

Whilst it was possible for Mick and Mardi to relax a little and enjoy being a family, Vietnam was never far from their thoughts. This was particularly the case on the 10th of April 1970 when newspaper headlines trumpeted the news… **"Diggers In Relief Bid - Under Heavy Attack"**. The accompanying article related the story of an Australian led an attack to relieve a besieged American Special Forces camp. The Australian leading the attack was Patrick Beale, Mick's mate and mentor from his 10 RSAR days.

Patrick, now a major, had deployed to Vietnam with the Australian Army Training Team, where he had been appointed the Commander of the 1st Battalion Mobile Strike Force, a unit made up mainly of Montagnard tribesmen. The Montagnards are an indigenous people of the Central Highlands of Vietnam, who, prior to the Vietnam War had little contact with Vietnamese people in the lowlands of the country. Indeed, the Montagnard suffered the same injustices inflicted on many indigenous peoples across the world. The Vietnamese considered them to be savages and on many occasions, endeavoured to force the tribesmen from their land. However, in spite of the sometimes, violent confrontations between the Montagnards and the Vietnamese, the tribesmen had aligned themselves with the South, and fiercely resisted the communist forces' advance into their territory. As the war progressed the Americans sought to harness the Montagnard aggression and direct it where they considered it would produce the best result against the communist forces. To this end American Special Forces had established a series of fortified camps along the Cambodian and Laos borders, and one of these camps was at a place called Dak Seang.

On the 1st of April, 1970, preceded by a heavy rocket and mortar bombardment, three Regiments of North Vietnamese troops numbering approximately 10,000 soldiers attacked the American camp at Dak Seang. In spite of repeated supporting air strikes against the communist force, the camp was in danger of being overrun, and on the 3rd of April, Patrick Beale's Battalion was ordered to attack the assaulting North Vietnamese to relieve pressure on the besieged camp.

A heavy fire fight ensued as the relief attempt developed, and Patrick's

Battalion took heavy casualties to gain a few hundred metres of savagely contested ground. However, while they did not succeed in breaking the siege, their efforts took some of the pressure off the Dak Seang defenders, enabling wounded to be evacuated and some resupply to be delivered. Throughout the battle Patrick led his men skilfully and resolutely and his leadership was recognised with the award of the Distinguished Service Order.

Back in Australia, Patrick's wife Denise was dismayed to learn her husband was involved in the fighting. She had believed Patrick was involved in training the South Vietnamese and that he would not be involved in combat. Anxious days passed before word was received that Patrick was safe...a common cost of duty to be endured by the loved ones of those deployed to a war zone.

Meanwhile at Puckapunyal, 2 RTB had graduated another intake of National Servicemen and Mick's Company was awarded the Champion Company award. Mardi and the children were thriving in their changed environment. Life was good, and the war and long periods of separation seemed very far away. However, their days at Puckapunyal were now numbered.

Mick was panelled for the 1972 April/May Infantry Company Commanders' Course, a sure sign he was at least being considered for promotion, and that in his near future duty was still waiting for another disbursement to be made. The time for the course soon arrived and once again, Mick packed his bags, kissed Mardi and the children goodbye and made his way to Ingleburn and the School of Infantry.

The Company Commanders' Course required its students to study the theory and doctrines associated with leading an Infantry Company. Brought to its most simple form the course involved a series of battlefield problems, which the students considered, moved imaginary troops around a map, and produced answers that hopefully agreed with the Directing Staff's solution. Most of the students had already experienced active service, and some like Mick had led a Company on operations. Inevitably some students produced solutions based on what worked in reality, often contradicting the theoretical solutions being taught by the Directing Staff. Unfortunately for any nonconforming students, the Directing Staff placed little value on the old military saying, "tactics are fine, but rightness is all". There was a clear message for the students…conform or fail. Mick passed the course and returned to Puckapunyal qualified for promotion to the rank of major.

Attaining the rank of major admits the officer to the senior ranks of the Army, a group referred to as having "Field Rank". It is an important step in an officer's career, particularly in an infantry Battalion, where an officer of Field Rank is a particularly formidable entity. The ill-informed may believe that promotion to major occurs as a matter of course. This is not so. Promotion to Field Rank is gained by experience and demonstrated ability. Junior officers who fail to demonstrate these qualities are not promoted to Field Rank and are often quietly encouraged to seek alternative employment.

In mid-1972 Mick's promotion was confirmed and the now *Major* Bawden considered the options for his next posting. A return to Vietnam was on the cards, but this was less likely as Australia had already begun to wind down its military effort in the war. The last Infantry Battalion, 4 RAR, had left Nui Dat on the 7th of November 1971. The remaining ground troops were now a handful of AATTV members. He could of course be posted to one of the nine Infantry Battalions, which seemed a good option for Mardi and the children. However, to paraphrase the hit song *You Can't Hurry Love*, Mick indeed would…*just have to wait*. It was while he waited for confirmation of his next posting, that he was presented with a more immediate duty to perform.

Mick was contacted by the Military Police (MP) regarding a situation that was developing with one of the corporals in Mick's Company. The corporal, a Vietnam veteran, had armed himself with a shotgun and locked himself in his married quarter. When the MPs approached him, he threatened to shoot them, and so they decided to employ the tried-and-true Army solution to any difficulty…the chain of command. This approach could see a problem passed either up, or down, the hierarchical system. At its best, this system ensured an issue was addressed at an appropriate level, at its worst the system enabled those who should have dealt with the issue to avoid it. In this particular case the MPs figured Major Bawden was the corporal's Company Commander, so he could sort the problem out. Mick Bawden:

"*I went to see the corporal hoping against hope that the situation was not as bad as the MPs described. Unfortunately, they had hardly exaggerated. As soon as I approached the corporal, he threatened to shoot me and then himself... not a good start. However, from that chilling introduction, the situation began to improve. It took a while, but I managed to convince him to hand over the weapon. As soon as he was disarmed the MPs promptly arrested him and took him away..."*

Mick never established the ultimate fate of the unfortunate corporal, a matter that still troubles him. Indeed, at that time there was little opportunity for him to consider such matters, for soon after this event he was posted at short notice as the Officer Commanding Support Company, 2nd Pacific Island Regiment (2 PIR).

2 PIR was located at Moem Barracks, Wewak, Papua New Guinea.

CHAPTER 16

*"And hail the advent of each dangerous day,
And meet the great adventure with a song."*[117]

New Guinea

IN 1972 PAPUA NEW GUINEA was still an Australian Protectorate; a condition some political observers claimed was in reality a thinly disguised colony. Certainly, Australia maintained substantial control of key aspects of the PNG administration, including the military, the largest portion of which was the Pacific Island Regiment (PIR). The Regiment consisted of two Battalions, 1 PIR located at Taurama Barracks in Port Moresby, and 2 PIR, Mick's destination, located at Moem Barracks in Wewak. Most of the officer and senior non-commissioned officer positions were held by Australians. As Mick had observed on his previous visit to the PIR, these appointments were not easily managed, as the PIR soldiers could prove to be a volatile lot. Indeed, it was this volatility that had led to Mick's sudden posting to the Regiment. There had been trouble in 2 PIR Support Company, necessitating the hasty removal of its Commander. However, the exact nature of the trouble was not made clear to Mick until after his arrival in-country. This did not concern him overly as in addition to command

---

[117] Julian Grenfell.

there was the added advantage to the posting...Mardi and the children would accompany him.

The Bawden family arrived in PNG on the 27th of October 1972. In a variation of their previous experiences with housing uplifts, Mick had first made a visit to the new posting, but then returned to Australia to accompany Mardi and the children on the day of their move. It is not a journey Mardi recalls with any pleasure:

"...*two-year-old Amanda didn't have a seat and was asleep on my knee and I missed out on a meal...*"

Six years had passed since Mick's first visit to the country and while he did not immediately notice any difference, PNG was in the process of undergoing significant social and political change as it moved inexorably toward complete independence from Australia. This move toward independence was supported by successive Australian Governments. As part of the process the House of Assembly of Papua and New Guinea had been established in 1964, and by 1968 a ministerial system of government with an Administrator's Executive Council adopted.

Australia still controlled PNG's International Affairs and all matters regarding the new nation's defence. However, by 1972, responsibility for PNG's International Affairs was beginning to transfer to local control. Defence, however, was still firmly an Australian responsibility. This was a sore point for many local politicians, as they believed the Australian Government was likely to use the PIR against its own people. There was in fact some basis for this concern. In 1970 the then Prime Minister of Australia John Gorton, had moved to have the PIR called out to deal with an insurrection on the Gazelle Peninsula, on the island of New Britain where separatists were illegally occupying land. Gorton's idea was rejected by his Cabinet, however the knowledge that such an action had been considered resulted in many PNG citizens regarding the PIR with some suspicion.

A nation thus poised on the edge of independence has the potential for volatility. However, if the Bawdens gave this possibility any consideration, the prospect of a great adventure in an exotic location, one which in many ways they could experience together, surmounted any concerns they may have held on the issue.

Mick's adventure began with an appointment to meet his new CO Lieutenant Colonel Lewis. It was during that meeting he learned his new posting had all the hallmarks of a poisoned chalice. Some weeks before his arrival, the soldiers of Support Company had mutinied. As mutiny goes it was a rather tame affair and basically involved the soldiers' refusal to leave barracks for early morning parade. While this may seem a trivial incident, in an organization where the disaffected are armed and trained to kill, it was not to be taken lightly. The Company Commander had been sent back to Australia, and Mick was now the man in charge. The CO made it clear he expected Mick to motivate the men of Support Company and have them return to being productive and trustworthy soldiers. It was a heavy expectation for it was clear to Mick that the members of his new command were unhappy. Mick Bawden:

"My briefing with the CO included news of the mutiny or 'sit down', and I was told to take the Company out into the bush for six weeks so that they could get to know me, and for me to form a bond with them so there would be no more mutiny in the future. I had the distinct feeling this was a tall order.

I left the CO's office deep in thought, and the first person I ran into in the corridor outside was the Battalion's Roman Catholic Padre, Austin Crapp. We exchanged introductions and pleasantries and in the course of conversation the Padre told me of an opportunity to build a schoolhouse in a remote village called Wogenara. I was quickly sold on the idea, for it seemed just the kind of task to refocus Support Company and to give the men a sense of purpose and pride."

Within hours of assuming command of Support Company, Mick began to plan to put Padre Crapp's idea of the new schoolhouse into practise. He recalls:

"...Support Company was well equipped to take on this task, aside from numbers of fit young men to labour on the building, I had discovered the Assault Pioneer Platoon Commander was a qualified Engineer.

A day or so after the meeting with the CO, the Padre and I set out on foot to visit Wogenara to carry out a reccie to see what needed to be done. On arrival at the village, we met the village schoolteacher Sister Mary Linda of the Holy Spirit Adoration Sisters, the female branch of the order of the

Society of the Divine Word or SVD. She was about 25 years of age, of German extraction with a string of degrees after her name that would have qualified her for all kinds of senior jobs in just about any part of the world. Instead, she had chosen a religious life and to work in an isolated PNG community. The only European in the village, Sister Mary Linda was very excited at the prospect of the new school building. I was excited too for I could see the task of building the new school was just the thing Support Company could succeed at.

A few days later I took the whole Company out to Wogenara. The soldiers carried in all of the supplies and equipment needed for the job and as soon as we got there, we started to build the schoolhouse. There was an initial problem when we used sand and gravel from a nearby river without first washing the stuff, apparently this was required to remove some kind of impurities that spoiled the concrete. As a result, the first batches of concrete we made were useless, but once we sorted that out the build went very smoothly.

So far as Support Company was concerned it was as I hoped. The job seemed to please the soldiers and it was obvious they were taking great pride in their work. When the building was finished, we returned to Moem Barracks in good spirits.

Unfortunately, while our work was successful, soon after we left Wogenara the situation in the village changed dramatically. Sister Mary Linda was sexually assaulted. The perpetrator of the assault was a "long long man" (one who was mentally deranged), and because of his condition the village community tended to tolerate his behaviour. Finding little support in the village Sister Mary Linda walked through the jungle to the SVD Mission at Wewak where she was initially cared for."

Duty assumes many shapes and sizes, as does the related costs.

The authorities were not as constrained by cultural morals regarding long-long men, and the perpetrator of the assault was soon arrested. In the ensuing period the Bawdens provided Sister Mary with a refuge:

"As the time for his trial drew near, Mardi and I were approached to have Sister Mary Linda stay with us until after a verdict had been reached. We readily agreed and I went to the mission and brought her to our house in

Moem Barracks. When I introduced Sister Mary to Mardi and the children, she was very emotional and hugged our six-year-old Byron for a long time. This surprised the lad and afterwards he kept asking why she had done that. It was of course a very stressful time for the poor woman, and I took her to the courthouse each day that she was required to give evidence. However, as time passed, she grew more relaxed. She often went swimming with Mardi and the children. Then when the trial was over, she asked to return to Wogenara to continue her work. So far as I know she is still somewhere in Papua New Guinea, she is an amazing person."

For Mardi, her PNG adventures commenced with taking possession of the family's married quarter:

"Married Quarter 51 was aptly named "Haus kokroach", for we shared the house with a large community of cockroaches of various makes and sizes. The building itself was a timber construction set on tall concrete poles, which allowed it to survive the many "guria" (earth tremors).

Beneath the house I grew a garden of peanuts, pineapple and I think some struggling potatoes. Through the louvre windows where the geckos clung to the fly wire permeated the sweet perfume of the canopy of frangipani trees after rain."

It was a far cry from the houses in Canberra and Puckapunyal, but as Mardi recalls there was a compensating factor…there was an entitlement for a servant:

"Our first servant or "Haus Boy" was a young man called Aaron. Early in our association he told us he wanted a bicycle to ride from his place to ours. He agreed to pay off the cost of the bike if we would first buy it for him…in our innocence we bought the bike and didn't see him again.

Our next Haus Boy was an older man named Gilbert. He made no demands but just got on with his work. He had a wife and a family at the village of Marprik, about 65 kilometres away. When he was with us he lived in the "Boy Haus" at the bottom of the garden. He ate a handful of peanuts for breakfast, and his only other meal of the day consisted of a huge mountain of rice with a "tin fish" on top, which he consumed mid-afternoon.

Gilbert did the housework including washing the dishes and our laundry. He made an immaculate job of the soldiers' starched juniper shorts and shirts. However, he had limited understanding of children's clothing, at one time reducing Byron to tears when he ironed the plastic "tweety bird" on the front of Byron's favourite t-shirt. I would turn on the back light after dinner about 9.00pm and his bare footsteps could be heard on the stairs when he came to wash up.

When we came back to Australia, I missed Gilbert, and I was sometimes heard to call out to him as I struggled with washing on the clothes-line in a high wind."

While these dramas were unfolding in PNG, back in Australia a drama of a different nature was unfolding. Riding the wave of anti-war/anti-conscription feeling, the Australian Labor Party's pre-election publicity was pushing the theme "It's Time". On the 2nd of December 1972 the majority of the Australian electorate agreed with this sentiment and the Australian Labor Party swept into office with an eight-seat majority. This victory had an almost immediate impact on the Army, as on the 5th of December the new Prime Minister announced the end of conscription. The immediate result of this announcement was profound, as National Servicemen voted with their feet and simply walked off base to return to their homes. As 1973 rapidly approached, Army Headquarters was faced with a massive rationalisation project, one which would meet the new Government's policies and realign Army units in order to meet the severe reduction in available manpower. Inevitably this meant the disbandment of some units.

There was some concern among former 9 RAR veterans that as their beloved Battalion was the last Battalion to be raised, it might well be one of those units to be stood down. However, while the Battalion avoided the ignominy of disbandment, it was nevertheless affected. In October 1973 it was linked with 8 RAR, to form 8/9 RAR, a new unit that honoured the ethos and achievements of both former units. On the other hand, Mick's previous unit 2 RTB, was one of the first units to be disbanded. Mick and Mardi received an invitation to a disbandment party. The 2 RTB officers knew there was no way the two could attend…a handwritten note on the bottom of the invitation read:

"It's the thought that counts…"

While they may have missed out on the party, to some degree Mick and other Australians serving with 2 PIR were shielded from the political ministrations occurring at home, for regimental life at Wewak hardly changed. It was a situation that would be short-lived. To begin with now that Vietnam and conscription had been removed from the Army workplace environment, there was a diminishing landscape of posting positions and promotional prospects for the remaining officers and soldiers alike. Competition for the more exacting and exciting postings, such as those on offer in PNG, became intense. In addition to these impacts the new Government's defence policy rejected "forward defence" where the nation deployed troops beyond Australian shores to combat threats, in favour of "continental defence". PNG remained the only major offshore posting for Australian soldiers who were keen for some kind of "operational experience" to enhance their résumé. Once PNG gained full independence this opportunity too would evaporate. It was a depressing set of circumstances for many professional soldiers, made worse by a feeling that Australian society neither supported them, nor understood the service they had provided to the nation during the Vietnam conflict.

No doubt Mick had a professional interest in the changing military situation, however there was little point in worrying about it. Besides, his regimental duties were more than enough to hold his attention. As he had predicted, the job at Wogenara had given the soldiers of Support Company a renewed sense of purpose. As a result, the Company was able to take on other tasks allocated by the CO. These tasks were largely influenced by the Australian Government's change in defence focus and the suspicions of the budding PNG national Government regarding the Pacific Island Regiment. During this time the Regiment's activities had a decreasing focus on training for war and increasing focus on "Aid to the Civil Power" operations.

Following the success of the Wogenara school project Support Company's next patrol was to Cape Gloucester. Cape Gloucester was the scene of a World War Two US Marine landing to capture Japanese airfields in the area, and the area remained littered with war relics and unexploded ordnance. Support Company's mission was to "show the flag" and to destroy as much of the unexploded ordnance as possible. Aside from these activities there was also time for some relaxing fishing with the local people.

The Company's next task was to build a wharf on the island of Tarawai. The wharf project was to provide a ship loading facility for the Islanders, who hitherto were required to row their marketable produce out to the ships lying at anchor off the coast. Working to a limited budget, it was decided to use local timber to construct the facility. A deal was negotiated with a local timber merchant who happily provided the necessary lumber. However, timber proved to be an unfortunate choice of building material, one that would introduce Mick and his officers to one of nature's most ferocious eaters…the Teredo Worm.

As the men of Support Company expertly went about their work, positioning heavy timber poles in the water then driving them into the sand beneath, and erecting the decking of the wharf, the Teredo Worms gathered for a feast. Sometimes referred to as the "termites of the sea", these worms play an important ecological role, by quickly and efficiently devouring submerged timber; however, for man-made wooden marine structures –the Teredo Worm is a catastrophe. They bore through submerged wood, efficiently undermining its structural integrity, ferociously consuming all they can find. The worms have been responsible for the demise of many wooden ships, small boats, and of course wooden wharves.

So it was that almost as soon as Support Company drove the first pylon into the water, these ferocious eaters of all things wooden began to bore into and through the submerged wood. Unaware of the situation developing beneath them, Mick and his men completed their work, and with some ceremony handed the completed wharf over to a slightly bemused island community.

Soon after Support Company had returned to barracks, the Tarawai wharf began to weaken, and finally collapsed into the waves where its pitiful remains were completely devoured by the ravenous worms. Sometime later Mick was escorting a visiting VIP on a tour of the area. He intended to show the visitor the shipping wharf as an example of Support Company's work but to his amazement the structure no longer existed!

The local timber merchant was summoned, and an explanation demanded. The answer was simple 'Teredo Worm…' Somewhat bewildered Mick inquired that if the merchant knew what would happen, why had he not told

Mick before the wharf was built. Again, the answer was simple... 'You didn't ask!'

Later, Support Company returned to the scene and effectively addressed this misunderstanding by rebuilding the wharf using steal pylons. The Teredo Worm's reaction to this is not recorded.

Following their feeding of the Teredo Worms, the Company was tasked to build a road at Oksapmin, a village in the Southern Highlands nestled at the foot of the massive geological feature of Hindenburg Wall. When Mick and Support Company visited, the area was in transition from the traditional way of life in favour of plantation crops and employment with a number of mining companies active in the area. Support Company's road greatly assisted population mobility.

Another major task undertaken by Support Company was to clear a log jam on the Green River. The Green River area was being logged for timber, some would say illegally, and the river was being used to float the logs to the coast where they could be retrieved for milling. On this occasion the logs had jammed in a solid mass, preventing navigation along the river. To get to the area the Company travelled by tractor, a slow and uncomfortable journey.

There were many other tasks including garrison duty at Vanimo on the West Irian border; a 60-mile patrol in the Southern Highlands from the major settlement of Tari in the Hela Province to Mendi in the Southern Highlands Province. There was also a patrol to Dagua-But for the purpose of assessing the tourism potential of the World War Two battlefields and airstrips, and to the remote coastal community of Aitape in the Sandaun Province.[118]

The destruction of World War Two unexploded ordnance was a constant and important task for Support Company. During the Second World War, Wewak was the site of the largest Japanese airbase on mainland New Guinea and it was repeatedly attacked by Australian and American air forces. In 1972 evidence of these attacks in the form of unexploded bombs of various sizes and of Japanese anti-aircraft shells were still in evidence around the

---

[118] On the 17th of July, 1998 Aitape made world news when the region was hit by two major earthquakes, followed by a series of tidal waves. Several villages 20 km west of Aitape were destroyed, leaving 2200 people dead and thousands injured and homeless.

area. On the airport grounds the main means of achieving the task was to gather any ordnance discovered and where possible move it to a central place for destruction. This was potentially dangerous work for many of the items found were beginning to degrade, to a point where any injudicious handling might cause them to detonate. However, it was also potentially dangerous for aircraft using the airport, and of necessity close liaison with the airport's air traffic control was needed to ensure any demolition work did not threaten low flying aircraft. Fortunately for all concerned the 2 PIR demolition teams were extremely well trained, and their Company Commander insisted on the most rigid safety precautions being adhered to. However, in spite of the best intentions of Mick and his team, accidents could not be totally avoided. As Mick recalls:

"We had a pile of UXBs[119] from the airport area ready to blow and I contacted the air traffic controllers for final clearance before lighting the fuse. They gave the all-clear, but at the last minute I saw this RAAF Caribou that seemed to be on its final approach. I radioed the air traffic folk again and they weren't concerned and said that once he landed, I was free to blow the lot. Well, the Caribou lumbered in and as soon as it disappeared beneath the level of the trees, I lit the fuse...only to see the bloody Caribou reappear above the trees, climbing toward the sky. There was a fearful bang as the UXBs went off and I swear the Caribou staggered in the sky, but it kept climbing..."

It seems the pilot of the Caribou was practising "bumps", practise landings where the pilot approaches the landing zone, the aircraft touches down followed by an immediate take off. Badly shaken, Mick vowed to be even more careful in all further demolitions. This additional care led to him laying demolition charges around a discarded Japanese helmet, the crown of which had been discovered protruding above the ground (*"well it looked like a bloody bomb"*)[120]. Then in 1975, in spite of the caution and respect Mick took in dealing with explosives, he was involved in another incident.

A request for assistance with an unexploded bomb was received from the nearby Brandi High School. Brandi High School was at that time a boarding

---

[119] Unexploded Bomb.
[120] Mick Bawden

school with a total student population of around 500. The school was noted for its academic achievements and the students were very active in art, drama and music. There was a heavy emphasis placed on agricultural pursuits as a field of study, and as a means of providing food for the students. To this end, the school had an area of land set aside for gardens and another area as a cow paddock on which grazed a small herd of cattle. The unexploded bomb that was to become the focus of another Support Company activity was discovered on the cow paddock, by a school worker. The worker was cutting grass in a swampy area of the paddock when he found a metal object which he and the school's headmaster identified as an unexploded bomb.

There was no undue alarm at the discovery. During the Japanese occupation of World War Two, the school's cow paddock had received its fair share of ill directed Allied bombs. The paddock was pock-marked with the craters of bombs that had exploded on impact, but some had been absorbed by the swampy nature of the paddock's ground and failed to detonate. Every now and then, one of these unexploded bombs would somehow work its way to the surface and the Army would be called on to remove it. These occasions had the potential for great tragedy…a misdirected foot, or a curious student, and the results were unthinkable. The school had indeed been lucky the bomb had been detected by someone with a strong serving of common sense. A call was made to the Barracks where, as it happened, Mick was the demolition officer on duty. Gathering a small team of his Support Company soldiers he hastily drove to the school to address the situation.

After an initial inspection, Mick identified the object he could see as a Japanese 50-pound bomb, and because of its condition he decided that the safest course of action was to destroy it in situ. Mick Bawden:

"The school's headmaster insisted on accompanying me to where the bomb lay. The ground was so boggy and wet that any attempt to move, or dig around the thing, might have set it off... I had three safety concerns, the first of which was a crowd of interested spectators who had gathered to watch the fun. The second concern being the cow paddock was directly beneath a busy flight path for the Wewak airport. The third consideration was the school's herd of cattle..."

The airport was contacted, and a flight scheduled to fly over the cow paddock air space, was delayed. The cattle were chased away to a distance considered to be safe, and the spectators dispersed. A small explosion was expected, but every reasonable precaution taken to ensure all involved were safe. The demolition explosives were set in place, a suitable fuse ignited, and Mick and the headmaster retired a safe distance.

The resulting explosion was far greater than anticipated, as the headmaster's wife, Laura Keating later recalled in a rather colourful description of the event:

"The noise was horrific. Wet mud flew high in the air and nearer residents later reported that some of it rained down on their roofs. Then immediately after the explosion there was shocked silence, followed by pandemonium... Junior students fled into the bush...the cattle stampeded and pigs in their pens screeched in terror and the school hens ceased to lay...

Uttering an original blend of blasphemy, obscenity and prayer Major Mick and the headmaster gingerly approached the scene of the blast and stood dry-mouthed and shaking on the edge of a deep black crater into which water had already begun to flow."

Fortunately, no one was hurt, and once Mick and the headmaster recovered from their shock, it was possible for them to see the funny side of the incident. Other members of the school community, however, were not amused, and while the headmaster and Mick retired to the headmaster's residence to calm their shattered nerves with a strong drink, a steady stream of complainants arrived at the headmaster's door.

It had been a harrowing experience for all. In his after-action consideration of the incident Mick assumed the 50-pound bomb must have been lying on top of a number of similar bombs, or perhaps one very large bomb. He was thankful he had not attempted to more closely investigate the bomb prior to demolition.

That incident was typical of the tasks undertaken by the 2 PIR demolition teams at that time, the fact that accidents were rare, a tribute to the soldiers' training and professionalism.

On the domestic scene Mardi had her own excitements to cope with. Earthquakes are a regular feature of PNG life, but are generally beyond the experience of most Australian housewives. She recalls:

"I remember my first guria[121]. I was washing my two babies in the bathtub. My friend was in the kitchen preparing the evening meal and her baby was at the end of the long passage in her carry basket on my bed. Suddenly the towels on the bathroom rail began swinging – the babies looked startled. My friend stood in the kitchen door looking astounded. I stepped into the passage halfway between her and the sleeping baby, now rocking with the momentum of the house, I wondered will I get the baby, or leave it sleeping.

Before a decision was arrived at, the crisis point had passed, and the oscillations decreased, and we wondered if it had all been in our imaginations..."

Earthquakes aside, at first glance a housewife's life in the PIR appeared ideal. Mardi's 1973 diary records a bevy of social engagements: yoga, tennis, art (painting), picnics and swimming at the beach. There were, however, other aspects of life that were less appealing and very different from what she was used to. Fumigating the house against cockroaches and mosquitoes, and dealing with tropical related illnesses and infections, were generally not part of the Bawden working schedule in Australia. There were other aspects of life to which she had become more accustomed. Her diaries are punctuated with military engagements… "Mick goes on patrol…" "Mick comes home…" "Dining-in Night…" "Parade" … This was the lot of the wife of a Regular Army soldier. Not a lot different from her previous experience in Puckapunyal and Woodside.

There were other distractions to regimental life. As the new Australian Government settled into power, Australian VIP visits like the one where the demise of the wooden wharf was discovered became a regular part of the 2 PIR schedule. Politicians and senior military officers, a few with legitimate reasons to visit PNG (but many who had not) arrived in a steady stream. Among the notable visitors at this time was the Minister for External Territories Bill Johnson. The Minister addressed the officers of the Battalion, telling them that after PNG independence, there would be no Australian external territories. If any of the assembled officers believed they had a chance of an extended tenure in 2 PIR, this announcement certainly put a

---

[121] Pidgin English word for "shakes".

dampener on their expectations. Another VIP visitor was the US Ambassador to Australia. This gentleman impressed the Battalion by arriving in his own aircraft. However, it was obvious many of the VIP visitors were quite simply taking advantage of their positions to visit an exotic location and escape the stress of Canberra, particularly in the winter. Climatically Wewak was a far more attractive location than the frost covered expanse of Australia's national capital. This category of VIP visitor had plenty of time for a little sightseeing, and in some cases time to go fishing. A keen fisherman himself, Mick used the barrack's small "tinny" to enable his own fishing expeditions, and so he was often the guide selected to take those VIPs with a desire to catch fish out on the sea for a day's sport. Mick recalls those occasions with some glee:

"Most like the Chief of the General Staff, General Hasset and Brigadier Norrie, Commander of the PNG Defence Force were well prepared with state-of-the-art fishing gear. They thought my fishing gear was barbaric compared with their equipment! Barbaric yes, but I landed more fish!"

It all sounds like fun, and to a degree it was. However, the cost of duty in PNG could be measured in time apart. Time apart from Mardi and the two children when Mick undertook frequent patrols into the bush, often for extended periods; and time apart from their extended families back in Australia. A visit by Mardi's mother Alma in 1973 helped, however, Mick's mother Sadie was too frail to make such a journey and sadly died on the 27th of August 1974. Time separated from loved ones represented a cost that could never be recouped.

In 1974 Mick's attention was diverted away from fishing and building houses and wharves, to a more unusual task for an Army officer. He was appointed as the Army representative on the Wewak-But Council. The Council was a similar organization to local government shire councils in Australia. The Army was one of the largest landowners in the area, and roads and community facilities were an important consideration for the organization, its members and their families. Mick recalls his time on the Council with affection:

"I was an appointed observer, with the brief to implement any assistance that the Army could provide. I enjoyed the role...they were good people to be with..."

It was an experience that was to stand him in good stead in the future.

Change was afoot for 2 PIR. In 1974 Mick left Support Company to become the Battalion second-in-command (Battalion 2ic). A Battalion 2ic has a complex and highly responsible life. On the one hand he is accountable for the overall administration of the Battalion, while at the same time being ready to assume command of the unit should the CO become ill or for some reason be called away from his command. Mick's Vietnam experience as Company 2ic, and as a Company Commander helped prepare him for this new role. Indeed, in a case of history repeating itself, soon after Mick was appointed as Battalion 2ic the CO, Lieutenant Colonel Lewis, was posted back to Australia, and the new CO was not immediately available to assume command. This left Mick in the position of "administering command". It was a similar situation, although a somewhat less dangerous one, to when he had assumed his appointment of 2ic D Company 9 RAR in Vietnam at Dat Do. No doubt with some nervousness Mick gritted his teeth and got on with the job.

Administering command of a Battalion is often a thankless task. The officer placed in such a position is restricted in the policy he may instigate to that established by the absent incumbent. In this case, as the new CO was yet to arrive, Mick was required to follow the policies established by the former CO. This fact aside he was, if only temporarily, in command of a Battalion. A copy of 2 PIR Routine Orders Part One dated the 5th of November, lists Major T.L. Bawden as: *"Commander 2nd Battalion The Pacific Island Regiment and Commander Wewak Area Moem Barracks"* ... a very satisfying list of titles.

The replacement CO was Lieutenant Colonel Jeffrey. This officer would go on to have a distinguished career in the service of Australia. At various stages of his military career, he commanded Australian Special Forces, and was Deputy Chief of the General Staff prior to retiring from the Army at the rank of major general. After his retirement he was appointed as Governor of Western Australia (1993 to 2000) and then as Governor General of Australia (2003 to 2008). When the new CO finally arrived at Moem Barracks he was well pleased with the job Mick had performed on his behalf. This, plus Mick's continued positive reporting of his performance by his various previous CO's, led to another well-earned opportunity. He received a signal from the officer career managers in Canberra, offering him a place at Staff College.

Selection to attend Staff College is a particularly significant event in a major's career, as attendance at the College prepares the officer for promotion to the rank of lieutenant colonel. The College had been officially opened in 1938 in Sydney. The course at that stage ran for a period of one week, and was attended by major generals, brigadiers, and colonels. By 1940, the course had been extended to 12 weeks duration, and was conducted at Duntroon in Canberra. By the end of World War Two, the course had again relocated to the School of Infantry at Seymour, Victoria and attendance extended to selected majors and lieutenant colonels. It relocated again in January 1947, this time to Fort Queenscliff, a Crimean War era artillery fort overlooking the entrance to Port Phillip Bay. By the 1970's, a major focus of the College was to prepare officers of the rank of major for promotion to lieutenant colonel. Students generally attended the College for a period of 12 months. Success was no guarantee of promotion, however, being able to use the post nominal "psc" (Past Staff College) provided access to plum staff positions within a variety of headquarters. Student places were hotly contested, and generally it was former Royal Military College Duntroon and Officer Cadet School Portsea graduates who vied for inclusion. Those who had gained their commissions through the CMF system were rarely considered. Therefore, it was a considerable honour for one, such as Mick Bawden, to be placed above those who may well have believed they had a God given right for selection.

Mick was panelled to attend the 1975 course, however, while he was pleased to have been selected, his circumstances had changed. Somewhat reluctantly he reached an unexpected decision:

"My mother had recently passed away and there were succession issues to be dealt with and the situation in which I found myself with my being selected for Staff College in 1975 complicated my life somewhat.

When the new CO arrived, he was well pleased with the work I had done administering command and he asked me to stay on in Moem Barracks. However, I felt I needed to go home, so I pulled out of Staff College and took long service leave."

Several unsuccessful attempts were made to have him reverse his decision regarding Staff College and to ensure he continued his career in the Army. However, Mick and Mardi's commitment to duty had taken a new direction, and family responsibilities were now foremost in their minds. The children's schooling was one issue they both felt would be best addressed from a more stable environment in Australia, and Mardi's mother, a widow since 1965, would benefit from her daughter's closer proximity. There was also an unspoken understanding, at least on Mardi's part, that Mick's ultimate desire in life had always been to become a farmer. In the end there was really no need for further discussion, Mick's long service leave from the Army was the beginning of the end of that part of his life, and on the 26th of February 1976 he resigned from the Regular Army to begin life as a farmer at O.B. Flat near Mount Gambier.

CHAPTER 17

"On this land there was an abundance of grass for sheep. This took my eye, as I could see a grand chance of doing well by grazing sheep. My wife was in agreement, so we accepted the offer of this property."[122]

Civilian Life Again

THEORETICALLY, OTHER THAN THEIR DUTY to each other, their family, and to the law of the land, the Bawdens were done with demanding duties. No one could say with any real justification that they had not done their bit for the nation, and few would have begrudged them time to pursue their private interests. However, once a sense of duty is embedded into a life, it is difficult to ignore. The return to civilian life was almost as exciting for the Bawdens as the move to the Regular Army had been, and for a time Mick was as happy as a pig in muck. Compared with his military life, farming was a far more relaxing lifestyle, and he took to it with great enthusiasm. Yet there were negative aspects too. He missed the comradeship and the challenges of military life, and early in 1977 he was provided with the opportunity to continue his new farming career and to at least partially renew his military life. He was approached to assume command at the local CMF training depot. Mick readily agreed, it felt like the right thing to do…a duty. Besides, it

---

[122] A.B. Facey, A Fortunate Life, p 297.

seemed appropriate that he end his military career where it had begun, with the part-time Army in Mount Gambier. In retrospect it was a move destined to fail.

During the second National Service scheme the CMF had offered an alternative means for young men to complete their National Service obligation. The options were 2 years in the Regular Army, or 6 years in the CMF. Many young men chose the 6-year alternative and as a result the CMF had greatly expanded, but at a cost. Prior to conscription the CMF had been a volunteer force, the influx of National Servicemen seeking the 6-year CMF alternative had largely replaced the volunteers. Thus, when the Government ended National Service, the majority of conscripts abandoned their units, and the CMF shrank from a numerically large organization to a mere fraction of its former size. Some units ceased to exist. This situation was further magnified when the Government commissioned Dr T. B. Millar to review the organization and purpose of the CMF.

At the end of his review the Millar Report was accepted by Government and steps were taken to implement the report's findings. The most obvious of these was the retitling of the CMF to that of the Army Reserve, but there were other conclusions reached by Dr Millar which were to have a dramatic impact on what remained of the CMF.

Millar concluded that the existing organization of the part-time Army could not be sustained. This was reasonably obvious to those who continued to serve within its ranks, as most units were now extremely top heavy. Many officers and NCOs had continued to parade after the end of conscription, but many of the soldiers they once commanded were gone. Millar's solution was to designate an organizational title to each Army Reserve depot, based on the number of people parading there, and to limit the command structure for the depot to a level appropriate to that number. Thus, if a depot had twenty or thirty people parading, that depot was designated as a Platoon, commanded by a lieutenant, with a sergeant and three corporals in the more junior leadership positions. The flaw in this conclusion was that most of those who continued to parade were officers and NCOs, and as the majority of these people were now surplus to requirement, they were expected to resign or accept postings to a unit away from their normal place of parade.

Mick was appointed as the Officer Commanding 43 Company, an organization that included around a Platoon's worth of Mount Gambier based soldiers, plus a slightly larger number of soldiers who continued to serve under "special conditions". Special condition soldiers attended two 14-day camps per year and did not attend weekly parades or weekend training activities. This mixture of enlistment conditions made 43 Company a difficult beast to manage as its members were rarely gathered in the same location at the same time. On assuming command of the Company, he appealed for assistance from Battalion Headquarters, and in the communication exchange that followed he formed the opinion that the headquarters interests lay in the metropolitan area, and not in assisting rural based units. He also objected to the Battalion mandated training program which he saw as unrealistic and lacking in imagination. With regards to training, he firmly believed that his own experience and knowledge would be invaluable to the Army Reserve and while this may well have been true, his suggestions were firmly rejected by the Adelaide based Army Reserve hierarchy. It all proved to be too much and eventually, frustrated and disappointed, Mick tendered his resignation. That final exit from the Army hurt a great deal more than he was prepared to admit.

Mardi on the other hand was unhampered by any particular expectations regarding her immediate past, and as a result enjoyed a somewhat happier time as she took the opportunity to further her studies:

"...I was thirty years old when we returned to Australia and went to live in the farmhouse at O.B. Flat. I enrolled at TAFE in Mount Gambier where I studied for the Art/Craft Certificate. However, being a farmer's offsider, I could only cope with one subject per semester. Half a day, one day a week for eight years I attended classes and I revelled in it. Drawing 1, 2, and 3, Spinning and Weaving and finally Art History were among the subjects I studied. It wasn't until 1982 that I completed the 10 subjects that constituted an Art/Craft Certificate. My certificate was presented to me by local MP Harold Allison..."

Indeed, her artistic talent blossomed into a commercially viable activity:

"My first commission was a 1950's limestone house. When I went to look at it, it was featureless...I looked about in dismay, caught a glimpse of the

nearby shearing shed, and said I would rather draw that. In the end I drew them both. O.B. Flat Rural School Spring 1979 was the final piece for Printmaking 1 (TAFE subject). I had used my art classes as an excuse for not taking a responsible position on the Mothers' Club for so many years so that I really wanted to do something artistically constructive to benefit that dear little one teacher school. I sold 38 of 50 prints at $15 each...half of which went into school funds."

Having put his attempt to renew his part-time Army career behind him, Mick's primary focus became the farm and through a combination of hard work and good management, he was able to eke out a reasonable living. In this endeavour he was fiercely supported by Mardi. Somehow between looking after the family, helping Mick on the farm and her studies, she found time to scheme a surprise party to mark Mick's fortieth birthday. It was a grand affair, modelled on the 'This Is Your Life' television program that was popular at the time. Old school friends and Army comrades attended, gleefully providing their contributions regarding Mick's past life. Many of those who were unable to attend wrote letters including the now Major General A.L. Morrison who wrote:

"I first met Mick Bawden in Adelaide in 1967 where I had been sent to raise the 9th Battalion, The Royal Australian Regiment; he had been busy for some days prior to my arrival preparing for the birth of the new Australian regular Battalion. We met at Adelaide airport on 13th November and after a short discussion I appointed him as adjutant. Mick was aghast; he wanted to lead soldiers and he prevailed on me to let him have a command. Finally, I agreed that he could lead Mortar Platoon.

Mick and his men spent almost three months at the School of Infantry at Ingleburn in New South Wales learning about mortars. When they returned to Woodside, they showed what a fine team they were, one that was to prove very successful in South Vietnam under Mick's leadership.

They were a fine team in other ways. Their haunt on off-duty days in Adelaide was the Gresham Hotel, of happy (!) memory. I never visited the place, but to this day I know the design and décor of the bar and surroundings – they were described to me by mortarmen as part of some heart-rending evidence that I heard in my Orderly Room. I hope the original members of the Mortar Platoon held a wake when the Gresham Hotel was demolished.

You were a good soldier, Mick, and I was very glad to have you in 9 RAR. I hope you never lose the twinkle of eye and the facial expression of astounded innocence.

A happy birthday is the fondest wish of all the Morrisons. Let me assure you – life does begin at 40."

Other non-attendees were Rod and Anne Curtis who in sending their apologies commented:

"Both Anne and I were rather pleased that we were not able to be with you tonight – our livers would not have stood the experience..."

From all accounts it was a great night, one that took some getting over.

It was not until 1980 that duty made another formal call on the Bawden family. An opportunity for service presented itself and Mick stood for election to the District Council of Mount Gambier to represent the O.B. Flat ward. He was successful, and drawing on his Wewak council experience, he entered into the cut and thrust of local government politics. He was pleased to find he was quite good at it, and he vigorously represented the rate payers of the O.B. Flat ward. He also sparred with the local newspaper The Border Watch, accusing the paper of inaccurate reporting of council deliberations. He earned further notoriety when he successfully moved a ban on smoking in the council chambers. Those of his fellow councillors who smoked tobacco were less than impressed, and in an exchange between Mick and one of the smokers who claimed Mick's anti-smoking motion infringed his civil liberties, Mick responded:

"It is everyone's right to give themselves lung cancer, but not their right to give others the disease... By not smoking in the chamber, you will be doing me a lot of good and I would suggest it will be good for you too."[123]

Most of the rate payers were well pleased with his efforts on their behalf. The positive comments and support he received, a welcome change to community attitudes that existed at the time, toward the Army and particularly service in Vietnam.

The cost of local government duty...time, effort and perhaps minor

---

[123] Border Watch 14/5/1981.

enmity from those in the community who bridled under the sometimes cutting sarcasm of the Bawden tongue. However, overall he found local government service was a gratifying experience, and in combination with his passion for farming, the future seemed to be full of promise.

In 1982 Mick and Mardi began to look for a larger property eventually finding a promising property in western Victoria, near the city of Hamilton. Known as "Monkani" the new property had most of the features the Bawdens desired, greater acreage, up to date improvements, and a larger house than their O.B. Flat farm. The purchase was successfully arranged, and the family prepared for yet another relocation.

Prior to the move, Mick resigned from the District Council of Mount Gambier, this action provoking a pleasant letter from the local Federal Member of Parliament, James R. Porter, thanking Mick for his service to the community:

"Dear Mr Bawden

I am writing to congratulate you on your achievements in local government.

Your record in the service of the people in the District Council area of Mt. Gambier is something of which you can be justly proud.

I offer my best wishes for the future."

The letter was signed by James R. Porter Member for Barker. The letter was far more than the Federal Government had offered Mick and his fellow Vietnam veterans following their more dangerous service in the national interests.

The relocation to Victoria was accomplished with minimal drama, and over the next few years Mick and Mardi became involved in a variety of community activities in their new location. Mick joined the Country Fire Authority, serving first as a communications officer and later as the captain of the local Brigade, and he continued his association with the RSL. Apart from supporting Mick and their children, Mardi found time to further develop her considerable skills as an artist. In 1982 she teamed up with fellow artist Sue Goodman for an exhibition at the 'Projects in Brown Street' gallery. It was Mardi's first exhibition but not her last. Further expositions of her work took place at the Hamilton Gallery and she followed these with a series of calendars with an assortment of drawings of twelve buildings mostly local woolsheds and other significant district structures. In addition to these pursuits, she joined the local branch of Rostrum, the public speaking association, and she managed to lower her golf handicap.

However, it soon became apparent that "duty" was not yet finished with Mick, or was it perhaps he had not finished with duty? In 1986 he made a return to local government when he was elected to the Dundas Shire Council where he served for 9 years, including a year as the Shire President. Being a councillor gave Mick a sense of purpose and of contributing to the community. His enthusiasm in this pursuit was not always fully appreciated by his wife. In her 1990 Christmas letter Mardi referred somewhat disparagingly to his activities in this regard, but also with a note of pride in his obvious skills in managing people:

"Mick has since reached the pinnacle of his local government career by being appointed chairman of the Regional Rubbish Tip Investigative Committee after which a knighthood will pale into insignificance. Last week he chaired a meeting of around 750 angry farmers' who were after the blood of the Wool Corporation, but he kept the reins tight and order was maintained..."

In 1996, following a state government initiative to reduce the number of shire councils across Victoria, numerous local government councils were amalgamated. The Shire of Dundas was consumed into a new and larger structure, the Shire of Southern Grampians. The new council was centred on the city of Hamilton and encompassed the townships of Dunkeld, Tarrington, Balmoral, Coleraine, Penshurst, Glenthompson, and the districts of Branxholme, and Byaduk. Mick was elected to the new council and was then elected as the inaugural Mayor. A bemused Mardi recorded the event in her 1996 Christmas letter:

"Our holiday to New Zealand in March was cancelled because Mick was nominated for the new local council. The City of Hamilton amalgamated with three rural shires to form the South Grampians Shire Council. There were 17 nominations for 7 seats, covering an area of 7000 square kilometres and doing the work of 36 previous councillors. On 10 March Mick was elected by the new councillors to be the leader..."

The cancellation of the New Zealand holiday was not the only cost of duty associated with the mayoral position, as Mick recalls his duties were particularly wide reaching and demanding:

"The Mayoral year involved 400 plus engagements including a visit by the Governor of Victoria, Debutante balls, family reunions, speaking engagements, and many, many committee meetings..."

The actual number of engagements belies the time spent in preparation for these duties, writing speeches, researching issues, and travel to and from the activities, to name but a few. For Mick the cost of duty was once again being measured in time and focus spent away from his family and his farm.

Mardi's duty at this time was different, yet hardly less costly. In supporting Mick and his mayoral related duties, her children were often placed second, as were her artistic pursuits. However, woe betide those who criticised her husband and his efforts. In her 1996 Christmas letter to family and friends she expressed some of her anger over Mick's lot, but also a fair degree of pride in how her husband was handling the situation:

"...Whichever way you want to put it he gets to wear it. He has learned through trial and error that it's always the same people whinging about each different thing so in latter days he has learnt to rest easier at night instead of worrying himself sick about every little problem."

Another 1996 issue that earned Mardi's ire was the removal of a decommissioned steam train that had been set up in the Hamilton Apex playground. Unfortunately, the train became a health hazard as it contained asbestos and was the dumping ground for all manner of dangerous and unpleasant trash. However, a large section of the community did not agree that the train was a problem and the old locomotive returned to its former location. They laid the blame for the unapproved removal of the train at Mick's feet and Mardi's anger exploded:

"...While the CEO was on leave his second-in-command, without reference to the council, paid someone to remove the train that stood in the Apex playground secreting used syringes and belching asbestos into the atmosphere. Well, the hue and cry sold umpteen dozen copies of the local rag across the entire Western District with little old grannies and tiny tots writing poems that brought a tear to the eye and an Apexian installed a train whistle

atop his dry-cleaning business that periodically lets out a shriek to keep the kettle of dissatisfaction boiling..."

The train issue was eventually resolved, but Mick drew most of the fire from disgruntled rate payers, with little support from his fellow councillors. As one rate payer noted:

"...When the fiasco of the train erupted around him, Mick at least had the guts to walk into a meeting of the Apex club and face the music! Unfortunately, he had no support from his council colleagues. It was most appropriate that Mick was also the only shire representative at the return of the loco..."[124]

Perhaps some of Mick's fellow councillors were unaware that accepting responsibility is another cost of duty that accompanied their office.

As a local government representative Mick was paid a small stipend, and as Mayor he received a little more than his fellow councillors. While this payment was better than nothing, it was hardly commensurate to the amount of work required of the Mayor.

The farm remained the Bawden family's main source of income it had to be worked and managed, but that enterprise presented its own problems which served to increase Mick's stress levels. Wool was the main stay of the Bawden income, but in the late 1980's and the early 1990's the price of wool plummeted. Family income was for a time augmented by the proceeds of a gravel pit located in one of "Monkani" paddocks. The gravel excavated from this pit was sold to the council to maintain the district roads, but then to add to Mick's stress the contract was not renewed. Then as if to prove the old saying that "things happen in threes", an investment in a Geelong based financial body went belly up destroying the family surplus savings. They experienced a slight upturn in fortune when the gravel contract was renewed, but as Mardi recorded in a 1990 Christmas letter to family friends...

"...things were looking a bit ordinary for a while. The farm, you may have guessed, is on automatic pilot with last year's wool still in the stores and this year's in the shed. We don't intend to give it away. Fortunately, the Mayoral Allowance allows us to eat..."

As if these events were not enough, Mick had purchased a new sheep dog

---

[124] Letter to the Editor, <u>Hamilton Spectator</u> 1999.

called Ben. At a purchase price of $600.00 he had every right to expect Ben to be a skilled and steady worker, however, as Mardi observed this was not the case:

"We had a mob of shorn wethers for sale and the carrier phoned to ask us to have them in the yard at dawn...all of this in the middle of shearing, with woolly sheep in the shed, and in the surrounding yards. So, we had to move each flock around to get to the paddock of shorn wethers and into the loading yards.

I am not an early morning person, so the prospect of a 5.30 a.m. droving exercise did not thrill me. On the other hand, Ben the sheep dog was full of enthusiasm. Mick who through the night woke every hour on the hour to beat the alarm clock into action, was toey. He was delivering cursory orders to me which I found difficult to hear, and sharp commands to Ben who was too excited to care what they were about.

Shorn sheep can run at about 100 mph, and Ben ran at about 101 mph, just enough to be right up their bums, and during a pause in the action where Mick had to stop while I shut a gate, Ben and the sheep disappeared from view. All the yelling in the world can't slow that dog down; Mick already red faced and angry tries to have Ben move a mob of woolly sheep to another yard to free the way for the shorn wethers, and Ben deals with these sheep the same way he had the others. Wham! The sheep are sent every which way, some jump over the plunge dip and with Ben's assistance the others join this lot cramming themselves into the dip. When I got there, with Mick yelling, "Oh Christ" in between, "You bastard, Ben", the two-foot wide, eight-foot deep, fourteen-foot-long concrete dip was chock-a-block full of sheep stacked on top of each other, and in the bottom of the dip I knew was eighteen inches of the most foul putrid, soupy brew of shit, dip, grease, worms, frogs, mosquitoes, et al. We had to let some of the other out of the yards before we could begin to rescue those trapped in the dip. Mick was furious still crying, "Oh, Christ" ...I was somewhat dazed, and Ben snapping his teeth, wagging his tail with an "isn't this fun" expression on his face..."

The sheep were eventually rescued, but not before Mick had to rescue his wife who in her efforts to assist in the freeing of trapped sheep from the dip, had herself become trapped by the weight of sheep and was in danger of being deposited in the putrid sump at the bottom of the dip.

Mick continued to have bad luck with expensive dogs. Some years later another dog called 'Fred' was purchased for the princely sum of $800.00. As Mardi recalled in another Christmas epistle, Fred proved to be a willing, if unlucky worker:

"Sandy and Helen Haig with Jordie went to the US for a holiday and asked us to baby sit their dog 'Rodney Hog the Dog'. We were in the habit of taking the dogs for a walk each day, and on this particular morning we decided to walk to the highway and back. Well, Fred, as was his want, went off trailing a delicious smell through a hole in the neighbour's fence and Rodney stayed on the roadside with us. Rodney sniffed out a hare and pounced on it and of course with the hare screeching and Rodney wrestling with it, Fred was alerted and desperate to be in on the kill, Fred took a flying leap over the fence. Unfortunately, he didn't clear the fence properly, let out a yelp, fell backwards to the ground, gave a shudder and promptly died..."

Veterinary exploration showed that Fred had had a weak heart. At first glance, Mick's issues with his sheep dogs appears trivial, even amusing. However, the dogs combined with the other farming hardships of the time were stress contributors the Bawdens could well have done without. Even so they acknowledged they were not alone in these difficulties, as Mardi acknowledged in a Christmas letter:

"...The whole of rural Australia is smarting at the local withdrawal of Government facilities. Jobs are lost so families move to the city seeking employment, schools lose pupils, classes are reduced, teachers are sacked, beds are closed in hospital. Wool prices are drastically low so farmers in our area aren't spending, shops close...goodness now I'm whinging...this is happening in all the little towns Australia wide..."

Whinging or not, there were indications that Mardi was finding Mick's off-farm activities more than a little frustrating, particularly when he made known his intent to stand for the Mayoral position again. In another letter to friends, she expressed her frustrations:

"...Oh poo, he can have it and to think he is willing to throw his cap in the ring for another twelve months of the mayoral position, he's mad..."

The issue of another 12 months as mayor was taken out of Mick's hands when council voted to limit the mayoral position to a 12-month stint. Although no longer Mayor, he continued to pursue his local government and other off-farm duties. However, on reaching his sixtieth year, with some serious prompting from Mardi, Mick came to the realisation that there was life to be enjoyed beyond the council, and he determined not to seek re-election.

A series of tributes followed his announcement as supporters and opponents recognised the effort he had contributed to local government. The Hamilton Lions Club awarded him the club's community service award (the Alan Holding award), and the Police Consultative Committee recognised his service as a Justice of the Peace and as a bail justice.

At the Shire Council meeting on the 12th of March 1999, the new Mayor provided a tribute to Mick and another retiring councillor John Myers. With regard to Mick, the Mayor stated Mick's distinguishing feature was his ability to chair groups and meetings, often involving diverse interest groups and councils. In a bittersweet moment Mick provided the following address in reply:

"...I wish to briefly reflect on what has been a most rewarding experience during which time I served with some truly dedicated and able people, both councillors and staff, It needs to be said that the great majority of council decisions evoke little or no interest from the public. For instance, the capital works budget adopted each year is always passed without comment, however the controversial issues such as the location of a mobile food van has cost the council many hours of debate within the chamber itself. This anomalous situation is brought about by the inordinate amount of time that this council seems to devote to the chronically dissatisfied who are a very small minority in our community..."

In conclusion, after providing particular thanks to John Myers who had served with him on the Dundas Shire Council and the Southern Grampians Shire Council, and wishing the council every success for the future, he said:

"If asked what attributes are required to be a councillor, I would have to say... commitment to the community, the ability to listen, endurance, tolerance, an understanding wife or partner, and last but not least... loyalty..."

And so Mick's period as a local government representative ended, and he immersed himself in farming activities.

At first glance, that period 1977 to 1998, Mick seemed to have been living an ideal life. He had a supportive wife, they had two vibrant children, a wide circle of friends, an enviable property, and he was engrossed in farming and community activities. However, in spite of all of this, his life had started to unravel.

Chapter 18

"I wish I could sleep with peaceful dreams,
Away from all the noise and screams,
Away from all the dead and dying,
Away from all the fear and crying.
I wish I didn't suffer from all war's ills,
Then I could live and sleep without those pills.
I wish for a slice of a long lost youth,
For war was a thief, the aftermath the proof".[125]

A Particular Cost of Duty

MICK'S SYMPTOMS WERE HARD TO spot, but they had begun to manifest long before he had resigned from local government. When he was out and about, he appeared happy and content…often the life of the party. However, away from the public eye a very different character had begun to emerge. His normally polite demeanour diminished, and a deeply cynical attitude to life and those with whom he came in contact began to emerge. He would be taken by sudden and uncontrolled rage, often at the most meagre of provocations. Then there were times of dark depression that threatened to overcome him.

---

[125] K. J. Maynard 2001, A Veteran's Wishes.

His immediate family and close friends were confused and worried by his behaviour…and so was he.

In spite of these symptoms, he made no attempt to curtail his community activities, indeed he increased them. Aside from his local government and the RSL activities he remained an active member of the local CFA Brigade, he joined the Hamilton P & A Society and was often the show day Ring Announcer. In addition to these commitments he was active in the Glenelg Pony Club where he served a term as District Commissioner. In fact, he may even have risen to greater heights as he was approached to consider standing for Parliament. Mick often joked that the offer was made on the basis that he was a former Army officer and that he had an attractive wife. However, Mick knew his limitations and the offer was refused. The very fact such an offer was made is probably an indication that the majority of the community were unaware of the internal turmoil he faced.

Like many men of his time, Mick believed mental illness was a sign of weakness, and the thought that he might be suffering some kind of psychological breakdown horrified him. Initially neither he, nor Mardi associated his difficulties with Vietnam and certainly not with Post Traumatic Stress Disorder, an affliction neither of them had heard of. Indeed, given a downturn in the rural economy, and the amount of effort he was putting into local government and his other commitments, overwork and worry seemed a more likely cause of his problems. Gradually though, signs began to emerge that the derivation of Mick's difficulties did in fact lie in his Vietnam service.

Along with the symptoms of irritability, anger, sleeplessness, fatigue, decreased confidence and self-esteem, came unexpected and adverse reactions to situations that triggered memories of incidents he thought he had put behind him. One such situation occurred at an early 9 RAR reunion to which the family and friends of 9 RAR members were invited. Mick recall that during that reunion he was confronted with an extremely awkward situation:

"During one of our operations one of our fellows had been shot in the head. He had been killed instantly and would not have known what hit him. Families though often feel they have to know how their son, or brother died,

and this was the case when the lad's father approached me and asked for details of how his son had died. I pretty much told him the truth...shot in the head, died instantly. However, my answer seemed to anger him, and he declared that I shouldn't treat him as a fool, he had seen his son's body on its return home and there was no wound on his head.

I was horrified! I blustered some sort of an apology and quickly withdrew...What I had forgotten was that during the war the American's had instigated a practise of 'rebuilding' the bodies of the dead prior to repatriation. The aim of this policy was to shield the families of the dead from the trauma of viewing the often horrible disfigurement associated with death in battle. In this case the forensic medical folk in Vietnam had repaired our man's head and so skilfully presented his body, his wounds had been invisible to the father.

It did me no good at all at the time, I felt absolutely wretched... I still feel the impact of that father's accusation today, and perhaps what hurts most is that I feel it was my own fault, and I should have approached the whole thing differently[126].*"*

At another similar occasion the bereaved sister of Bernd Bender, the 9 RAR soldier killed in a catastrophic claymore mine explosion, posed a similar question to Mick regarding her brother's death. However, the memory of Bender's death and its aftermath were too terrible to recall and Mick was unable to provide her with an answer:

"I just told her I didn't know, there was no way I could relive that particular incident. I think one of the others told her what had happened and after that she seemed relieved, but I couldn't tell her..."

At the time few in the medical profession, let alone Mick Bawden the individual, were aware that the feelings of guilt, anxiety and depression that Mick experienced following this incident, were symptomatic of an insidious injury known as Post Traumatic Stress Disorder, or PTSD.

The lack of diagnostic knowledge regarding this injury would not be addressed for some time. What was becoming clear though was that Vietnam

---

[126] Years later at another Battalion reunion Mick saw the father of the dead soldier again. By that time the man had learned the truth and he apologised to Mick for his previous outburst.

had left a dent in the soul of many veterans of the war, and slowly Mick came to realise that he was one of those so afflicted.

It seemed such a hopeless situation. For those veterans who sought help, the common treatment offered was Valium or other sedatives, along with vague assurances that they would eventually recover. Cold comfort indeed…

Strangely the organization that might have been expected to assist the Vietnam veterans was reluctant to address the needs of Australia's newest group of war veterans. This was the Returned and Services League, Australia (RSL). The RSL had been formed after World War One with the purpose of:

"… preserving the spirit of mateship formed amidst the carnage and horror of battle, to honour the memory of the fallen and to help each other whenever required".[127]

After World War Two this work continued with the additional aim of:

"…promoting mateship and providing outstanding advocacy, welfare commemoration and community services".[128]

However, after the Vietnam War, the RSL was less than enthusiastic in pursuing these aims on behalf of the Vietnam veterans. A few individual RSL clubs welcomed the Vietnam men and women, but at the national level, influential groups within the organization sought to play down the Vietnam veterans' combat experiences, and there were claims the Vietnam conflict was not a real war. This attitude alienated many of the Vietnam veterans from the organization, and some would never forgive the RSL for what they saw as a rank betrayal of the organization's stated aims.

There seemed little the suffering Vietnam veterans could do, but endeavour to forget the war, and to accept the scant treatment and advice that was available regarding their injuries. Some, however, were not prepared to be ignored, and these veterans took an active stance. In 1979 they formed a lobby group titled the Vietnam Veterans' Action Association (VVAA) with the aim of presenting the Federal Government with a variety of concerns regarding the health of Vietnam veterans.

The initial work of the VVAA focused on claims associated with the American use of chemical herbicides during the war. The herbicides known

---

[127] rslvic.com.au/about/rsl-history/
[128] rslvic.com.au/about/

as Agent Orange had been used to defoliate large areas of the Vietnamese countryside to deny the enemy forces cover. At the time, the Americans claimed the chemicals used were not harmful to humans or animals and did not contaminate water or food crops. However, by the end of the war there was strong evidence that contact with the chemical caused various types of cancer, and had resulted in birth defects in the children of veterans and the Vietnamese population. In addition to claims regarding Agent Orange, the VVAA argued that physical disorders associated with the war were exacerbated by psychological disorders among many Vietnam veterans. These claims were all firmly rejected by the Australian Government.

By 1981 the Vietnam Veterans' Action Association had morphed into the Vietnam Veterans' Association of Australia (VVAA) and under this new title a prolonged campaign of lobbying and protest to Government was pursued. The VVAA argued that the Government and its relevant departments were inadequately catering for the special physical and mental health treatment needs of Vietnam veterans. However, the Government remained unmoved and a variety of issues strengthened the Government's resolve.

One of these issues was founded in the doctrine of both major political parties. In the post-Vietnam war period, the ALP and the Liberal Party promoted multiculturalism as a key issue of their ideological platforms. The issues raised by VVAA were seen as being counter-productive to this philosophy. Even the ANZAC legend was seen in some political quarters as being contrary to political moves to embrace multiculturalism. ANZAC Day itself became a contested political feature of Australian identity and national discourse, attendances at commemorative ceremonies were down, and indications were that they might soon cease altogether. Government had no intention of reinforcing the ANZAC ethos by any public recognition of the Vietnam veterans, so there were no moves to erect memorials to the Vietnam conflict, or to recognise their claims regarding Agent Orange or mental health issues.

Another issue for politicians of all persuasions was their perception that the electorate was apathetic toward the fate of Vietnam veterans. Indeed, the majority of Australians at the time believed there were more important things to worry about than the claims of the Vietnam veterans. For many, the heightened Cold War tensions and a variety of anti-war movements were far more deserving of their interest than what was often seen as the whingeing claims of the VVAA. Others were unwilling to address the issues left behind by what they saw as a "lost war". The general public apathy served to deepen the hurt and rejection many Vietnam veterans felt. As one veteran stated:

"It's not that I was ashamed I was in Vietnam, but I'd been given the feeling I should be ashamed. I mean it was obvious at that time we were going to lose, so you had no comeback. For a man that was a dedicated Australian, and thought I was doing the right thing, it was very hurtful... We were fighting a war that was not only unpopular, no one had a clue where we were. Young blokes of twenty were dying for their country through no choice of their own, and the people didn't know and couldn't care less..."[129]

Safe in the knowledge the electorate was disinterested, successive Governments remained indifferent to most of the VVAA claims. The claim regarding stress related injuries was one that the Government firmly rejected, a decision that was strongly supported by the RSL. The RSL contended that stress had always been synonymous with combat and that the veterans of the First and Second World Wars and of the Korean War experienced similar trauma and stress to those of the Vietnam conflict. Further to this, the RSL claimed special treatment for Vietnam veterans was unnecessary, as existing services to treat war related injuries and illness were entirely adequate.

In an attempt to counter their critics, the VVAA pointed out the uniqueness of the Vietnam conflict, showing that statistically the infantryman in the Vietnam conflict experienced around 300 days of continuous combat like conditions. This opposed to a World War Two infantry soldier who experienced around 60 days of continuous combat. Therefore, they argued the number of combat stress related injuries were likely to be far higher among the Vietnam veterans.[130] It was an argument that failed to move their detractors. However, events overseas provided VVAA and its veteran supporters with a glimmer of hope.

---

[129] Nicholas Bromfield, Welcome Home: reconciliation, Vietnam veterans, and the reconstruction of Anzac under the Hawke Government, University of Sydney.

[130] Posttraumatic Stress Disorder (PTSD) A Vietnam Veteran's Experience, vvaa.org.au/experience.

By 1980 American research into similar claims made by American Vietnam veterans, had recognised a new condition which they titled Post Traumatic Stress Disorder (PTSD), as a legitimate psychological condition. The American research demonstrated that a soldier may develop PTSD as a result of an extreme or catastrophically stressful life event. However, this evidence failed to move the Australian Government and it remained reluctant to recognise PTSD as a legitimate condition.

Cynics might claim the Government's reluctance in this matter was based on a desire to avoid compensation payments to veterans. While there may be some validity to this belief, a major issue for both the Australian Government and the Australian medical profession was the lack of an agreed identifiable cause of the condition.

In the past, stress related injuries suffered by soldiers were referred to by a myriad of titles including: Shell Shock, Battle Exhaustion, Nervous Syndrome, Gross Stress Reaction, even Post-Vietnam Syndrome. The symptoms for each of these defined conditions are quite similar and included headaches, nightmares, hallucinations, distressing and intrusive memories, hysterical disorders, such as mutism and paralysis, amnesia, and even 'personality loss'.[131] However the recognised causes of these injuries tended to be quite specific. For example, shell shock was associated with exposure to prolonged artillery bombardment. Gross stress reaction was generally associated with participation in a particularly prolonged and violent battle. For PTSD, however, while the symptoms were similar, the cause of the injury was seen as quite another matter.

The most widely accepted cause for PTSD was that the sufferer had experienced "an extreme or catastrophically stressful life event". On the face of it this seems a reasonable definition, after all, battle would seem to be "an extreme, catastrophic and stressful life event". However, for Government and military authorities the definition was far too broad as it might be seen to include any traumatic incident from a car accident, to a situation experienced during combat. This is not to say that veteran claims for stress related injury were disbelieved, but claims regarding PTSD as a specific injury continued to be treated with extreme caution. So the authorities' attitude toward PTSD

---

[131] bl.uk/world-war-one/articles/shell-shock

remained unchanged. The same however, could not be said for public opinion.

The work done by VVAA to publicise the effects of Agent Orange and the mental health of Vietnam veterans had struck a chord with the public, and support for the Vietnam veterans' claims grew. Reluctantly, but with an eye to the ballot box, the Government acknowledged that VVAA claims needed to be addressed. In 1982 the Federal Cabinet announced that Vietnam veterans were to be provided with a limited, special counselling service. The new service was to be known as the Vietnam Veterans' Counselling Service (VVCS), and it would facilitate veterans' access to existing services. In addition, the wives and children of Vietnam veterans would have access to Repatriation General Hospitals for emergency treatment. The costs of non-insured veterans seeking emergency treatment in country hospitals would be met by the Department of Veteran Affairs. These initiatives did not mean the Government had fully accepted PTSD as a condition, but it was a start.

Like most Vietnam veterans Mick was well pleased with the achievements of the VVAA, however he was uncertain as to how the Government's announcement regarding the VVCS would apply to him. He remained reluctant to claim his symptoms as war related particularly when compared to those who had been wounded by bullet, mine or shrapnel. Besides, even if he were to attribute his condition to war service, he believed the new VVCS facilities were located some distance from the farm, too far away for a busy farmer to visit for some kind of casual inquiry. Then sometime later while listening to the ABC regional radio station of 3WV[132], he made an interesting discovery.

The subject of 3WV's program that day was the VVCS. The program explained the circumstance which had led to the creation of the amenity and highlighted the services offered to veterans. However, what really pricked Mick's interest was the announcement that the VVCS had an office a few miles away from "Monkani" at Horsham. He recalls what was to be a life changing moment:

"I rang the office in Horsham and spoke to a lady to find out more. To my surprise she immediately made me an appointment, not for me to go to her, but for her to come to me at the farm. That meeting changed my life, and my

---

[132] A regional ABC Radio station of the time.

interaction with VVCS continues to this day. I cannot speak more highly of them! Through that service I have met so many caring people since that time, who have helped me cope with my problems I could not have done it without them."

Soon after his meeting with the VVCS representative, Mick commenced a course of counselling treatment. This course was basic by standards of the therapies available to veterans of later deployments, but at least it provided him with strategies to gain a reasonable night's sleep and to cope with the anger and flashbacks. Perhaps at that time one of the most important factors for him was that VVCS acknowledged that his condition was stress related to his service in the war, a particular cost of duty. However, exactly what his condition could be called, no one was prepared to say. In addition to commencing his course of treatment, Mick also agreed to acting as a "First Point of Contact" for Vietnam veterans in his local area. In the absence of Government or official RSL response to the crisis facing many Vietnam veterans, the VVCS determined to provide a nation-wide system of contacts for veterans who were seeking help. The VVCS concept for this system was that the First Point of Contact appointees would direct the veteran toward the VVCS who in turn would assist the veteran to an appropriate avenue of help. In addition, the First Point of Contact appointees were identified to the police, health related organizations and community service groups who in the course of their duties came in contact with veterans in crisis. Generally, the troubled veteran was pleased to be able to talk with a fellow veteran, a person who had shared similar experiences to their own.

Over the next few years, in his capacity as a First Point of Contact, Mick assisted numerous Vietnam veterans to make contact with VVCS from where ultimately, they received assistance. There were also several incidents when he was approached by people claiming to have fought in Vietnam but in fact had not. The majority of the cases Mick addressed, both for genuine and fraudulent[133] claims, were straight forward, and he gained a strong sense of purpose in performing this duty. However, on two occasions he was presented with more complex problems.

---

[133] Identification of fraudulent claims became much easier after a Nominal Roll of all those who had served in Vietnam was published.

Late one night he received a phone call from the Hamilton police requesting his assistance. Mick Bawden:

"A Vietnam veteran had barricaded himself in a room of a local motel. The police told me that the man was armed with two rifles, and they wanted me to come and disarm him. I agreed to go and have a look at the situation. I was accompanied by a rather reluctant policeman, and I must admit I was not feeling all that confident either.

The policeman told me that the fellow in the motel room had recently gone through a marital breakdown and was very angry with the world. It all sounded so similar to the situation I had faced with the corporal at Puckapunyal.

On approaching the motel room, I saw that the fellow was seated, with a rifle across his knees and another at his feet. After some talking, he agreed that I could enter the room and it was then I noticed that the rifle on the floor didn't have a bolt in it. I pointed this out to him, and he acknowledged the fact, but then chilling pointed out the weapon on his knees did have a bolt, and he assured me it was loaded. The few minutes were not the easiest of times, but eventually he agreed to hand over both weapons, and the police moved in and took him away. Once again I received no feedback on what happened to the poor fellow."

Not unreasonably, Mardi was more than a little concerned at this turn of events in her husband's work with VVCS, and she asked him why he would get involved in these situations. His response that he just hoped to help save someone's life was hardly satisfactory…perhaps his real reason may have been that he not only sympathised with these men, he empathised with them, a case perhaps of … *"there but for the grace of God, go I"*.

On another occasion he was contacted by a representative of the Salvation Army who expressed concern about the welfare of another Vietnam veteran. This veteran had also suffered a marital breakdown and according to the Salvationist was living in squalor. Mick recalls the event:

"When I arrived at the fellow's house, the first thing I noticed was how untidy and unkempt the garden area was. He was in quite an agitated state, apparently working on his car, but I was alarmed to see a vacuum cleaner positioned close to the exhaust of the car. On questioning him as to what he

was doing, he swore he was cleaning the car out as it was about to be repossessed. This explanation did not reassure me, and I wondered why he would take an interest in cleaning his car when everything else was in such disarray. It seemed to me he had a more sinister plan in mind involving the vacuum cleaner and the car's exhaust.

I got him away from the car and we went inside the house. Inside was a total mess, with dogs running around and damaging the furniture while they searched for something to eat. We talked for a while and he seemed to calm down and after a time I left him alone. For a short time after that I was able to help him financially, but he was clearly very unwell and I understand, he was shortly thereafter admitted to the Heidelburg Repatriation Hospital."

Mick's experience in these matters was not unique. Across Australia other First Point of Contact appointees faced similar situations, and sometimes those situations did not end peacefully…another cost of duty

It was clear to the VVCS and the veterans themselves, that the war had been a major factor in their feelings and behaviour, but others, including the Federal Government remained to be convinced. Indeed, the Government and the nation's medical experts did not formally acknowledge the existence of PTSD until 1995. In that year, DVA in collaboration with the University of Melbourne and Repatriation Medical Centre, established the "Australian Centre for Posttraumatic Stress Disorder" it was a major step forward in the recognition of the Vietnam veterans' plight. The new Centre's mission was to:

"…improve the recognition and treatment of PTSD and related conditions within the veteran population".[134]

However, even with the establishment of this Centre, progress in treating the veterans remained slow, a factor attributed to the need to properly train practitioners in the diagnosis and treatment of the condition[135]. This deficit in skill had a marked impact on Mick's case, as DVA did not officially identify his condition as PTSD until 1999. Being able to put a name to his particular cost of duty was a small consolation, but at least it was something.

---

[134] Opcit
[135] Opcit

CHAPTER 19

"Go where glory waits thee,
But still, while fame elates thee,
Oh! still remember me."[136]

Recognition

IT IS DOUBTFUL THAT THE initial treatment Mick received would have been available had public attitudes to the war not changed. The VVAA can rightly claim to have been a major contributor to that change, as their representation to Government had awakened a sense in the public psyche that the Vietnam veterans had received a very raw deal. This change in public attitude had not gone unnoticed by the Federal Government and Prime Minister Hawke sought to take advantage of the change to heal the rift that had developed between the Vietnam veterans and the country that had sent them to war. It may be argued that the Prime Minister's actions in this matter had an eye to the electorate. This cynicism overlooks the fact that Hawke's actions certainly assisted in improving the availability of treatment of Vietnam veterans with war related injuries. Hawke believed he needed a more visible indicator of his Government's intent regarding Vietnam veterans, but at first he was unsure as to how this could be

---

[136] Thomas Moore

achieved. However, when he was approached with the idea of a Welcome Home March for Vietnam veterans to be conducted in Sydney, he readily agreed. Prime Minister Hawke:

"I firmly believe that the October parade will be the culmination of a long process of reconciliation and community acceptance of its obligations to the veterans of Vietnam. I believe we must honestly acknowledge that our involvement in Vietnam did cause deep divisions in the Australian community. But whatever our individual views on the merits of Australian involvement, we must equally acknowledge the commitment, courage and integrity of our armed forces who served in Vietnam".[137]

A healing sentiment…and no doubt there were votes in it too, in either event the march was scheduled for the 3rd of October 1987 and on the appointed date some 25,000 veterans marched through Sydney streets to the cheers of several hundred thousand spectators. Mick, however, did not make the journey to Sydney. He found the occasion too much to bear, the memories too raw for him to take part. So he stayed at home and tearfully watched the event on TV with Mardi.

The Welcome Home March was a marked success and provided a public face of a new deal for Vietnam veterans, but that deal did not provide an instant panacea for their problems. Some quarters of Government still resisted veteran claims, particularly those regarding Agent Orange, and DVA processes remained methodical and painfully slow.

While the VVAA promoted the veterans' cause to Government, individuals were also contributing in this regard to their local community. The lack of community acknowledgement for the service the Vietnam veterans had performed in the name of the nation was one of the more painful costs of their duty. In addressing this community failure Mardi played her part championing the veterans' cause. Following the family move to Western Victoria, she had become an active member of Rostrum and on several occasions used that venue as a means of educating her fellow orators on the issues faced by Vietnam veterans and their families. In one particular oration

---

[137] Welcome Home: reconciliation, Vietnam veterans, and the reconstruction of Anzac under the Hawke Government Nicholas Bromfield University of Sydney. auspsa.org.au

competition she titled her discourse "Over The Hill" and used a parody of the nursery rhyme "Ten Little Ducks', to illustrate the impact of the war from the perspective of a veteran's wife:

"Ten little ducks went out one day,
Over the hills and far away,
Mother duck said 'Quack, quack, quack, quack,
But only nine little ducks came back.
Ten little soldiers marched away one day
Over the hills and far away
Ten young wives cried 'please come back'
But only nine wiser old men hobbled back."

She went on to highlight the unfairness of the treatment of the veterans referring in particular to 9 RAR:

"Thirteen months, five days and three hours. It seemed like an eternity. After twelve months of preparation for war, a whole Battalion of some eight hundred men, after a little more than ten days aboard HMAS Sydney, were flung back into society with not so much as a 'hello, welcome home' and virtually told 'there, get on with your life and be normal.' They were young men then and they buried trauma deep within their psyche, but they were changed forever. The stroke of the political pen that in a year had stripped idealistic teenagers of their youth, had made cynical old men of them."

Her audience listened politely, but she didn't win the competition. Perhaps only those who have waved their partners off to a war zone, to wait long months for their return, and who have witnessed the cost duty had exacted on their partners, could really understand the message in her speech. In her closing remarks she referred to an event that was to take place on the 3rd of October 1992…the dedication of the Australian Vietnam Forces National Memorial. Mention of that event possibly prompted some interest among her audience, for hitherto such an event had been unthinkable.

The success of the 1987 Welcome Home March had demonstrated a general change in attitude by the public and Government toward the Vietnam veterans. In 1988 the Federal Government announced its support for a project to build the Australian Vietnam Forces National Memorial. Coupled to this announcement, in August of that year the first official Vietnam Veterans'

Day was held. Both the Memorial project and the Vietnam Veterans' Day were strongly supported...times had certainly changed.

A site on Canberra's ANZAC Avenue was selected for the memorial, and a competition for the design of the memorial conducted. However, in a demonstration that times had not completely changed the memorial was not totally funded by Government and a public appeal for funding the Memorial was established. To this fund the Federal Government gave a total of $250,000, the remainder of the final cost of over $1.2 million came from public donation and corporate sponsorship. Following an address provided by Mick to their year, Hamilton VCE students Melanie Kenny and Melissa Green raised almost $900.00 for the memorial. This donation was an example of the change in attitude of many young Australians to the Vietnam War and its veterans. This change was not lost on Mick, and prior to his attendance at the Memorial dedication, he gave an interview to the local newspaper:

"Most of these men (the Vietnam veterans) went off to fight because they were told by their elders and betters that that is what their country needed them to do. Their fathers and grandfathers before them had done the same thing, but when they came back their sacrifice was acknowledged, and their wounds salved. Not so with the Vietnam veterans.

It has taken 25 years for this healing process to begin. We (the veterans) need that collective embrace from our country so that a reconciliation can take place...

It's gestures like that (the $900.00 raised by the VCE students) that have made this memorial mean so much..."

The Dundas Shire Council also donated $1000.00 to the memorial appeal and presented an Australian flag to Mick which they asked that he carry at the head of the parade with other similarly awarded flags. There were a few raised eyebrows when Mick politely declined this request and proposed an alternative solution. While acknowledging the council were attempting to do him a great honour, they failed to understand the compelling obligation he felt to march with his comrades of 9 RAR. His counter proposal was that Mardi should carry the flag, an idea that was based in the recognition of another debt...another cost of duty. Mick Bawden:

"*I felt it was a gesture to Mardi and to the wives and families of all veterans who 'kept the home fires burning' while we were away, and of the support they have provided in the years that followed...*"

His proposal was accepted by the council, and with Mardi he prepared for their journey to Canberra. However, in spite of his enthusiasm for the memorial, once again the fear of his wartime memories threatened to de-rail Mick's attendance at the dedication ceremony. Just in time, the therapy he had been receiving and the support of friends and former comrades eased his anxiety. One friend, Ken Dungey took up his pen and composed some heartfelt prose which he presented to Mick before he and Mardi left for Canberra:

To Mick and Mardi and thousands like them, Canberra 3rd October 1992

Don't be afraid
This stone is for you
It is the sob that has lain within you
For twenty-five years:
The primal scream you couldn't give
Because you were afraid (you knew)
No-one would hear.
You see:
No-one said, "Well done, that lad",
No-one said, "This is our son who tried for us".
We never said, "You did not fail".
We just forgot
And left you in limbo land.
Unreal
This stone is for you.
It is a touch stone
To release your primal screaming.
It is our collective breast, and it is ready to receive you.
You can sob now.
This time we will hear.
We have seen your sacrifice
And we know what you did.

These words were extremely evocative for Mick and for Mardi, along with Ken's wife who had formerly been married to a Vietnam veteran.

The 3rd of October 1992 finally arrived…it was a great day for the Vietnam veterans, when over half of their number travelled to Canberra for the event. This time Mick was one of them, and Mardi later recalled the event in another speech to Rostrum:

"We were in Canberra on October 3rd with thousands of other veterans of that infamous war and they were symbolised by the medals on their chests, the flags and the tears.

Mick's Battalion had a reunion the night before and there they were… the voices hadn't changed, the shouts, the laughter… the smiles and just in case a name escaped, the name tags, if you could read through the tears without your glasses. The average age of National Servicemen who served in Vietnam was now 48 and the majority reached for their specs.

A sprinkling of grey hairs, lines finely etched, balding pates and rounded paunches, but the essential characteristics hadn't changed. Hugs, kisses, handshakes, introductions to new wives, recounting adventures, catching up on the progress of children, photos…"

Some had travelled vast distances to attend the reunion and the next day's march and the dedication ceremony. For some 9 RAR veterans the reunion was the first time they had seen one another since they had returned home from the war. However, one individual at the reunion received Mick and Mardi's special attention:

"…in the midst stood a pretty 24-year-old woman with red hair, pale skin and a tentative somewhat bewildered look, holding hands with an equally awkward young man.

But let me digress for a minute. Harry Musicka has now become a legend. He was one of those young men who in 1968 "took a weekend off to marry a sweetheart."

Kay and Harry were married after their baby was born. It was a time when life was lived in the fast lane, crammed with every sensation and emotion extractable from living, one experienced a delirious appetite for fulfilment because we simply didn't know what fate had in store for us. It was pre-embarkation leave and the whole Mortar Platoon was invited to the

Oakbank Pub to celebrate. Mick was Platoon Commander, so we were there for the wedding and christening. Sandy was 14 weeks old when Harry left, and Harry had been gone two months when he was killed..."

Mick had felt Harry Musicka's death particularly keenly, for it was he who had arranged for Harry to be transferred into the Mortar Platoon. Then there was the promise he had made to Harry's mother that he would look after her son. The guilt he felt was palpable. As the years had passed Mick and Mardi had maintained contact with Harry's widow and they had watched his child, Sandy, grow into a fine young lady. They had lost contact with Sandy when she moved to Western Australia, but there she was at the Canberra reunion, living evidence of yet another cost of duty. Mardi remembered:

"...this young woman standing in the midst of the joyous reunion holding the hand of the awkward young man, was Sandy, the child of Harry Musicka, come from Perth to carry his flag. As Mick and I introduced ourselves, he cried, I cried, she cried, and we all cuddled each other. When I finally stood back, wiping away the tears there were more men and women by our side waiting to introduce themselves. Thus, she was welcomed into the hearts of this family of 9 Battalion."

The morning of the dedication started early for the veterans and their families, and the impact the day was to have on them would be profound. For Mick and many of his comrades there was a feeling that their service was at last being appropriately recognised. Later he wrote of the experience:

"It was a pilgrimage of the faithful from every State in Australia. They came to pay tribute to those who served, suffered and died in the Vietnam War. They came in many shapes, sizes and in varying physical and mental conditions, but all had made some sacrifice in order to be there and were richly rewarded for having done so, not in the material sense, but for those who marched the length of ANZAC Parade, the continuous applause was a reward of the richest kind..."

Much later in another speech to a Rostrum audience Mardi tried valiantly to have them understand the feelings of that day:

"...Mick and his long-time friend Patrick (Beale) went off to the dawn service together where 508 green candles were lit and held by relatives and *friends of the fallen, where the WOK WOK of a single lone helicopter punctured the silence of the dawn causing prickly hair on the necks of the veterans to stand up spontaneously in silent salutation to the memories of that dreadful war. To quote the words of Brigadier Colin Kahn, "It was a war that was predictable, the same as most other wars, in the contrasts that the war seemed to throw up in starkest relief. For we experienced cruelty but at the same time unbounded love and compassion; fear yet unequalled courage, the realisation of the impermanence of life, at the same time the desire to preserve one's own life – we saw the comparisons of other ways of life with our own, and the realisation that despite our imperfections Australia really is God's country."*

9 a.m. saw more than 10,000 people shoulder to shoulder on Reid Oval under the banner of their units preparing to march the 1.6 kilometres along ANZAC Parade. The 508 flags for the fallen and flags representing the donor organizations who had supported the memorial fund, marched together. I carried a flag for the Shire of Dundas – we strode six abreast between the crowds on either side of the road, silent except for a slow handclapping, most were weeping, small children had paper flags they forgot to wave...

As they peeled off to march past again with their units, we donors wound up our flags and joined the crowds on the sidelines – and so they kept coming. The disabled in open Land Rovers – Michael and Jenny our friends from Woodside days – we went to their wedding after Vietnam – his back gives him hell – they yelled to me from a padded seat on high. AATTV with whom Patrick served. Geoff and Marylin Whitney from Hamilton materialised out of the crowd, grabbing me by the hand and then John Francis from Portland arrived. I saw Geoff Joseph with his unit. We stood together as two hours of people marched by, all the support groups, engineers, admin, stores, navy that took them, tankies that fired in front of them and finally the Battalions 1 to 9; then the medical teams, policemen, Americans, Kiwis and South Vietnamese, each group peeling off to become the lengthening crowd, cheering, shouting salutations, marchers diving into the crowd to embrace a friend then rushing back to continue the parade. There were men in wheelchairs, men with wooden legs struggling to keep up but determined to make the distance, men with seeing-eye dogs. Someone yelled, "up the old red rooster" and a chorus responded, "more piss". They marched together the debonair and dishevelled, the composed and the shaken, the injured and the strong Vietnam veterans brothers in arms and this was their day.

To those who went to Canberra on that special weekend, their wounds were salved, to those who didn't go, there is a tangible shrine to which they can make their pilgrimage whenever they feel ready to receive the nation's blessing."

The dedication of the Memorial may well have salved the veterans' wounds and the relief experienced by those who attended intense, but their wounds were far from being healed. Indeed, the general health and wellbeing of the Vietnam veterans remained in alarming decline. Studies showed that a variety of physical health ailments were much more prevalent among veterans than in the wider population, and with regards to veterans' mental health the results of these studies was even more alarming. It was revealed that at the time the memorial opened, approximately half of the Vietnam veteran community were taking some form of medication for mental health issues, with PTSD most strongly associated with these diagnoses.

It has been argued that the Hawke Government's initiative in recognising the Vietnam veterans with the Welcome Home March and the Memorial in Canberra, was more symbolic than any tangible effort to address veteran health. That Prime Minister Hawke's desire was to heal national divisions, and to admit the Vietnam veterans to the "ANZAC legend", any benefit to veteran health was simply a spin off.[138] These arguments regarding symbolism were reinforced when the Government determined to maintain the momentum of the new attitude toward the veterans, and in 1998 the Government initiated a new program titled "Their Service our Heritage". This program provided funding for community projects to recognise veterans' service.

Symbolism it may have been, but it was also important acknowledgment at a local level for the Vietnam veterans. A small group of Western Victorian Vietnam veterans, enthusiastically supported by Councillor Mick Bawden, applied for a grant under this program, to erect a Vietnam War memorial to

---

[138] Opcit

be located in Hamilton. Their application was successful and a memorial consisting of three blue stone boulders, each with a bronze plaque... one for the Navy, one for the Army and the third for the Air Force, were erected in Lonsdale Street, Hamilton. The 'Their Service our Heritage' scheme provided $3000.00 for the project, with the remainder of the total cost of $5000.00 raised through public donations. The local support for this project was confirmation that Australian society had fully accepted the nation's part in the Vietnam War and that the veterans of that war deserved their place in Australian military history. There were other indicators too. Attendance at ANZAC Day ceremonies was on the increase, many young Australians were making pilgrimages to the Gallipoli Peninsular to attend the Dawn Service with an almost religious zeal. Others trekked the Kokoda Track in tribute to the Australians who had fought along its length in World War II, and Vietnam Veterans' Day was being observed by many, if not with the same zeal reserved for ANZAC Day, at least with a greater understanding. And so the Hamilton Vietnam Veterans' project was supported with much more enthusiasm that it would have been a decade earlier.

The dedication took place on the 3rd of October 1998. Pat Beale, Mick's long-time mate unveiled the memorial. Pat had stayed on in the Army reaching the rank of brigadier, and when Mick asked him to open the Hamilton memorial he had readily agreed. The dedication ceremony attracted around 100 ex-service personnel and around 250 members of the public. The organizers were well pleased with the turn out, but Mick was disappointed to note that most shire councillors were conspicuously absent from the event...aside from himself, only the Mayor attended. Perhaps this poor council attendance was an indication that not everyone's attitude toward the Vietnam War had changed. There were still those who remained staunchly anti-war and anti-military, and others who were quite simply apathetic, so long as the war, any war, and anything to do with war did not impact on them they were happy. This aside the memorial was a victory of a kind, a reminder to those who pass it on their daily lives of the cost of duty some of their fellow citizens had paid on the nation's behalf.

Chapter 20

"An elegant sufficiency, content
Retirement, rural quiet, friendship,
Books,
Ease and alternative labour, useful life,
Progressive virtue, and approving
Heaven!"[139]

Letting Go

IN THE PERIOD IMMEDIATELY FOLLOWING Mick's resignation from the council, the farm became the focus of Bawden family life. It was bloody hard work, and when in 2001 Mick tentatively floated the idea to Mardi of retirement from the farm, he was hardly surprised when she responded to the idea with enthusiasm, feelings she expanded on in her Christmas letter:

"...*What a fabulous year it has all turned out to be! The best season ever, shiny, fat sheep, feed everywhere. TL (Mick) is determined to precipitate his retirement and is selling off the stock while the prices are fantastic. All the wethers went on a boat trip, 1000 ewes were found a good home on another farm...*

We have put the place on the market and the plan is we will stay here and

---

[139] James Thomason

lease the land to some young farmer...no more shearing, crutching, dipping, drenching and whingeing...Whoopee!..."

Travel was the Bawdens next passion, a desire made easier to consummate by a sharp rise in the price of sheep, and early in 2001 the couple had made their first "civilian" overseas trip. Mardi recalled the experience:

"...Mid-August we left the wintery (rainless) shores of home, via Honolulu and on to Vancouver..."

They spent 10 days in Canada with Mardi's long-time friend Barbara Wyn—Edwards (nee Hulm), before flying on to the United Kingdom:

"Flew to London on 1st September to be greeted by Amanda (daughter) at Heathrow...She drove us to Warwick where we stayed while she went to work at Leamington Spa. By this time we received emails from home telling of inches of rain that fell as soon as we left..."

They spent 4 happy weeks travelling the length and breadth of England and Scotland, mainly by train, managing on one trip to create a security alarm when Mick accidently left his backpack at a railway station. They caught up with friends from the Army days, Brian and Margaret Cloughley and spent some days with them. It was a wonderful holiday, and at its end they both declared they were hooked on travel.

In August 2002, Mick's resolve to retire faced a reality test. The sale of the farm went through and they moved to Hamilton. However, while Mardi loved living in the town, Mick was far from happy. It was as though his identity had been completely stripped away...when he left the Army, he had immediately identified as a farmer...when he left local Government he could still identify as a farmer...but now he had left the farm....For months he wallowed in his own misery, declaring he hated living in Hamilton and proposing Nelson, a small village at the mouth of the Glenelg River, as an alternative, but one that was staunchly resisted by his wife.

It was only another call to duty that began to lift him from his dark mood. Still an active CFA member, during the summer of 2002/2003 he deployed four times, in various capacities, to fight bush fires in New South Wales and North Eastern Victoria. During the same period, he completed his qualifications for fire management, skills that are recognised anywhere in the world. In addition to this service Mick had maintained an active role in the Hamilton branch of the RSL and in 2001 was elected President, a position he held until 2007. A trip to Tasmania in May 2003 further improved marital morale, and in October of the same year the award of an Order of Australia Medal boosted Mick's spirits. The citation for the award read:

"For service to local government, to the welfare of veterans and their families, particularly through the Vietnam Veterans' Counselling Service, and to the community through firefighting organisations."

It was most gratifying to have his civilian service recognised…so many who perform civic duties receive little more than their name recorded on a dusty honour board in a town hall or civic chambers. Mick's award was gratifying, thoroughly deserved and maybe went some of the way to repaying the cost he incurred pursuing his civic duties. Once again life seemed to be pretty good.

The marriage of their daughter Amanda in November 2003 was another positive event, even though Mardi managed to swipe the centre post of the car port in the SAAB, and the bride was 17 minutes late at the church. Living in Hamilton remained a contentious issue. Mick saw the two storied, five bedroomed Hamilton residence, as a mausoleum in which the two of them rattled around in, only useful when the married children made a rare visit. On the other hand, Mardi enjoyed her circle of friends and living in the town kept her in close touch with the local artistic community. It took a while but slowly Mick's grumbling wore Mardi down, and eventually she agreed to explore the possibility of a move, but only on the condition any house they chose had to be acceptable to both of them. This condition seemed a tall order given Mardi's artistic taste and Mick's pragmatic approach to housing. However, late in 2005 a dwelling with distinct possibilities in the tiny Victorian township of Nelson, was found. As Mardi recalls:

"…this house is the only one that came close to acceptable to both of us, but it didn't have a shed, or a room for a studio, but all this has been overcome. Mick bought a boatshed on the river and the original builder of the house has attached a room on the western side of the house that looks as if it was always meant to be…

Hence, we have our little purple house with the roof that resembles an ocean wave. Mick calls it a water tank chopped in half and lying on its side (no imagination)..."

While the purchase of the house was being finalised, the couple attended the 2006, 9 RAR reunion in Perth, placing the car on the train and then after the reunion, driving back to Victoria.

There was further travel in 2007 when they joined a party of Mount Gambier people and journeyed to the "Deep North", visiting Cairns, Port Douglas and many and varied exotic tourist destinations in the region. March 2008 saw the intrepid pair journey to central Australia, Alice Springs, Uluru and the Olgas. Then toward the end of the year, along with a number of 9 RAR veterans, a more distant destination was selected...Vietnam.

For Vietnam veterans suffering from PTSD such a trip seems to have all the hallmarks of Aversion Therapy, or its offshoot Interoceptive Exposure, but without the controls and support of a clinic or a hospital. Such therapies are designed to help the sufferer to directly confront their fears and bodily symptoms such as anxiety, anger, an increased heart rate and shortness of breath.[140] With a therapist on hand the sufferer has support and expert advice to assist them through the symptoms. Such support was unlikely to be readily available on a trip to revisit the very country where their PTSD had its genesis. This was a factor that was not lost on either Mick or Mardi:

"...I had mixed feelings about going as did Mardi. We stayed overnight at Tullamarine and at about 0530 we went across the road to cancel our flight bookings, fortunately the terminal wasn't operating yet, so that we had another change of mind and after some mental agony, proceeded with the trip...not a good start!"

After such a worrying beginning the trip rapidly improved. In her 2008 Bulletin, Mardi recorded fine food, and good company which in combination soon dampened the concerns they had felt at Tullamarine:

"...we travelled from north to south of the country. We flew from Sydney to Saigon (Ho Chi Minh City), changed planes and on to Hanoi where we stayed in the Hilton Opera Hotel for two nights. Saw Uncle Ho[141] lying in

---

[140] ncbi.nlm.nih.gov/pubmed/1741730
[141] Communist revolutionary leader of the North Vietnamese during the Vietnam War. He died in 1969.

state (seems everyone has to do it). We had a gorgeous young man guiding us; he worked for Indochina Travel through whom we were booked. His name was Binh and would you believe it, the Aussie blokes dubbed him "Wheelie". I have to say that he spoke good English once we tuned into his accent, and he had a good grip on Aussie humour. He was 30 and had been to university in Ho Chi Minh City, but has yet to visit Australia. Every time we got into the bus there was a bottle of cold water and a "wet-one"[142] for hand wash. Oh, the food, I just loved it, lots of rice and noodles, stir fried vegies, pork, chicken, beef and fish. Pho (pronounced fur) is a favourite – chicken noodle soup – but their version is much, much more than the packet job as we know it."

There may have been the odd eyebrow raised at the seemingly compulsory visit to view Ho Chi Minh's body, but if so, it was soon put behind them, and the body of the former enemy leader was viewed with respect. Mardi Bawden:

"We travelled down the coast – a night in a junk in Ha Long Bay was a favourite stop over, and shopping in the marketplace in Hoi An in torrential rain was a treat for the Adelaide girls who had forgotten what real rain was like. At this time the threat of a typhoon lingered. In Hoi An we stayed at the Hoi An Beach Resort which was a little way out of town with the sea over the road and the river on the other side. The dining room looked through a curtain of orchids hanging from the pergola to the dragon boats on the river...just exotic..."

Mardi recorded that next, they visited Ho Chi Minh City, formerly Saigon. This was more familiar territory for Mick and his fellow veterans...not that many of them had spent much time in the South Vietnamese capital, but at least it was in the south of the country where they had operated:

"Next stop Ho Chi Minh City where the traffic was horrendous. We had a room on the 10th floor of the Palace Hotel, with a balcony which overlooked a corner where eight roads merged around a workstation in the middle. Some men were erecting a fountain sculpture in what I assume is going to be a pond, it had a tin fence around it and some shelter atop and the workers slept under it...in the middle of the road! Literally millions of motor bikes, buses,

---

[142] Disposable hand towels.

cars, taxis, all honking their horns and people jay walking through the middle of it as if they were on a Sunday stroll! It was hair-raising to cross the road. The first time Mick and I crossed the road on our own (on a pedestrian crossing), Mick was two steps from the gutter when he leapt, so joyful that he had made it, and fell on a lad on a scooter. 13 stone[143] of himself, fell on top of a 7 stone[144] lad...knocked the lad out cold, he had a helmet on, and the bike continued on by itself for a few feet. It took a minute for the lad to come around and then he sat in the gutter holding his head. I guess his eyes were still spinning when our guide came on the scene and sent us to the hotel while he took control of the situation. Mick had a few bruises to elbow, hip and leg, and henceforth remained very uncertain about crossing the road."

When the idea of the trip had first been mooted, Mick had some definite objectives that he wanted to achieve and activities he wanted to take part in, and he was keen to achieve these. Mick Bawden:

"...9 RAR ex diggers support an orphanage in Baria and there was to be a presentation of toys clothing and cash to be given at a function on a particular day and Mardi and I wanted to attend! Which we did and it was a very moving experience.

I wanted also to visit the 9 RAR supported school at Nui Dat and we made some presentations to the children.

Also, I was curious to see how the province had repaired the damage of the war and if possible, attend a memorial service for our KIA soldiers at Nui Dat..."

On the second last day of the visit the party arrived at Nui Dat, the former location of the Australian Task Force. Little remains of the former base where up to 5000 Australians once lived. The remains of the Luscombe Airfield that the Australian Engineers built is still evident, but even the feature from which the base took its name Nui Dat, which means dirt hill, had been quarried and cut away. Each veteran had his own thoughts as they entered the area, a moment made more evocative by the presence of a number of their former foes. Mick Bawden:

"Finally, on 20 November, the 40th anniversary of the arrival of 9 RAR in

---

[143] 82 kilograms
[144] 44 kilograms

Vietnam, we held a service on a hill in Nui Dat with an interpreter and members of the North Vietnamese Army. We said "sorry" and they said "sorry" and that both of us were only being the best soldiers that we could for our Governments. Tears flowed spontaneously. Then everyone hugged each other and with arms around each other group photos were taken."

For Mick, the moment with a former enemy was uplifting, even liberating:

"I was embraced by an ex-Viet Cong at a memorial service at Nui Dat who with great emotion said to me through the interpreter... 'We are both servants of our country'...That statement of logic was worthy of many hours of remedial assistance..."

Duty and its associated cost knows no boundaries and takes no account of nationality.

The next day the Australians flew home.

CHAPTER 21

You can't stop the future
You can't rewind the past
The only way to learn the secret
...is to press play.[145]

The Way Ahead

THE COST OF DUTY FOR the Australian servicemen and women who deployed to the Vietnam War, and for their families who waited hopefully for their return is difficult to calculate. None of them are the same people they were before the crucible of war interrupted their lives. For some, the experience has strengthened them and better prepared them for life after the war. Others have been utterly destroyed by their involvement and have withdrawn from family and the community to live a life apart. An alarming number have taken their own lives. The direct impact of the war aside, there can be little doubt that the cost of duty they endured was unfairly increased by the negative attitude of successive Governments, and a large section of the Australian community, had toward their service. It took a herculean struggle by the Vietnam veterans themselves to redress that wrong. Because of that

---

[145] Jay Asher, Thirteen Reasons Why. goodreads.com/work/quotes/2588213-thirteen-reasons-why

struggle, the majority of Vietnam veterans and their families, often in spite of war related injuries, have been able to live successful and productive lives. Mick and Mardi Bawden are typical of this group. In spite of the bad times they sometimes endure, such as when PTSD makes an uninvited visit, life has been and remains fairly good. Both have enjoyed success in their chosen fields of civilian endeavour, and they continue to contribute to the community. Retirement has not exactly suited Mick, and he remains actively involved in the Country Fire Authority. While there are no signs that his sense of this particular duty have diminished, there are signs he may be battling to pay the cost it demands. In January 2018 while attending a fire at the nearby district of Mumbannar, he took a tumble from the Nelson fire tanker injuring a shoulder. It was a painful injury necessitating his evacuation from the fire front, and regardless of his flippant comments concerning the accident, it shook him up, and in 2019 he was forced to consider a less active CFA role. The fish in the Glenelg River are still occasionally in danger of his hooks and he still manages to grace the tennis court with his presence.

Mardi continues to pursue her artistic interests, augmenting her drawing skills with the camera and she has become a keen photographer. Her garden is another pastime she enjoys, the once windswept plot around the Nelson house now produces prodigious blooms which have often provided inspiration for new photographs and drawings. Golf remains as a keen interest, she still plays tennis, and until relatively recently…hockey. However, she is still on duty, supporting and fiercely protecting her husband whenever his spirits darken, and the nightmares return.

Mick is immensely proud of his wife. He once wrote of her:

"Mardi has been with me through all the journey. Her smile and charm are precious, not to mention her artistic talents and ability to go from sheep yards to a Council function on very short notice. I am a life member of her fan club."

Their two children, Byron and Amanda lead successful professional lives. Byron is an economist working out of Sydney and London. He was married to Samantha and the couple have two children…Sophie and Hamish. Sadly, the couple have divorced and as a result Mick and Mardi see less of Byron's children than they would like.

Amanda, a psychologist and management consultant, is married to Matthew Caulfield, and they have three boys…Tom, Luke, and Jonathan. As a result of Amanda's purchase of a beach house at Allestree, just to the northeast of the Victorian town of Portland, Mick and Mardi have seen much more of these grandchildren. The beach house is a relatively short drive from Mick and Mardi's Nelson home and when Amanda and her family are in residence, the grandparents make frequent visits to revel in their grandchildren's company. This relationship has provided several learning experiences for Mardi (known to her grandchildren as "Nana Mard") one of which occurred when Tom was at the tender age of three:

"We were out somewhere, and Tom had to go to the toilet, so I found a loo and took him inside. As I lifted him up on the seat, I said to him… 'push your whistle down so it doesn't splash out'…He looked me in the eye and said, 'Nana Mard, Tom the Tank Engine has a whistle, I have a penis!"

Note to Nana Mard…the modern child calls a spade a spade, and a penis a penis.

On a darker note, to date there is no cure for PTSD. In every sufferer the injury remains like taut sinews in a naked body. In Mick's case, it is hidden most of the time by the twinkle of eye, and the facial expression of astounded innocence that Alby Morrison found so endearing. Yet given the right (or should it be "wrong") set of circumstances the epidermis is stripped away and the concealed tension and fear he sometimes experiences is starkly revealed. As a result, when the idea of this book was first presented to Mick, he refused to participate on the grounds it would revive memories he was trying to forget. After some additional pestering he gave his reluctant assent, and some initial research began. Progress, however, was short-lived and after around 3 months of answering questions via e-mail, and a series of lengthy telephone calls, he found the process too painful and at his request the project was cancelled. Five months later he renewed contact saying he had changed his mind and asking if the work could be recommenced. Aside from the length of time it has taken to write the work, the research involved is an intrusive process and one that has at times reopened old wounds. It is doubtful that Mick has enjoyed the experience, but with Mardi's support he has managed to persevere.

The 9 RAR Association is another important interest for the couple. The

Association comprises of former members of the Battalion and their families, and until recently regular reunions and other social activities were conducted. Importantly, the Association has kept the former members of the Battalion in contact with each other, providing a means of mutual support when the going gets tough. Sadly, age and illness has impacted their ranks to such an extent that regular reunions are no longer viable. Nevertheless those who are able, maintain annual visits to the gravesides of their comrades who died in action. To Mick the graveside visits are a sacred trust:

"...I do this because of the quality of the men with whom I served. Honour was and still is important to them; they were simply the bravest men I have ever known and my bond with them has to do with absolute trust in each other..."

The graveside pilgrimages have provided an indication of wider, less obvious membership of the 9 RAR family. Some years ago, Mick and Mardi travelled to Whyalla for the pilgrimage to Lance Corporal Rick Abraham's grave. Rick Abraham had been killed in action in July 1969 during Operation Matthew. After the brief ceremony Mick and Mardi visited the World War Two corvette HMAS Whyalla which has been established in a dry dock as a tourist attraction for the city. Their guide for the visit was an attractive young lady and during the course of the visit she asked Mick and Mardi what had brought them to Whyalla. On providing an explanation their guide fell silent, before explaining that Rick Abraham had been her first boyfriend.

On another occasion at the end of a day's fishing along the Glenelg River, Mick was cleaning his catch prior to going home, when a man approached him. The man had noticed a Vietnam veterans' sticker on the rear window of Mick's car and a conversation followed:

"We exchanged small talk. He was from Ardrossan just having a look around. He had seen the Vietnam veterans' sticker on my car and asked if I had been in Vietnam. When I told him I had, he then asked which Battalion I had been with and when I told him 9 RAR, he looked at me with an incredulous expression on his face. It turned out he was the brother of one of our blokes, Barry Plane, who had been killed on Operation Goodwood..."

Following that chance meeting, Mick ensured a sizeable group of 9 RAR veterans travelled to Ardrossan for the anniversary of Barry Plane's death.

The Bawdens keep in regular contact with Harry Musicka's widow and with his daughter Sandy in Perth, also Bernd Bender's sister in Wangaratta, Rick Abraham's family in Whyalla, and Bruce Plane's brother in Ardrossan. They are determined to maintain these contacts as long as they are able. Sadly, it would seem that very soon the Battalion reunions will cease, not through lack of interest, but rather through a lack of members. For time has taken its toll on the members of the original 9 RAR who made it back to Australia. In the years since the Battalion's return home some 213 of them have died, including their original CO Alby Morrison AO, DSO, MBE. After the Battalion's return to Australia the much-loved CO and father of 9 RAR remained in the Army reaching the rank of major general before his retirement in 1981. He died in 2008 at the age of 81.

Mick and Mardi were part of a huge crowd of mourners who attended General Morrison's funeral which was conducted at the Royal Military College Duntroon. At the service an ensemble from the RMC Band played the Gilbert and Sullivan tune from the comic opera The Pirates of Penzance "The Modern Major General". The tune provides a parody of a 19th century major general who had a well-rounded academic education, but who lacked military knowledge. In contrast, Alby was indeed a well-educated man, but that was where any similarity between him and Gilbert and Sullivan's General ended. Of all those who had the honour of serving with him, but most particularly the men of 9 RAR, militarily Alby Morrison had few equals. In providing the eulogy, General Peter Cosgrove said:

"I know that those many people here today will excuse me if I pause in my account of Alan's great service to Australia, to dwell for a minute or two on that time we in 9 RAR spent under his command. You see, it is our conceit, our conviction that after his family, within that great sweep of his wonderful Army career, Alan loved us best of all."[146]

Greatly saddened, Mick and Mardi returned home certain in the knowledge General Cosgrove's words regarding Alby's love for 9 RAR were absolutely true.

---

[146] A eulogy for the late Major General Alan Lindsay Morrison AO, DSO, MBE by General Peter Cosgrove (RETD) at the Chapel of St Paul, Duntroon, 14 May 2008.

At the time of writing most of the remainder of 9 RAR are now in their mid to late seventies, however, while what's left of their hair may be grey, their vision dimmed and they might not hear as well as they once did, the 9 RAR spirit that Alby Morrison worked so hard to create and maintain, is as strong now as it was when they were in their twenties.

Mick and Mardi's addiction to travel has continued and they are now able to tick off a bucket list of places and events they had long planned to see and experience…Scotland and Ireland were high on the list. In Scotland they attended the Edinburgh Military Tattoo a stirring occasion for a retired Scottish dancer (Mardi) and Mick a former member of an Australian Regiment with an affiliation with the Seaforth Highlanders (the Royal South Australia Regiment). They visited the Isle of Skye and marvelled at the rugged beauty of the place. In Ireland their visit coincided with the coldest summer on record, but in between rain and sleet they still managed to kiss the Blarney Stone and to drink ample quantities of Guinness. Another journey took them to France, to visit old friends Margaret and Brian Cloughley, in Burgundy. The view from Margaret's kitchen window became the subject of another of Mardi's skilful drawings. In 2017 the more adventurous destination of Norfolk Island became a port of call. The thick walls of the long-abandoned prison provided the two tourists with a stark reminder of the island's dark convict past, but they were captivated by the island's rugged beauty, and its inhabitants' unique lifestyle. New Zealand has been another holiday destination for sightseeing and even driving Go-cart-like contraptions at alarming speeds down the Luge at Rotorua.

Aside from their overseas excursions there have been regular visits to family, and they remain determined to attend as many 9 RAR reunions and grave side remembrance services for the Battalion KIA as they can. Most recently Mick was asked to read the eulogies at the 50-year commemoration services for Operation Goodwood, an operation which cost 9 RAR heavy casualties. The services were conducted at Murray Bridge, Centennial Park and Ardrossan. There have also been speaking engagements at ANZAC Day services particularly at schools in Hamilton where he sought to highlight the futility of war. Familiar themes in these addresses have been, education, remembrance, and the evil of war. Mick Bawden:

"Wars are not precipitated by soldiers rather they are declared by political leaders and their prosecution is carried out by soldiers who in doing so suffer the most casualties.

Long after the war is over, continuing physical and mental pain is experienced by those who fought the war, whilst the politicians who decided that the war should take place are forgotten by history.

Australia's soldiers swear an oath on enlistment part of which states that "They will well and truly serve the sovereign in the military forces of the Commonwealth".

This service was reflected in such places as Gallipoli and Flanders in World War One, Greece, Libya, Egypt and New Guinea in World War Two where in total 100,000 lives were lost.

It is difficult indeed to find even a tenuous link with the loss of 8000 lives on the Gallipoli Peninsular and a threat to Australia's security, but serve they did and continued to do so in Korea, Malaya and South Vietnam where less lives were sacrificed but the difficulty to establish a link with a threat to our security continued.

Soldiers served and suffered casualties in all these campaigns so that peace would ultimately prevail, and it has!

The uncensored coverage by the media of the Vietnam War has shown the public how brutal, senseless, and wasteful war can be and the public reaction and questioning of the campaign was instrumental in politicians ending our involvement.

The present, after all, is the sum of the past and the peace we enjoy now is the fruit of much human striving and sacrifice, not a small part of this sacrifice has been and still is borne by Australia's service personnel whom we honour today.

A sceptic might contend that Mick's thoughts on the futility of war while commendable, demonstrate the relevance of an old French truism:

"Plus ça change, plus c'est la même chose" ...the more things change the more they stay the same."[147]

Certainly, since the Vietnam War there have been periods of relative

---

[147] Jean-Baptiste Alphonse Karr the French critic, journalist and novelist November 24,1808–September 29,1890.

peace, and yet when politicians have judged it to be appropriate, Australian servicemen and women are readily deployed to overseas conflicts where their duty still propagates great cost. However, instead of the negativity that greeted returning Vietnam veterans, contemporary veterans returning home receive a more positive reception from Government and the general public. The Department of Veteran Affairs provides an improved level of support, although the Department's methods are still the subject of complaint from some disgruntled younger veterans. Much of the scepticism regarding PTSD is no longer evident, however, sadly some politicians and senior military figures persist with the notion that that particular affliction is a sign of weakness in the individual.

There is evidence to suggest that politicians and some sections of the population remain more interested in symbolic gestures than in the provision of genuine welfare and care for those who have paid the cost of duty. For example, in 2018, the Sir John Monash Centre at Villers-Bretonneux, an additional memorial to those World War One soldiers who fought and died in France, was opened…the cost of the new memorial $100 million. In 2019 the Government released plans for an extension to the Australian War Memorial in Canberra…the estimated cost $500 million. Approached by the ABC Television Program 'The Mix' regarding these Government backed initiatives, former Chief of the Defence Force Admiral Chris Barrie commented that in his opinion rather than building more memorials to the dead, the money would be better spent funding the treatment and care for soldiers who are suffering from PTSD from our most recent conflicts.[148] To date both major parties have ignored Barrie's remarks and support the spending on the memorials. A misanthropic view of this decision would say that there are possibly more votes in the number of families whose relations served and died in World War One, than with the number of modern veterans and their families suffering the effects of PTSD.

On the other hand, if the cost of duty paid by members of the armed forces is to be remembered, some form of education or tangible reminder is necessary. John Schumann's song "I Was Only 19" went some way toward

---

[148] ABC Program 'The Mix' 2019.

this end, the evocative lyrics providing an insight into the reality of war and the cost of duty:

Mum and dad and Danny saw the passing out parade at Puckapunyal
It was a long march from cadets
The sixth Battalion was the next to tour and it was me who drew the card
We did Canungra and Shoalwater before we left.
And Townsville lined the footpaths as we marched down to the quay
This clipping from the paper shows us young and strong and clean
And there's me in me slouch hat with me SLR and greens
God help me
I was only nineteen.
From Vung Tau riding Chinooks to the dust at Nui Dat
I'd been in and out of choppers now for months
And we made our tents a home, V.B. and pinups on the lockers
And an Asian orange sunset through the scrub.
And can you tell me, Doctor, why I still can't get to sleep?
And night-time's just a jungle dark and a barking M.16?
And what's this rash that comes and goes, can you tell me what it means?
God help me
I was only nineteen.
A four-week operation, when each step can mean your last one on two legs
It was a war within yourself
But you wouldn't let your mates down 'til they had you dusted off
So you closed your eyes and thought about somethin' else.
And then someone yelled out contact, and the bloke behind me swore
We hooked in there for hours, then a God almighty roar
And Frankie kicked a mine the day that mankind kicked the moon
God help me
He was goin' home in June.
And I can still see Frankie, drinkin' tinnies in the Grand Hotel
On a thirty-six-hour rec. leave in Vung Tau
And I can still hear Frankie, lying screaming in the jungle
'Til the morphine came and killed the bloody row.
And the Anzac legends didn't mention mud and blood and tears

And the stories that my father told me never seemed quite real
I caught some pieces in my back that I didn't even feel
God help me
I was only nineteen.
And can you tell me, Doctor, why I still can't get to sleep?
And why the Channel Seven chopper chills me to my feet?
And what's this rash that comes and goes
Can you tell me what it means?
God help me
I was only nineteen.[149]

Without reminders such as this, the physical memorials and the days of special remembrance the cost of duty made on the public's behalf, it is all too quickly forgotten, and the Vietnam War provides an example of this forgetfulness. Many younger Australians have no knowledge of South Vietnam, or of any Australian involvement in a war in that country. This lack of knowledge was highlighted in 1999 during the planning of logistic support for INTERFET[150], the Australian led intervention in East Timor. A highly experienced and qualified logistician was identified on the Reserve List of Officers and action was taken to reactivate him to enable his input to the planning process. The identified officer was a Vietnam veteran and his return to the fold required his security clearances to be reviewed and updated. As a part of that process, he was required to complete a questionnaire provided by a young public servant who dwelt somewhere in the bowels of the security world in Canberra. A particular section of the officer's response to the questionnaire caused that young public servant some consternation. The questionnaire asked if the officer had travelled abroad in the last 30 years, and if so to which country? The officer answered "yes" to the first part of the question, and "South Vietnam" to the second. The completed questionnaire was then e-mailed to Canberra but hours later it was returned by the young public servant with these additional questions:

Where is South Vietnam? and

Did you travel there for business or pleasure?

---

[149] John Schumann, "I was Only 19".
[150] International Force East Timor.

Well may we say, "Lest we forget", because nothing will ever reduce the call of duty or remove its concomitant costs.

ACKNOWLEDGEMENTS

I WOULD LIKE TO ACKNOWLEDGE the following folk:
My wife Ella for her endless patience and for accompanying me on long drives to meet and interview Mick and Mardi Bawden.
Dawn Sims for her work with initial proof reading and editing.

Also in their own words the Bawden family;
This book is the result of a considerable collaboration between the author, Max Carmichael, and my wife Mardi and I. Over a considerable number of telephone calls, e-mails, and face to face interviews, not to mention proof readings, selection of photographs and fact checking, between the three of us 'The Cost of Duty' *has finally been published.*

It is a little confronting to see your life presented in print, and at times I almost found the work too much to endure. However, Mardi and I trust that on reading this book, the reader will gain some idea of the costs endured by Vietnam veterans and their families, and indeed the veterans and families of other conflicts to which Australia has committed its young men and women.

All photographs were supplied by Mick and Mardi

About the Author

Max Carmichael CSM* RFD*

MAX CARMICHAEL WAS BORN IN country Victoria, and spent most of his formative years in boarding school. On leaving school he has worked in a variety of fields including agriculture, education, the Australian Army (including three operational deployments), and the Australian Public Service.

Other titles by Max Carmichael are *"In Kilted Company, a story of Part-Time Soldiering"*, *"With Skill and Fighting, Craftsmen of the Australian Army 1942 – 2014"*, *"Attack on the Black Cat Track"*, and *"The Map of Honour"*.

Max is now retired and lives with his wife in Ballarat. His interests include writing, reading, gardening and Australian Cattle Dogs.

*Conspicuous Service Medal
**Reserve Forces Decoration

BIBLIOGRAPHY

ABC Program 'The Mix' 2019

Australian Army Legal Corps, Justice in Arms: Military Lawyers in the Australian Army's First Hundred Years, Angus and Robertson.

Author unnamed, A History of Kokoda Barracks Canungra 1942 – 2002.

Bruce Picken Fire Support Bases Vietnam (Big Sky Publishing 2012).

Edited by Garth Pratten and Glyn Harper, Still The Same Reflections on Active Service from Bardia to Baidoa (Army Doctrine Centre Headquarters Training Command, 1996).

Enoggera Barracks, Brisbane: 9 RAR Association, 1992. First Edition, The 9th Battalion Royal Australia Regiment Vietnam Tour of Duty, 1968 – 1969, On Active Service.

https://www.5rar.asn.au/poems

http://www.freewebs.com/9rar-rvn/apps/photos/album?albumid=1111002

https://www.sites.google.com/site/9rarsa/in-memoriam

http://www.awm.gov.au/cms_images

http://www.nashoaustralia.org.au/Honour%20Roll.htm

https://en.wikipedia.org/wiki/Battle_of_Hat_Dich#CITEREFAWM_95-1-4-136

http://www.vietnamroll.gov.au/VeteranDetails.aspx

https://vwma.org.au/public/search?utf8=%E2%9C%93&query

http://lachlanirvine.tripod.com/poetry

https://vwma.org.au/public/search?utf8=%E2%9C%93&query=Gordon+Sorrensen&commit=

http://www.hmassydney.com/library/sydney3/intheirownwords.html account by Jim Dickson

https://www.bl.uk/world-war-one/articles/shell-shock

http://www.vvaa.org.au/experience.htm#INTRUSIVE%20THOUGHTS/FLASHBACKS, Posttraumatic Stress Disorder (PTSD) A Vietnam Veteran's Experience.

Ian McGibbon, New Zealanders' Vietnam War: A History of Combat, Commitment and Controversy, (Exisle Publicity 2010).

John Schumann, "I was Only 19".

LTCOL Fred Fairhead (RTD), A Duty Done, http://rarasa.org.au/wp-content/uploads/2014/12/A-Duty-Done.pdf

Max Carmichael with Frank Benfield and Kerin Joyce, With Skill and Fighting – Craftsmen of the Australian Army 1942 – 2014, pp 88,89 (CopyRight Publishing Company Pty Ltd 2014).

Michael Brander, The Making of the Highlands, Book Club Associates London 1980.

Mike Coleman, Payne VC, ABC Books 2001.

Nicholas Bromfield, Welcome Home: reconciliation, Vietnam veterans, and the reconstruction of Anzac under the Hawke Government, University of Sydney.

Phillip Caputo, A Rumour of War (Owl Books).

Richard "Barney" Bigwood and Andrew Bigwood, We Were The Reos: Australian Infantry Reinforcements in Vietnam, (Xlibris Corporation 23 May 2011)

https://www.aihw.gov.au/getmedia/8182c820-d3cf-47e7-ac1f-3203c85126c9/p1055d-dapsone.pdf.aspx?inline=true

VOLUNTARY GUIDES BACKGROUNDER Number 05 Issue #4 - Part 2 of 2 January 2010 Vietnam War 1962-1975.

1 Psychological Unit, Deployment Guide, printed July 2000.